WHY DID JESUS DIE?

WHY DID JESUS DIE?

DICK TRIPP

WIPF & STOCK · Eugene, Oregon

WHY DID JESUS DIE?
What the Bible Says About the Cross

Copyright © 2014 Dick Tripp. All rights reserved. Except for brief quotations in critical publications or reviews, no part of this book may be reproduced in any manner without prior written permission from the publisher. Write: Permissions, Wipf and Stock Publishers, 199 W. 8th Ave., Suite 3, Eugene, OR 97401.

Originally Published in New Zealand by
Castle Publishing
PO Box 68 800
Newton, Auckland, NZ
info@castlepublishing.co.nz

Wipf & Stock
An Imprint of Wipf and Stock Publishers
199 W. 8th Ave., Suite 3
Eugene, OR 97401

www.wipfandstock.com

ISBN 13: 978-1-62564-242-4

Manufactured in the U.S.A.

To John Stott

whose Bible teaching and encouragement in my
formative days as a Christian laid a great foundation
for understanding the Scriptures and whose faithfulness to
the cross over a lifetime has been an example for so many.

Foreword

The cross is the centre and heartbeat of the biblical faith. It is the hallmark of evangelical orthodoxy, which has empowered the Church throughout its history in worship and in times of persecution, and is the central motif for world evangelisation. It is surprising, therefore, how few books on the cross have stood the test of time. During the twentieth century, James Denny's *Death of Christ* (1903), Leon Morris's *Apostolic Preaching of the Cross* (1955) and John Stott's *The Cross of Christ* (1986) are among the few outstanding works.

Now in Dick Tripp's *Why did Jesus Die? What the Bible Says About the Cross* we have a work of outstanding and lasting worth – an amazingly comprehensive reference to all the biblical texts that point to Christ's death, its meaning and significance for today's Church.

In Part I he traces the progressive revelation of God's saving work from Genesis to Revelation. He takes us through the images of the cross in the Old Testament from the tree of life to the Passover, to the bronze serpent in the wilderness, to the Day of Atonement, to Israel's Suffering Servant in Isaiah and the Psalms.

Continuing in the New Testament, Dick Tripp takes us through the centrality of the cross in the Gospels, the Acts and the New Testament Letters and Revelation. Throughout, there is constant cross-reference to both Testaments, to the Church's commentators throughout its history and to contemporary Christian writers - a mine of fact and interpretation to inspire the heart of any preacher and teacher of Scripture.

In Part II he relates the cross to the theme of the Trinity, the love and justice of God, to suffering and resurrection and to other religious Faiths.

Dick Tripp's treatment of the cross as Christ's atonement for sin brings together Christ's identity with God his Father and with suffering and sinful humanity. He outlines the benefits of reconciliation and forgiveness, justification and sanctification, adoption and union with Christ in victorious living. For here the cross reveals both the character of God and the purpose of Christ's incarnation – that 'Christ died for our sins according to the Scriptures'.

The Cross is shown to be the symbol of Christ's saving act, universally recognised in every church and publicly displayed on the clothing of believers. Jesus promised that when he is lifted up he will draw all people to himself (John 12:32). Dick shows that the cross is a magnet drawing people of every culture by his redeeming love.

I unreservedly commend this book to pastors as a study guide for preaching on the cross and to all who seek to live out in daily life Jesus Christ as Saviour and Lord.

Bruce Nicholls

Rev. Dr Bruce J. Nicholls was a career missionary in India working in theological education and in pastoral ministry with the Church of North India. He was also Editor of the *Evangelical Review of Theology* for 18 years and is now Editor of the Asia Bible Commentary series.

Contents

Preface	13
Acknowledgements	15
Introduction	17

Part 1
What the Bible says about the cross — 25

Old Testament images of the cross — 27
- The tree of life — 28
- The serpent's fatal wound — 29
- Thorns – symbol of the curse — 32
- Our nakedness covered through the shedding of blood — 32
- A God who is prepared to die — 34
- The Father's sacrifice — 35
- Passover – safe beneath the Lamb's blood — 37
- Bitter waters made sweet — 40
- The smitten rock – God in the dock — 40
- Animal sacrifices — 44
- Day of Atonement – the rent curtain — 48
- The bronze serpent – look and live — 51
- Isaiah's Suffering Servant — 53
- The Psalms — 60
- Death leading to resurrection — 64

The cross in the Gospels — 69
- Emphasis on the passion and cross in the Gospels — 69
- Hints and references to the cross before its occurrence — 70
- The Last Supper — 83

Gethsemane	86
The trial	91
The crucifixion	97
The burial	109
The resurrection	112
Between resurrection and ascension	113
The cross – the focus of prophecy	114
The cross in Acts	**119**
The cross in the New Testament letters	**125**
Christ's death "for our sins"	126
The blood of Christ	128
The cross in Paul's letters	**135**
The cross and sin	138
The cross central in Paul's preaching	139
Our identification with Christ in his death	140
Our identification with Christ in suffering	144
The cross and the wisdom of God	144
The cross and the challenge of godly living	145
Christ's death and our death	146
The death of Christ and his exultation	147
Benefits of the cross	**149**
Forgiveness	149
Justification	150
Salvation	157
Reconciliation	159
Redemption	163
Sanctification	167
Propitiation	169
Adoption	172
The cross in Hebrews	**177**
The cross in Peter	**183**
The cross in 1 John	**187**
The cross in Revelation	**191**

Part 2
Related Issues   195

The cross and the Trinity   197
The cross and the love of God   205
The cross and the justice of God   211
The cross and suffering   219
Why Easter Saturday?   227
God's "Yes" of Easter Day   233
The cross and history's reversal of values   237
Why the cross is not popular   239
The cross and discipleship   247
The cross and other religions   253
The cross and our response   257

Preface

Why write a book on the cross? Since having first experienced the forgiveness and love of Jesus nearly 50 years ago, I have become more and more convinced that understanding the significance of the cross is important for a healthy perception of what Christianity is all about. It shapes the key issues – how you become a Christian, how you grow as a Christian, how you can find certainty in your relationship with God, and how you can be sure about where you are heading in the life beyond death.

However, I have another reason for writing this book. Over the last 100 years, there have been endless debates in the name of "scholarship" surrounding what we can really know about Jesus, what he really taught, and what he achieved – if indeed such a person ever actually existed. Today, with the prominence and influence of the mass media, the situation is even more confusing. The media tends to focus on the sensational and so highlights beliefs that would not be accepted by the vast majority of Christians. The result is a mass of misinformation that can confuse ordinary people and make them suspicious of Christianity.

One of my main purposes in writing this book is to let the Bible speak for itself. The wonderful God that the Bible describes didn't plan to make it difficult for us to understand his central message. He has given us a book that holds plenty of clues as to its divine inspiration and that contains an essential story that is not hard to understand. Though the Bible contains parable, symbolism, poetry and other literary styles, it usually means exactly what it says. The reader has every right to disagree with what it says, but no one has a right to say that it says something that it doesn't – even if they do so in the name of "scholarship".

My goal is simply to open up the Bible, and focus on its teaching about the cross. The Bible contains a mass of material that can be daunting for someone sincerely seeking the truth. Key passages can easily be missed if someone doesn't know where to start. I have sought to clarify the Bible's central message in a manner that makes it impossible to miss. God planned the universe and the creation of a race of humans with whom he could enjoy a loving relationship both in this life and in eternity. My belief is that those who seriously consider this message, will not find it easy to resist its appeal. It is a message that can satisfy the deepest longings of the human heart.

Dick Tripp

Acknowledgements

I wish to thank the many folk who have given encouragement and advice in writing all the titles in this series. Particularly I would thank my wife Sally for sharing her computer skills and her patience; my son, Tim, for his creative cover illustration, Alison Simmons for her thorough and particular proofreading, and Bruce Nicholls for his generous foreword and encouragement. Above all, I wish to thank any who may have prayed for this ministry.

Introduction

Wherever you find Christians, you find crosses. There are huge crosses towering in the Alps and Andes. There are little crosses that hang around people's necks. Crosses are found on spires and gravestones, at roadsides, on dashboards and shelves. There are Celtic crosses, Crusader crosses, crosses of St Anne, and Coptic crosses. They are made of gold, silver, bronze, plastic, wood and stone. Churches have traditionally been built in the form of a cross. And, of course, there is no counting the frescos, mosaics, icons, and oil paintings that have the crucifixion scene for their subject.

The only corporate ceremony that Jesus commanded his followers to observe, the Lord's Supper, celebrated every Sunday in thousands of churches, focuses on the cross with its central symbols, bread and wine, portraying his body broken and his blood shed. The ceremony he gave us for initiation into the Christian faith, baptism, symbolises our dying and rising with Christ.

Malcolm Muggeridge wrote in *The Observer* on 26 March 1967:

> One thing at least can be said with certainty about the crucifixion of Christ: It was manifestly the most famous death in history. No other death has aroused 100th part of the interest, or been remembered with 100th part of the intensity and concern...

Why Did Jesus Die?

For eighteen hundred years the cross has been the major symbol of Christianity. It has not always been so. The earliest Christian motifs seem to have been a peacock (symbolising immortality), a dove, the athlete's victory palm, or in particular, a fish (the letters of the Greek word for "fish" being an acronym for Jesus Christ, Son of God, Saviour). However, it seems certain that, at least from the second century onwards, Christians not only drew, painted and engraved the cross as a pictorial symbol of their faith, but also made the sign of the cross on themselves or others. From then it increasingly dominated all other symbols of Christianity.

When one considers the horror with which crucifixion was regarded in the ancient world, the adoption of such a symbol seems very odd indeed. Crucifixion was possibly invented by the Persians and was taken over from them by the Greeks and Romans. It is probably the cruellest method of execution ever practised because it deliberately delayed death until maximum torture had been inflicted. Victims could suffer for days before dying. The modern hangman's rope or electric chair are tame by comparison. Cicero, in his defence of the elderly senator Gaius Rabirius in 63 B.C., declared:

> The very word "cross" should be far removed not only from the person of a Roman citizen, but from his thoughts, his eyes and his ears. For it is not only the actual occurrence of these things [sc. the procedures of crucifixion] or the endurance of them, but the liability to them, the expectation, indeed the mere mention of them, that is unworthy of a Roman citizen and a free man.

To the Jews it was equally abhorrent, but for a different reason. They made no distinction between a "tree" and a "cross", and so applied to crucified criminals the terrible statement of the law that

Introduction

"**anyone who is hung on a pole** [or tree] **is under God's curse**" (Deuteronomy 21:23).

Why then have Christians chosen this as the central symbol of their faith? One of the reasons is because of who they believe the person dying on that cross really was. In my booklet *Was Jesus Really God?* I spell out some of those beliefs. It is because they believe he is all that he personally claimed to be that New Testament scholar Tom Wright can say, in his recent book *Simply Christian*:[1]

> The death of Jesus of Nazareth as the King of the Jews, the bearer of Israel's destiny, the fulfilment of God's promises to his people of old, is either the most stupid, senseless waste and misunderstanding the world has ever seen, or it is the fulcrum around which world history turns.

The second reason, however, and why Christians believe the second of these options, is because of what he achieved by his death, and that is what this book is all about. Martin Luther declared, "If you want to understand the Christian message, you must start with the wounds of Christ." Theologian Emil Brunner said in his book *The Mediator*, "He who understands the Cross aright… understands the Bible, he understands Jesus Christ." He then quotes Luther:

> Therefore this text – "He bore our sins" – must be understood particularly thoroughly, as the foundation upon which stands the whole of the New Testament or the Gospel, as that which alone distinguishes us and our religion from all other religions.

---

1 SPCK, 2006, ©. This book has been described as the most thrilling attempt to re-express the heart of the Christian faith and the transformation it offers to every area of personal and social life since C. S. Lewis's *Mere Christianity*.

Why Did Jesus Die?

Christians believe that there is wonderful power in the cross. John Stott, in *The Preacher's Portrait*, says:

> It has power to wake the dullest conscience and melt the hardest heart, to cleanse the unclean, to reconcile him who is afar off and restore him to fellowship, to redeem the prisoner from his bondage and lift the pauper from the dunghill, to break down the barriers which divide [people] from one another, to transform our wayward characters into the image of Christ and finally to make us fit to stand in white robes before the throne of God.

The influential bishop Leslie Newbiggin, in his book *Journey in to Joy*, tells of the experience that brought him into the Christian faith. He says:

> As I grow older I am less inclined to be dogmatic about many things. But there are a few things about which I am sure. I am sure about Jesus Christ…
>
> Forty-two years ago there was a student at Cambridge who was not a Christian believer, but was very much concerned about the way the world was going and his responsibility for it. This student decided to spend a good part of his first long vacation working with the miners of the Rhondda valley in South Wales, who had been rotting in unemployment and misery for a decade. The experiment was not a success. But one night, overwhelmed by the sense of defeat and of the power of evil in the world, there was given to him a vision of the cross of Jesus Christ as the one and only reality great enough to span the distance between heaven and hell, and to hold in one embrace all the variety of humankind, the one reality that could make sense of the human situation. I was that student.

Introduction

Over the last two thousand years there have similarly been millions of people who have found in the cross of Christ the meaning of life. Through it they have found forgiveness for the worst of sins, peace of mind, a purpose for living, perseverance under the greatest of trials and hope for a glorious future beyond death. This being the case, what is it that makes the cross so significant?

People have had their theories about the cross: the *penal theory*, developed in the Reformation era and still the one most accepted amongst evangelicals; the *subjective theory*, originating with Peter Abelard, a medieval monk; the *classic theory*, popularised by Swedish theologian Gustav Aulen in his book *Christus Victor*; the *ransom theory*, popular in the early church period; the *satisfaction theory*, originating with Anselm (1033-1109). For those who wish to delve in detail into such things I would commend John Stott's magnificent book *The Cross of Christ*.[1]

However, the purpose of this book is not to look at theories of why Jesus died, but rather to let the Bible speak for itself. It is not written primarily for sceptics, but for those seeking the truth about the meaning of life and what the Bible actually says. Apart from such subjects as the nature of God and his moral governance of the world, the cross is arguably the major theme of the Bible, certainly of the New Testament, followed closely by the resurrection of Jesus and his coming return to judge the world and welcome his people. The emphasis is such that one could well say Jesus' prime purpose for coming into the world was to die. As the eminent preacher R. W. Dale put it, "While he came to preach the gospel, his chief object in coming was that there might be a gospel to preach." In symbol, metaphor, story and by direct statement, the Bible constantly illuminates the significance of this event and indicates that what Jesus did on the cross has reference to every human being.

---

1 Inter-Varsity Press, 1986, ©.

Why Did Jesus Die?

Many people have died horrible deaths, sometimes voluntarily for some great cause, or out of love for others, but Christians have always believed there was something different about the death of Jesus. This difference is due to a number of things – who it was that did the dying, why his death was necessary and what it achieved. As regards to who he was, in the booklets *Is Jesus Really God?* and *Understanding the Trinity*, I have given the biblical and historical evidence for believing that Jesus was no ordinary man but the Second Person of the divine Trinity of Father, Son and Holy Spirit, who took human flesh and blood in the womb of Mary. In other words, though Jesus' death was a very human death, the one who was doing the dying was the creator of the universe. And as theologian James Packer put it in an article in *Christianity Today*, "As his life was a divine person's totally human life, so his dying was a divine person's totally human death." As regards to why his death was necessary and what it achieved, that is what the rest of this book is all about.

In the 1993 film *In the Line of Fire*, Clint Eastwood played the part of Secret Service agent Frank Horrigan. As a young agent he was assigned to President Kennedy on that fateful day in Dallas in 1963. When the assassin fired, he froze in shock. For 30 years afterwards he wrestled with the ultimate question for a Secret Service agent: Can I take a bullet for the President? In the climax of the movie, Horrigan does what he had been unable to do earlier: he throws himself into the path of an assassin's bullet to save the chief executive.

Secret Service agents do such things because they believe the President is so valuable to the world that he is worth dying for. Obviously, they would not do it for just anyone. At Calvary, Christians believe, the situation was reversed. The President of the Universe actually took the bullet for each of us. As the Scriptures declare, he died "**for the sins of the whole world**" (1 John 2:2). That is how much he values you and me.

Introduction

The cover of a recent *Newsweek* asked the question: "Who killed Jesus?" Mel Gibson understands who. In his magnificent but gut-wrenching film *The Passion of the Christ*, which prompted the question, the hand that holds the spike being nailed through Christ's hand is that of Gibson. Rembrandt understood who. In his painting *The Raising of the Cross*, the soldier pulling it up is Rembrandt.

Professor Albert A. Trevor, in his *History of Ancient Civilisation*, says:

> In the later years of Tiberius, probably soon after A.D. 30, occurred in Judea an event unnoticed by Romans, the Crucifixion of Jesus. Yet this seemingly insignificant affair was to become the central event in future Western history and the despised Galilean was destined to triumph over all the gods and emperors of the Roman world.

Christians would go further and say that it was not only the central event in future Western history, which it indeed was, but it is the central and most important event in all of human history. Anglican scholar, Bishop Stephen Neill, put it like this:

> In the Christian theology of history, the death of Christ is the central point of history; here all the roads of the past converge; hence all the roads of the future diverge.

If you want to understand why Christians should think this way, then read on to see what that wonderful book, the Bible, has to say about it. R. V. G. Tasker, in his foreword to James Denney's classic book *The Death of Christ*,[1] says:

---

1 The Tyndale Press, 1951, ©. Quotes by Denney are all taken from this book unless otherwise stated.

The 'theology which helps us to evangelise' is the theology which recognises 'the centrality, the gravity, the inevitableness and the glory of the death of Christ', wherein the unity not only of the New Testament but also of the entire Bible is to be found. To put the emphasis anywhere else; or to use the language of the New Testament about Christ's death in a sense other than that given to it by the New Testament writers, is to debase the Christian religion and paralyse the life of the Church. On the other hand, to recognise the death of Christ for what the New Testament asserts it to be is, in Denney's view, to possess the essential clue to a proper understanding of His person, of the purpose of His incarnation, of the working out of His vocation during His earthly ministry, and of the influence He has had upon all who have accepted Him as Saviour.

Denney himself says: "The simplest truth of the gospel and the profoundest truth of theology must be put in the same words – 'He bore our sins.'" After you have read this book, you may judge for yourself whether these statements represent indeed an accurate reading of the Bible.

Soon after posting his 95 Theses on the church door at Wittenburg, Luther declared that the only person who deserved to be called a theologian was he "who comprehends the visible and manifest things of God seen through suffering and the Cross." My hope is that not only will theologians be encouraged to keep this truth central in their teaching, but that preachers will find here many useful sermon outlines for proclaiming the heart of the gospel, and those who are still searching after the truth will find their quest abundantly satisfied.

Part 1:
What the Bible says about the cross

Old Testament images of the cross

The Bible is an amazing collection of 66 books, 39 in the Old Testament and 27 in the New Testament. These books were written over a period of about 1200 years, in three different languages, in several different countries and in many different literary styles – for example, history, parable, poetry, drama, prophecy, vision, oration, epigram. However, one of a number of reasons why Christians believe that God himself was involved in the process – involving people chosen and equipped by himself for the task – is the way the whole corpus holds together. It is remarkably consistent in the way it presents the character of God and his dealing with mankind throughout history. It is consistent also in its picture of the nature of human beings, their accountability to God, their potential and their perversity.

Another way in which the Bible is consistent is in the meaning it gives to various symbols and images. The Bible often uses images, metaphors, symbols, and stories or parables to illustrate spiritual truths. It is interesting to note the number of times in the Gospels that the disciples, or others, misunderstood Jesus because they took him too literally when he was using a story or metaphor to get across a truth. Sometimes these images from the Old Testament are spoken of as "types". Douglas Moo, in *The Epistle to the Romans*, defines types as "those Old Testament persons, institutions, or events that have a divinely intended function of prefiguring."

The Old Testament is mostly the story of God's dealings with the Israelites, the descendants of Abraham, over a period of some 1500 years, as he prepared them for his personal coming into the world in the person of Jesus Christ, the second member of the divine Trinity.[1] However, there is a very real sense in which the Old Testament could be said to be God's Picture Book, a book that illustrates, often in quite vivid ways, the truths that are made more explicit in the New Testament through the coming of Christ.

Some of the most significant images given to us in the Old Testament look forward to the cross and in some way illuminate its meaning. Often these images are referred to by writers of the New Testament. It is always easy to get carried away with interpreting images. Some of the Church Fathers in the early centuries after Christ tended to do this. However, a good guide is to see how the New Testament writers interpreted them. If we believe that God had a hand in giving us the Bible, then we can expect some consistency here. So let's go exploring in the Old Testament to see what we can find.

The tree of life

The "tree of life" is mentioned a number of times in the Bible. It occurs first in the Garden of Eden (Genesis 2:9; 3:22,24). It is found in four of the pithy sayings of Proverbs (3:18; 11:30; 13:12; 15:4). It occurs again in Revelation as one of the symbols found in the Eternal City (2:7; 22:2,14). It seems obvious, in Genesis and Revelation at least, that this stands for that quality of life which we enjoy when we have a relationship with God. This was the life that humans lost when they turned from God and forfeited their fellow-

---

1 I have explored the question of why Christians believe that God is a Trinity of persons, Father, Son and Holy Spirit, and how this makes sense, in the booklet *Understanding the Trinity*.

ship with him, symbolised by being driven from the Garden and no longer having access to the tree of life (Genesis 3:22-24). In the New Testament, this life is called "eternal life" and is given as a gift when we put our faith in Jesus (e.g. Romans 6:23).

It is significant, however, that in the New Testament the cross is four times spoken of as a 'tree' (Acts 5:30; 10:39; 13:29; 1 Peter 2:24 – literal translation). This, no doubt, is related to the statement in the Old Testament that "**anyone who is hung on a pole** [or tree] **is under God's curse**" (Deuteronomy 21:23). Paul, when quoting this verse, explains that Christ bore that curse on our behalf, "**becoming a curse for us**" (Galatians 3:13). The Greek word used for "tree" in these instances is *xulon*, which is the usual word for dead wood or timber. The normal word for living wood in the New Testament is *dendron* (from which comes our word "rhododendron" – "rose tree").

When the tree of life is mentioned in the New Testament, the Greek word is always *xulon*, not *dendron*. It is the "dead tree of life". I see here a clear reference to the cross. It is Christ crucified (and risen again) who offers us life. One could well say that the "dead tree of life" is Christ himself, the one who forever bears in his risen body the scars of his suffering (John 20:20). "**God has given us eternal life, and this life is in his Son. Those who have the Son have life; those who do not have the Son of God do not have life**" (1 John 5:11,12).

The serpent's fatal wound

"**I will put enmity between you and the woman, and between your offspring and hers; he will crush your head and you will strike his heel**"(Genesis 3:15).

These words of God to the serpent at the beginning of the human story have from early times been recognised by Christians as a symbolic reference to the ongoing struggle between Satan and humans and foreshadows the means by which he will ultimately be defeated. Revelation 12:9 speaks of "**that ancient serpent called the devil, or Satan**" (cf. Isaiah 27:1). The word "Satan", in both the Hebrew and Greek, means literally "The Adversary".

The above verse from Genesis implies that it is the offspring of the woman who will eventually crush Satan's head – that is, give him his death blow. The Hebrew word for "offspring" is literally "seed" and can be taken either in the singular or plural. No doubt it could have a collective significance (as in Romans 16:20), but many would see here a reference to Christ. The personal pronoun "he" of this verse is allowed, but not required, by the Hebrew, but is used in the LXX, the first Greek translation of the third century B.C. Paul uses a similar interpretation of the word "seed" in Galatians 3:16 when referring to the Old Testament prophecy concerning the seed of Abraham.

In dealing Satan his death blow, the descendant of the woman would also suffer – "**you will strike his heel**". Interestingly, the one instance of a crucified person that has yielded to the archaeologist's spade has been the discovery in a cemetery north of Jerusalem in 1968 of a crucified male whose right heel bone was pierced medially by a nail (see Psalm 22:16; Luke 24:40).

The New Testament has little to say about the cross being a battleground between Christ and Satan in which Satan is defeated, though it is mentioned. Shortly before the event, Jesus said, "**Now is the time for judgement on this world; now the prince of this world will be driven out. And I, when I am lifted up from the earth, will draw all people to myself**" (John 12:31,32). Satan is "driven out" in the sense that he no longer has the power to keep people from being drawn to Christ. The clearest reference is Paul's statement in Colossians, "**God wiped out all the charges that were against us for disobeying the law of Moses. He took them away** and nailed them to the cross. There Christ defeated all the powers and forces. He let the world see them being led away as prisoners when he celebrated his victory" (2:14,15). Though the activities of the evil one are still too obvious in the world, the point at which he is defeated by the cross is his power over those who put their trust in the crucified and risen Saviour. In this sense the New Testament describes him as "bound" (Matthew 12:25-29; Revelation 20:2).

Another hint of this battle between Christ and evil comes in the magnificent scene in the throne-room of heaven in Revelation 5. "'Do not weep! See, the Lion of the tribe of Judah, the Root of David, has triumphed. He is able to open the scroll and its seven seals.' Then I saw a Lamb, looking as if it had been slain..." (vv. 5,6). Christ has triumphed over all the forces of evil, from whatever source. How has the Lion of Judah triumphed? He did so as the Lamb who was slain. And as this passage goes on to explain, it is "by [his] blood" that the Lamb has "purchased for God members of every tribe and language and people and nation" and "have made them to be a kingdom and priests to serve our God, and they will reign *on the earth*"[1] (vv. 9,10), thereby implying that this defeat of evil will eventually lead to the restoration of all creation.

Many would see the battle between Michael (Christ?) and Satan described in Revelation 12:7-9 as that which took place on the cross. This makes sense as it is immediately followed by the statement that "They [believers] triumphed over him by the blood of the Lamb" (v. 11). What Satan took as a great victory proved his greatest defeat, as through the cross Jesus provided the means for our total forgiveness and Satan can no longer accuse us before God (v. 10). Mel Gibson hints at this aspect of the cross, the defeat of Satan, in his film *The Passion of the Christ*.

The battle still rages, but the final outcome is assured through

---

1 Italics mine.

the death and resurrection of Jesus. Believers may begin to experience a foretaste of that victory through their trust in him. The kingdom of this world will be taken from Satan and "**become the kingdom of our Lord and his Messiah, and he will reign for ever and ever**" (Revelation 11:15).

Thorns – symbol of the curse

The result of the curse that God pronounced on the ground after Adam and Eve's disobedience was that it produced thorns (Genesis 3:17,18). There are a number of significant references to thorns in the Bible. In the Parable of the Sower it is thorns that represent the attractions of this world, those things that prevent people from hearing the word of God (Mark 4:7,18,19). Paul speaks of his illness, whatever it was, as a "**thorn in my flesh, a messenger of Satan**" (2 Corinthians 12:7).

Do we see in the "**crown of thorns**" (Matthew 27:29; Mark 15:17; John 19:2) a picture of Satan's final attempt to exert his authority over Jesus? Christ did indeed redeem "**us from the curse of the law by becoming a curse for us**" (Galatians 3:13). Because he endured the consequences of this curse, Isaiah can look forward to a glorious future when "**You will go out in joy and be led forth in peace; the mountains and hills will burst into song before you, and all the trees of the field will clap their hands. Instead of the thornbush will grow the juniper, and instead of briers the myrtle will grow**" (55:12,13).

Our nakedness covered through the shedding of blood

"The Lord God made garments of skin for Adam and his wife and clothed them" (Genesis 3:21).

Christians have often recognised here a simple illustration of the

Old Testament Images of the Cross

gospel. Adam and Eve had tried unsuccessfully to cover the shame of their nakedness with fig leaves (Genesis 3:7). God provided, at no cost to them, a better way, but a way that involved the death of the one from whom the covering came.

In a number of places in the Bible our outer garments are given as a picture of the state of our heart or our standing before God. For instance, Isaiah declares, "**All of us have become like one who is unclean, and all our righteous acts are like filthy rags**" (64:6). The prophet Zechariah describes a vision in which the high priest, Joshua, is accused by Satan. Joshua is dressed in filthy clothes. However, "**the angel of the Lord**" says, "'**Take off his filthy clothes.**' Then he said to Joshua, 'See, I have taken away your sin, and I will put fine garments on you'" (3:4).

In the New Testament, Paul describes the experience of becoming a Christian as putting "**off the old self with its practices**" and putting "**on the new self, which is being renewed in knowledge in the image of its Creator**" (Colossians 3:9,10). He says, "**clothe yourselves with the Lord Jesus Christ**" (Romans 13:14). In Revelation, believers in glory are said to be those who have "**washed their robes and made them white in the blood of the Lamb**" (7:14).

An illustration of this principle comes to us from the story of the crucifixion itself. We are told that the robe that Jesus wore was "**seamless, woven in one piece from top to bottom**" (John 19:23). Here we have a beautiful picture of the sinless perfection of the Son of God. However, when he came to the cross he shed his seamless robe as "**God made him who had no sin to be sin** [or "sin offering"] **for us**" (2 Corinthians 5:21). What happened to the robe? It was gambled for and taken home by one of the rough soldiers who had nailed Jesus to the cross – and it cost him nothing. To complete the verse above – "**God made him who had no sin to be sin for us,** *so that in him we might become the righteousness of*

Why Did Jesus Die?

God"[1] (2 Corinthians 5:21). This is the great transaction of the New Testament. He took the consequences of our sin that we might be regarded as righteous before God. Lloyd Douglas's magnificent novel *The Robe* tells the imaginary story of this garment of Jesus and the transforming effect it had on those who later possessed it.

Paul takes this illustration further still when he speaks of the new glorified body we shall receive at the resurrection as a new suit of clothes, when "**what is mortal**" will be "**swallowed up by life**" (2 Corinthians 5:1-4).

"**My soul rejoices in my God. For he has clothed me with the garments of salvation and arrayed me in a robe of his righteousness**" (Isaiah 61:10).

A God who is prepared to die

God made several great promises to Abraham: that Abraham would have a son in his old age; that his descendants would be as uncountable as the stars; that they would possess the land of Canaan and that through his "seed" all nations of the earth would be blessed (Genesis 12:1-3; 15:4-7; 22:15-18). In chapter 15 God seals his covenant with Abraham with a ceremony that was no doubt familiar to Abraham and typical of the culture of that day when two persons entered into a lasting agreement. The parties to the covenant would divide the bodies of certain animals in two and walk together between the parts, indicating by this that if either broke the covenant, then they would be prepared to suffer the same fate as the slaughtered animals. In this instance it is God alone who seals the covenant and moves between the slaughtered animals.

I can do no better here than quote theologian Miroslav Volf, from his book *Exclusion and Embrace:*

---

1 Italics mine

Abraham cut the sacrificial animals in two, and "a smoking fire pot and a flaming torch" – both symbols of theophany – passed between the halves (15:17). The unique ritual act performed by God was a pledge that God would rather "die" than break the covenant, much like the animals through which God passed died (Ratzinger 1995, 205f.; Westermann 1981, 271). The thought of a living God dying is difficult enough – as difficult as the thought of a faithful God breaking the covenant. At the foot of the cross, however, a veritable abyss opens up for the thought. For the narrative of the cross is not a self-contradictory story of a God who "died" because God broke the covenant, but a truly incredible story of God doing what God should neither have been able nor willing to do – a story of God who "died" because God's all too human *covenant partner* broke the covenant.

Frederick Buechner illustrates this truth beautifully: "Like a father saying about his sick child 'I'll do anything to make you well', God finally calls his own bluff and does it."

The Father's sacrifice

In Genesis 22 we read a story which is one of my favourite illustrations of the cross. God had kept his promise to Abraham by giving him a son, Isaac, in his old age. Abraham must have had much joy as he watched the lad grow. However, one day the Lord gives Abraham a terrible command: "**Take your son, your only son, whom you love – Isaac – and go to the region of Moriah. Sacrifice him there as a burnt offering on a mountain I will show you**" (v. 2). We can hardly imagine the struggle that must have gone on in Abraham's heart. But his trust in God is such at this point in his life that he obeys. The writer of Hebrews tells us that "**Abraham** reasoned that God could raise the dead" (Hebrews 11:19). How else could God's promise be fulfilled – "**my covenant I will establish with Isaac**" (Genesis 17:21).

A clue to the significance behind this story lies in the statement that it was to take place in the "**region of Moriah**". In 2 Chronicles 3:1 we are told that Solomon built the temple of the Lord on "Mount Moriah". So the "region of Moriah" was no doubt the area around Jerusalem. In John 8:56 Jesus makes the puzzling statement that "**Abraham rejoiced to see my day; he saw it and was glad**". In what sense did Abraham see the day of Jesus? I love a suggestion of the famous evangelist, D. L. Moody. Maybe, as Abraham stood with his knife raised in his hand, ready to slay his one and only son, God gave him a vision down the corridors of time. What he saw was a glimpse of the eternal Father offering his only Son for the sins of the human race, perhaps on that very same spot, approximately 1,800 years later.

In the story of Abraham, the son was spared and God provided a substitute, a ram. Abraham named the place "**The Lord Will Provide**" (Hebrew *Jehovah-jireh*). God's only Son (John 1:14,18; 3:16) was not spared, though in his case it was followed by the resurrection. We are the ones who deserved to be on the cross, but God has provided the perfect substitute.

As Isaac carried the wood to the place where he was going to be sacrificed (v. 6), so Jesus was compelled to carry his own cross to the place of execution (John 19:17).

This raises the interesting question as to who suffered most through the experience of the cross, God the Father or God the Son? An interesting statement occurs twice in the story of Abraham: "**The two of them went on together**" (22:6,8). The New Testament constantly emphasises that both the Father and the Son were involved in the decision that led to the cross. Jesus spoke of it as a voluntary decision on his part. "**No one takes my life from me, but I lay** it down of my own accord. I have authority to lay it down and authority to take it up again. This command I received from my Father" (John 10:18). He spoke also of his love for his friends in laying his life down for them (John 15:13,14). However, the New Testament puts much emphasis on the Father's love in sending his Son to die for us. "**God so loved the world that he gave his one and only Son…**" (John 3:16). "**God demonstrates his own love for us in this: While we were still sinners, Christ died for us**" (Romans 5:8). "**He loved us and sent his Son as an atoning sacrifice for our sins**" (1 John 4:10). Both the planning and execution of our salvation were the work of both the Father and the Son. The writer of Hebrews speaks of the involvement of the Holy Spirit as well. "**How much more, then, will the blood of Christ, who through the eternal Spirit offered himself unblemished to God, cleanse our consciences from acts that lead to death, so that we may serve the living God!**" (9:14).

Passover – safe beneath the Lamb's blood

The first 12 chapters of the book of Exodus tell the story of how God brought the children of Israel out of slavery in Egypt after ten acts of judgement on Pharaoh and his people. The last of these judgements was the most terrible of all, when the eldest son in each family died. However, God provided a means of averting the judgement for the Israelites who were prepared to trust him. Each family was to take a year-old male lamb with no defect. On the 14th day of the month, the first Israelite month of Nisan, the lamb was to be slaughtered, roasted and eaten with bitter herbs. But, before the meal, its blood was to be put on the sides and tops of the doorframes of the houses where the meals were held. When God passed over the land in judgement the homes where the blood was present would be spared. "**The blood will be a sign for you on the** houses where you are, and when I see the blood, I will pass over you. No destructive plague will touch you when I strike Egypt" (Exodus 12:13).

The Israelites were commanded to keep this ceremony as an annual memorial on the 14th Nisan, in remembrance of how God had delivered them from Egypt. This was the beginning of their nationhood. It is still kept by the Jewish people today as their major annual ceremony. Since the destruction of the temple in Jerusalem in A.D. 70, the Jewish people have not sacrificed living animals, but the shank bone of a lamb is present on the table at the Passover as a reminder of the lamb's significance.

Paul declares in 1 Corinthians 5:7, "**Our Passover lamb is Christ, who has already been sacrificed.**" We are safe from judgement when we put our trust in the one who shed his blood for us. "**There is now no condemnation for those who are in Christ Jesus**" (Romans 8:1). The fact that the lamb was to be male and without defect adds to the symbolism. Also, the first Passover was to be celebrated "**with your cloak tucked into your belt, your sandals on your feet and your staff in your hand. Eat it in haste; it is the Lord's Passover**" (Exodus 12:11). This was to be the beginning of their journey to freedom. When we commit our lives to the crucified and risen Saviour, it is the beginning, and only the beginning, of our journey to spiritual freedom. A life of living for him lies ahead. The fact that it was to be eaten in haste implies the urgency of the occasion. There is no more important decision we will make in this life than our response to Christ. Before the lamb died they could not go. After the lamb died, they could not stay.

Jesus was crucified at Passover. It seems from John's Gospel that Jesus would have been hanging on the cross at the very time the Passover lambs were being slaughtered in the temple in preparation for the evening meal (18:28). This would have meant that the Last Supper with his disciples, held the night before, was not a Passover meal. However, the other Gospels make it appear as if the Last Supper was indeed the Jewish Passover (Matthew 26:17,18). The answer may well lie in the fact that it was a meal held the day before in preparation for the Passover, or that different Jewish groups celebrated the Passover on different days, in which case the Passover could have been celebrated on both days. I believe there is some evidence for this. There is no mention of the presence of a lamb, and I like to think that it was a true Passover meal but that Jesus deliberately excluded the lamb, as he was the one to be sacrificed on this occasion.

John the Baptist had declared at the very beginning of Jesus' ministry, "**Look, the Lamb of God, who takes away the sin of the world!**" (John 1:29). Now the time of fulfilment had come when symbols would give place to reality. "**He took the cup, gave thanks and offered it to them, saying, 'Drink from it, all of you. This is *my*[1] blood of the covenant, which is poured out for many for the forgiveness of sins**" (Matthew 26:27,28). This is why Christians now celebrate the "Lord's Supper" or "Holy Communion" in place of the Passover, to commemorate our spiritual deliverance from the consequence of our sins through the Lamb of God. The description of Jesus as the Lamb surfaces again in the book of Revelation, where it is used as his title 29 times. In heaven we will always know him as the one who sacrificed himself for our sins.

Terry Virgo, in his excellent book *God's Lavish Grace,* has a very pertinent comment to make concerning the security we have in Christ when we trust in his blood shed for our sins:

> Notice incidentally that the blood was to be placed on the *outside of their houses.* The blood was for God to see, not for their benefit. The blood was not to make them feel good or feel safe.

---

[1] Italics mine.

The blood was not for their feelings at all. The blood was to satisfy God. It was for his eyes alone, just as later the blood of atonement would be offered in the Holy of Holies where no other man was present. God said, "When I see the blood I will pass over you" (Exodus 12:13). We have peace, not because we feel good, but because God is satisfied with the blood. Only he can evaluate the worth of the blood of the lamb. Because he is satisfied, we have peace.

Bitter waters made sweet

At the very first stopping place on the Israelites' journey out of Egypt, a curious event happens. The water of the place is bitter and undrinkable. The people complain. Moses prays, and the Lord shows him a piece of wood which Moses throws into the water and it becomes sweet (Exodus 15:22-25).

Maybe it is not too fanciful to see in this piece of wood a picture of "the old rugged cross". The story of a God who suffers *with* his people, sharing their most hurtful experiences, and suffers *for* them, even to the extent of bearing the consequences of their sins on a wooden cross, is a story that can bring sweetness into the most bitter of human trials. I explore this theme further, and give personal examples, in the booklet *If There Is a God, Why Is There So Much Suffering* and in the book *Life After Death: Christianity's Hope and Challenge*.

The smitten rock – God in the dock

Exodus 17 tells the story of how the Israelites arrive at Rephidim in the desert and find no water to drink. The people complain, Moses cries out to the Lord, and the Lord tells him to walk on ahead of the people with the elders and his staff in his hand. "**I will stand there**

Old Testament Images of the Cross

before you by the rock at Horeb. Strike the rock, and water will come out of it for the people to drink" (v. 6).

God is spoken of as a rock many times in the Bible (e.g. Deuteronomy 32:4; Psalm 28:1; 62:2). In using the journey of the Israelites through the wilderness as an analogy of our spiritual journey as Christians, Paul says, "**that rock was Christ**" (1 Corinthians 10:4). It was necessary that the Son of God should be smitten on our behalf before the living waters could flow. Perhaps it is appropriate to quote here the words that Jesus cried out when present on one occasion at the Jewish Feast of Tabernacles: "'**Let anyone who is thirsty come to me and drink. Whoever believes in me, as Scripture has said, streams of living water will flow from within them.' By this he meant the Spirit, whom those who believed in him were later to receive**" (John 7:37-39).

Edmund Clowney, in his book *The Unfolding Mystery*, gives a fascinating insight into this story. We read that the people "quarrelled" with Moses (Exodus 17:2). Unfortunately, the word "quarrelled" does not adequately express the Hebrew word used. It is a legal term and would be better translated "they lodged a complaint with Moses." The word is the root of *Meribah*, the name given to the place of this incident. It describes the institution of a lawsuit and is used by the prophets to express the lawsuit that God brought against Israel because they broke his covenant (e.g. Micah 6:1-8).

It is initially against Moses that the people bring their charge, for allowing them to perish in the wilderness. However, Moses points out that their real complaint is against God (v. 2). God is the Judge of all the earth, and in response to Moses' prayer he indicates that the case would be heard. Moses is to bring his staff, the symbol of his authority, and the elders are to be present as witnesses (v. 5). What follows is one of the most amazing incidents in the Bible. We would expect God to act as the judge, but in this instance God places himself in the dock and Moses is appointed as the judge. God identifies himself with the rock by standing "beside" it, though a more natural translation would be that he stands upon it. In the Psalms that commemorate this event, the name "Rock" is used for God (Psalm 78:15,20,35; 95:1,8). Moses, acting as the judge, lifts his rod. Someone found guilty of a crime in Israel could be sentenced to lie down and be beaten (Deuteronomy 25:1-3). Moses cannot strike the heart of God's shekinah glory. God commands him to strike the rock with which he is identified.

Clowney continues:

> Is God then guilty? No, it is the people who are guilty. In rebellion they have refused to trust the faithfulness of God. Yet God, the Judge, bears the judgement; He receives the blow that their rebellion deserves. The law must be satisfied: if God's people are to be spared, He must bear the punishment.

Clowney then adds a significant comment: "Before God gave His covenant at Sinai, He pledged His presence at Calvary."

There is another story that is connected to this event at Meribah. In Numbers 20, we read how the Israelites again have no water. Again they quarrel with Moses, Moses prays and once more God instructs him to stand before a rock. However, on this occasion there is an important difference. There is no suggestion that this is to be a court of law and Moses is not commanded to strike the rock, but merely to speak to it. But Moses disobeys and strikes the rock twice, and though abundant water is provided, God rebukes Moses for his disobedience and tells him that, because of it, he will not personally enter the promised land.

Why the difference from the previous account? When we turn to the New Testament, particularly the book of Hebrews, the answer becomes plain. What Jesus suffered on the cross, because of its sufficiency to deal with the problem of sin for all time, cannot, will not, nor ever needs to be, repeated. In the New Testament there is a little Greek word *hapax* or *ephapax*. It has a very definite finality to it, meaning "once for all". It is used seven times of what Jesus did "once for all" on the cross, five of these in Hebrews (Romans 6:10; Hebrews 7:27; 9:12,26,28; 10:10; 1 Peter 3:18).

The writer of Hebrews gives three reasons why this event could only happen once. First, because of who Jesus was. "**God sent his Son to bring his message to us. God created the universe by his Son, and everything will someday belong to the Son. God's Son has all the brightness of God's own glory and is like him in every way. By his own mighty word he holds the universe together**" (1:2,3). Later he explains that Jesus became human in order to be like us as well as like God. He could then become a faithful high priest on our behalf, representing us in the presence of God (2:14-18).

Second, because of what his sacrifice achieved. The animal sacrifices of the old covenant were only looking forward to the cross and could never, of themselves, take away sin. Therefore, they were continually repeated. The sacrifice of Christ, however, can "**cleanse our consciences from acts that lead to death, so that we may serve the living God!**" (9:14. See also 7:27; 9:25-28; 10:11-13).

Third, because of its eternal significance. This was confirmed by his resurrection from the dead. "**Because Jesus lives forever, he has a permanent priesthood. Therefore he is able to save completely those who come to God through him, because he always lives to intercede for them**" (7:24,25). His "once for all" sacrifice has purchased an "**eternal redemption**" and an "**eternal inheritance**" for us (9:12,15). The Rock only needed to be struck once.

It is fitting to finish here with a quote from the seventeenth century Bible Commentator, Matthew Henry:

> These [rivers of living water] flow from Christ, who is the rock

smitten by the law of Moses, for he was made under the law. Nothing will supply the needs, and satisfy the desires, of a soul, but the water out of this rock, this fountain opened. The pleasures of sense are puddle-water; spiritual delights are rock water, so pure, so clear, so refreshing – rivers of pleasure.

Animal sacrifices

The first seven chapters of the book of Leviticus describe the offerings that God prescribed for his people at Mount Sinai. These consisted of burnt offerings, fellowship offerings (traditionally "peace" offerings), grain offerings, sin offerings and guilt offerings. When a person, or group, became conscious of having broken God's law and sought forgiveness, they would bring a sheep, goat or bullock, depending on the circumstances, to the priest to offer as a sacrifice. They would place their hands on the animal's head as a sign that they were being identified with it. Though they could know nothing of the sacrifice yet to be made by the Saviour of the world, they were acknowledging in this act not only their guilt, but also that God had provided a substitute, one that would suffer the consequences of their sins in their place.

Again, it is the writer of Hebrews who spells out the prophetic and temporary nature of these ceremonies. Hebrews is steeped in Old Testament imagery. From beginning to end, by direct quotes and allusions, it explains the essential themes of the Old Testament as they are now fulfilled in the New. It may be helpful here to point out the structure of this letter. In Hebrews 1:1-3 he (or she – we don't know who wrote this letter) gives the reasons why Christ is greater than the prophets. In 1:4-2:18 he gives reasons why Christ is greater than the angels. In 3:1-4:13 he gives reasons why Christ is greater than Moses. But from 4:14 to 10:31 he shows how Christ is greater than Aaron, the first high priest of the old covenant, and fulfils in reality all those functions that were symbolised in the ministry of Aaron.

Whereas the high priest of the old covenant had to offer sacrifices for his own sins as well as for those of the people, Christ, though tempted, was without sin (4:14-5:3). Whereas the priest of the old covenant offered sacrifices repeatedly, as they could never really take away sin, Christ's one sacrifice was sufficient to do this for all time (7:26-28; 10:11-18). Whereas the priests of the old covenant were replaced because of death, Christ lives forever (7:23-25). Whereas the high priest of the old covenant could enter the central court of the tabernacle (or later the temple), the Holy of Holies, Christ **"entered heaven itself, now to appear for us in God's presence"** (9:24). God has now established a new covenant with his people and there is now **"no longer any sacrifice for sin"** other than this one (10:18,26).

Paul adds an interesting point when he indicates that Christ's sacrifice was equally sufficient for those who had faith under the old covenant as for those who came after, as God **"left the sins committed beforehand unpunished"** in anticipation of the atoning sacrifice yet to come (Romans 3:25,26 – see also chapter 4). Maybe we could liken the Old Testament sacrifices to a "cover note" such as is provided by insurers. If you insure your car, then the insurer may provide you with a cover note which is valid in case of accident until the proper document comes through.

In the different sacrifices offered, it is appropriate to see symbolism pointing to different aspects of Christ's sacrifice. The burnt offering, in which the whole animal was totally consumed on the altar, points to the totality of Christ's offering of himself for us. The fellowship or peace offering points to the one who reconciled us to fellowship with God, **"making peace through his blood, shed on the cross"** (Colossians 1:20). The sin and guilt offerings point not only to the fact that we all experience guilt as the result of our actual personal sins, but that we are "*by nature*[1] **objects of God's wrath**" (Ephesians 2:3). We have a natural bent towards self-centredness, rather than God-centredness. The cross is sufficient for both these aspects of sin. However, the writer of Hebrews does not make distinctions between the various sacrifices, but points to the atoning significance which is common to them all. They represent a divinely appointed way of dealing with sin in order that it may not bar fellowship with God, and thus all point to the cross.

A common concept used in this connection is that of "bearing sin". For instance, Aaron, the high priest, is said to "**bear the guilt involved in the sacred gifts the Israelites consecrate**" (Exodus 28:38). The scapegoat is said to "**carry on itself all their sins**" (Leviticus 16:22). Isaiah's Suffering Servant is said to "**bear their iniquities**" (53:11). It may be helpful here to quote from a sermon of Arthur T. Pierson in *A Treasury of Great Sermons on the Death of Christ*, compiled by Wilbur M. Smith:

> If we examine from Genesis to Revelation, we shall find four senses in which the words "bearing sin" are used; first representation; second identification; third substitution; and fourth satisfaction. If we take those four conceptions: representation – one standing as a representative before God; identification – one being made identical with those he represents; substitution – one substituted in the place or stead of others; and satisfaction – a furnishing of a satisfying atonement on behalf of others; we have the scope and meaning of these four words.

Christ's death for us encompasses all four meanings. He is the "**last Adam**" or "**second man**" (1 Corinthians 15:45,47) and our "**advocate**" (1 John 2:2) who acts and speaks as our *representative*. He is *identified* with us and we with him in his sacrifice. "**One**

---

1   Italics mine

died for all, and therefore all died" (2 Corinthians 5:14). Paul can declare, "**I have been crucified with Christ**" (Galatians 2:20). He is our *substitute*, taking our place before the judgement bar of God. The Greek of Mark 10:45 is literally that he gave his life as a "ransom instead of" many. And his death *satisfies* the demands of a holy God to the extent that he is now "**able to save completely those who come to God through him**" (Hebrews 7:25).

A further point worth noting is that when they brought their animals for sacrifice, the Israelites had to make sure that the animal they brought was "**without defect**" (e.g. Leviticus 4:3). David Pawson, in the series *Unlocking the Bible, vol 1,* comments on this:

> They offered to God compensation. The word atonement actually means "compensation". So if you atone for something, you offer something as compensation. Both the sin offering and the trespass [or "guilt"] offering are compensation offerings to God involving blood: as a compensation for the bad life the offerer has lived, they offer to God a good life that has never sinned.

I comment further on these Old Testament sacrifices in relation to Jesus' sacrifice in the chapter "The cross in Hebrews".

Before leaving the subject of the symbolism that is inherent in animal sacrifice, it is worth noting the way the New Testament writers, particularly Paul, apply this to our Christian discipleship. There is no sense in which any human being can offer his life for the sins that another has committed against God. Only the one who is both fully God and fully human can do it. However, those who have experienced the reconciliation that is offered through the cross can offer their lives to God in gratitude. In this sense the New Testament speaks of all Christians as priests (1 Peter 2:5,9; Revelation 1:6; 5:10). The sacrifices we offer to God out of gratitude for what he has done for us are our bodies (i.e. lives – Romans

12:1), our material gifts (Philippians 4:18) and our praise and good works (Hebrews 13:15,16). Paul can speak of the converts of his evangelistic ministry as his sacrificial offering to God (Romans 15:16), and even his martyr's death as a drink offering that is poured out on the sacrifice as was prescribed in the Old Testament (Philippians 2:17; 2 Timothy 4:6 – see Numbers 15:5).

Day of Atonement – the rent curtain

The Day of Atonement, on the tenth day of the seventh month, was one of the seven major feasts prescribed for Israel.[1] The ceremonial ritual to be performed on this day is detailed in Leviticus 16. Between the Holy Place, where the priests worshipped, and the Most Holy Place, where the presence of God was focused, was a thick curtain. No human could venture beyond this curtain, as none were fit to enter the presence of God. However, there was one exception. On the Day of Atonement the high priest was to sacrifice a bull for his own sins and a goat for the sins of the people. Taking the blood of each beyond the curtain, he sprinkled it on the cover of the ark of the covenant – the wooden box that held stones on which were inscribed the Ten Commandments. He had bells around the hem of his garment. At least the worshippers outside would be able to hear him moving around and know that he had not been struck dead in the presence of the Holy One.

Again, it is the writer of Hebrews who describes the significance of this ceremony. The presence of the curtain and the fact that none could go beyond it indicated that "**the way into the Most Holy Place had not yet been disclosed**" (9:8). The problem of the sins that prevent us from enjoying a relationship with the living God

---

[1] In the book *Life After Death: Christianity's Hope and Challenge* I have detailed the symbolic significance of each of these feasts.

had not yet been dealt with. However, at the very moment when Jesus finally gave up his spirit on the cross, "**the curtain of the temple was torn in two from top to bottom**" (Matthew 27:51). No doubt this was the result of an earthquake, which is also mentioned in this verse. Imagine the consternation of the priests in the business of preparing the Passover lambs, when, for the first time ever, they are looking into the Most Holy Place, the very presence of God. If a human had torn the curtain, the fabric would have been rent "from bottom to top". But salvation through the cross is all God's doing. There is a further point of telling significance – it was the Jewish custom for a father to rend his garment on the death of an eldest son.

In chapters 9 and 10 of Hebrews the writer enlarges further on the significance of this for you and me. Using this symbolism from the Day of Atonement, he declares, "[**Christ**] **did not enter by means of the blood of goats and calves; but he entered the Most Holy Place once for all by his own blood, having obtained eternal redemption**" (9:12). The curtain is rent forever. The way is now open for any person, whatever they might have done or been in the past, to come into the very presence of God, if they will. "**Therefore, brothers and sisters, since we have confidence to enter the Most Holy Place by the blood of Jesus, by a new and living way opened for us through the curtain, that is, his body, and since we have a great high priest over the house of God, let us draw near to God with a sincere heart in full assurance of faith, having our hearts sprinkled to cleanse us from a guilty conscience**" (10:19-22). This means, of course, that Christian conversion and becoming a follower of Jesus is not just a matter of repentance and seeking forgiveness. It involves full reconciliation and a willingness to live in that relationship every day. If that is our desire, then we are encouraged to take full advantage of the invitation and have the right, indeed obligation, to live seven days a week, 24 hours a day, enjoying fellowship with God. That is his desire, and it was made possible at tremendous cost.

The writer goes on to point out the serious consequence of rejecting the offer. "**Anyone who rejected the law of Moses died without mercy on the testimony of two or three witnesses. How much more severely do you think those deserve to be punished who have trampled the Son of God underfoot, who have treated as an unholy thing the blood of the covenant that sanctified them, and who have insulted the Spirit of grace? …It is a dreadful thing to fall into the hands of the living God**" (10:28-31). In other words, no one will be ultimately condemned because of how big a sinner they were. They will be condemned for refusing the offer of forgiveness and reconciliation.

There is one other ceremony associated with the Day of Atonement that is worthy of mention. The goat that was sacrificed by the high priest, the blood of which was sprinkled on the ark of the covenant in the Most Holy Place, was not the only goat involved. The high priest was to take a second goat, traditionally called the scapegoat, and lay his hands on its head, confessing over it all the sins of the people. This goat would then be taken into the desert where it would be set free, carrying the sins of the people with it (Leviticus 16:9,10,20-22). Though the resurrection of Christ from the dead on the third day never comes sharply into focus until it actually happened, there are a significant number of hints through the Old Testament that his death would not be the end of the story. We will look at some of these briefly later. But it is the *living* Christ, still bearing the marks of his identification with our sins in his risen body, who now offers us the benefits of his death. The same symbolism is evident in the ceremony prescribed for the cleansing of those with skin diseases, when a living bird was to be dipped in the blood of another that had previously been sacrificed and then released in the open fields (Leviticus 14:3-7).

The bronze serpent – look and live

In Numbers 21 there is a curious story that is another of my favourite images of the cross. The people complain against God and Moses: "Why have you brought us up out of Egypt to die in the wilderness? There is no bread! There is no water! And we detest this miserable food!" (v. 5). The Lord sends poisonous snakes among the people and many die. Moses prays and the Lord tells him to make a snake of bronze and put it on a pole. "**Anyone who is bitten can look at it and live**" (v. 8).

As we have seen, the snake is one of the symbols for Satan in the Bible. There is a real sense in which we have all been bitten. "**All have sinned and fall short of the glory of God**" (Romans 3:23). Consequently, we are all under the sentence of death. "**The wages of sin is death**" (Romans 6:23). However, the Lord has provided One who was himself wholly identified with our sin. On the cross "**God made him who had no sin to be sin for us**" (2 Corinthians 5:21). I don't think there is a clearer picture of this principle in the Bible than in this story in Numbers 21. Though we can never fully understand all that took place on Calvary, it seems as if, in those awful three hours when "**darkness came over all the land**" (Matthew 27:45), as God looked down on his Son, all he saw were the sins and rebellion of the human race. Now all that remains for us to do is to look with the eye of faith and live. Jesus referred to this story and specifically related it to his cross in his discussion with Nicodemus. "**Just as Moses lifted up the snake in the wilderness, so the Son of Man must be lifted up, that everyone who believes may have eternal life in him**" (John 3:14,15).

I can imagine the kind of excuses Israelites may have made for not taking advantage of the offer of healing provided by the bronze serpent. Some no doubt thought it was too simplistic or ridiculous; some perhaps thought they were not really as ill as others might be, or that they had a better cure; others may have been too lazy to journey across the camp to where the snake was erected and just hoped things would turn out all right – excuses no different from those today who reject the forgiveness offered through the gospel.

I love the story of the conversion of Charles Spurgeon, the great Baptist preacher. When he was 15, he set off on the morning of 6 January 1850 for a church service. Hindered by a violent snowstorm, he turned down a side street and ended up in a Primitive Methodist Chapel. No more that fifteen people made up the congregation. As the minister didn't appear, no doubt snowed in, "a very thin-looking man, a shoemaker or tailor", agreed to do some preaching. He took as his text Isaiah 45:22, "**Look unto me and be... saved, all the ends of the earth**" (Authorised Version). He spun out the text for ten minutes or so, emphasising the idea of looking to Christ for salvation, before running out of steam. Then he noticed Charles sitting under the gallery and, no doubt knowing him to be a stranger, fixed his eye on him and said, "Young man, you look miserable." In his autobiography, Spurgeon continued:

> Well, I did, but I had not been accustomed to have remarks made from the pulpit on my personal appearance before. However, it was a good blow, struck right home. He continued, "and you always will be miserable in life, miserable in death – if you don't obey my text; but if you obey now, this moment, you will be saved." Then lifting up his hands, he shouted, as only a Primitive Methodist could do, "Young man, look to Jesus Christ. Look! Look! Look! You have nothin' to do but to look and live." I saw at once the way of salvation. I know not what else he said – I did not take much notice of it – I was so possessed with that one thought. Like as when the brazen serpent was lifted up, the people looked and were healed, so it was with me. I had been waiting to do fifty things, but when I heard that word, "Look!"

what a charming word it seemed to me… There and then the cloud was gone, the darkness had rolled away, and that moment I saw the sun; and I could have risen that instant and sung with the most enthusiastic of them, of the precious blood of Christ, and the simple faith which looks alone to Him.

Spurgeon looked to Jesus and left the chapel a changed person, understanding the gospel. He was so joyful that when he reached home his family said, "Something wonderful has happened to you," and he was eager to tell them about it.

Two years later he became pastor to a handful of believers at Waterbeach, in Cambridgeshire. Within another five years he was the best-known minister in London, and so began a ministry that extended around the world through the printed sermons which came weekly from the press. Such was the place that he had come to occupy in people's hearts that in his last illness, "for twelve days the attention of the civilized world was centred in the testimony borne, not only to the servant of God, but to the Gospel he preached, in column after column of almost every newspaper."

Isaiah's Suffering Servant

Isaiah is one of my favourite books of the Bible as it contains so much prophecy that anticipates the coming of the Saviour. Scholars have debated endlessly about whether all the writing in the book comes from the pen of the prophet Isaiah. Whether the book has one author or more, it is such a wonderful book that I am sure the Lord had a hand in putting it all together. At the beginning of chapter 40 there is a change of theme. The last 27 chapters are written in poetic form and there is much more emphasis on the Lord's greatness and the deliverance of his people. There is also considerable emphasis on the glorious future he has prepared for his people.

Why Did Jesus Die?

This means that the book naturally falls into two sections of thirty-nine and twenty-seven chapters. It is fascinating that there are thirty-nine books in the Old Testament and twenty-seven in the New. If we take the final twenty-seven chapters of Isaiah, they can be divided naturally into three sections of nine chapters each by the phrase, "'There is no peace,' says the Lord, 'for the wicked'" (48:22; 57:21). If we take the central chapter of the central group of nine chapters, then we have Isaiah 53 which, as we shall see, focuses on the sufferings of Christ for us, the heart of the New Testament message. Whether the Bible translators in the last half of the seventeenth century knew what they were doing when they first put the Bible into chapters and verses I have no idea. But it is certainly a remarkable set of circumstances and is one of the many kinds of hints that point to a divine hand behind the writing of these books.

The author of the final section of Isaiah has four passages[1] that speak of a figure whom the Lord describes as "**my servant**" (42:1; 49:6; 52:13). He will be God's agent, "**my chosen one**" (42:1; cf. 49:7) upon whom "**I will put my Spirit**" (42:1). "**He will bring justice to the nations**" (42:1). Through him God will establish a covenant with his people, "**and a light for the Gentiles [non Jews], to open eyes that are blind, to free captives from prison and to release from the dungeon those who sit in darkness**" (42:6,7). The third of these passages mentions his unjust sufferings. When brought to trial he does not resist his accusers but depends on the Lord to vindicate him. "**I offered my back to those who beat me, my cheeks to those who pulled out my beard; I did not hide my face from mocking and spitting. ...It is the Sovereign Lord who helps me. Who will condemn me?**" (50:6,9).

However, it is in the last of these passages (52:13-53:12) that the

---

1   42:1-9; 49:1-9; 50:4-9; 52:13-53:12.

Old Testament Images of the Cross

full focus is on his sufferings – sufferings he will endure to bring forgiveness, justification and peace to his people. As this passage plays such an important part in the New Testament understanding of the sufferings of Christ, indeed, in Jesus' own understanding of his ministry, I shall spend some time looking at that influence. Biblical scholar F. F. Bruce, in *The Books and the Parchments,* said:

> There is little or no evidence that anyone attributed the sufferings [of this passage] to the Messiah before the coming of Christ… The Tradition preserved in the Targum, while it identifies the Servant with Messiah, interprets his role as that of a champion of Israel against the Gentiles. If this was the view current in the first century, we can understand how the proclamation of a suffering and crucified Messiah was a stumbling-block to the Jews.

This also helps to explain why, when Jesus talked to his disciples about his coming death, "**they did not know what he was talking about**" (Luke 18:33,34). It took the resurrection and Jesus' own explanations (Luke 24:26,27,45,46) to help them understand, though that was sufficient for them to do so very quickly!

Joachim Jeremias, in *Eucharistic Words,* stated that "No other passage from the Old Testament was as important to the Church as Isaiah 53." John Stott, in *The Cross of Christ* (pp. 145-147) gives an excellent summary of the influence of this passage in the thinking of the New Testament writers. Matthew quotes verse 4, "**he took up our pain and bore our suffering**" with reference to Jesus' healing ministry (8:17). In 1 Peter 2:22-25 Peter has echoes of verse 5, "**by his wounds we are healed**"; verse 6, "**We all, like sheep, have gone astray**"; verse 9, "**nor was any deceit in his mouth**" and verse 11, "**he will bear their iniquities**". Verses 7 and 8, about Jesus being led as a sheep to the slaughter and being deprived of justice and life, were used by Philip to tell the Ethiopian eunuch "**the good news about Jesus**" (Acts 8:30-35).

There are two other significant statements by Jesus that have echoes of this chapter. In Mark 10:45, Jesus says, "**The Son of Man did not come to be served, but to serve, and to give his life as a ransom for many**". The "Son of Man" is a figure who appears in Daniel 7:13,14. He would come "**with the clouds of heaven**". He would be given "**authority, glory and sovereign power; all peoples, nations and men of every language worshipped him**". In an interesting twist, Jesus connects this with Isaiah 53:12, "**he bore the sin of many**". Jeremias has argued that "many" here is not exclusive (many, but not all) but, in the Semitic manner of speech, inclusive (the totality, consisting of many). In other words the "many" were the godless among both Jews and Gentiles, "a (Messianic) concept unheard of in contemporary Jewish thought."

Stott adds the following comments:

> Careful students of the gospels have detected numerous references by Jesus himself, sometimes only in a single word, to Isaiah 53. For example, he said he would be 'rejected',[1] 'taken away'[2] and 'numbered with the transgressors'.[3] He would also be 'buried' like a criminal without any preparatory anointing, so that (he explained) Mary of Bethany gave him an advance anointing, 'to prepare for my burial'.[4] Other allusions may well be his description of the stronger man who 'divides up the spoils',[5] his deliberate silence before his judges,[6] his intercession

---

1 Mark 9:12; cf. 53:3.
2 Mark 2:20; cf. 53:8.
3 Luke 22:37; cf. 53:12.
4 Mark 14:8; cf. 53:9.
5 Luke 11:22; cf. 53:12.
6 Mark 14:61; 15:5; Luke 23:9 and John 19:9; cf. 53:7.

Old Testament Images of the Cross

for the transgressors[1] and his laying down his life for others.[2] If these are accepted, then every verse of the chapter except verse 2 ('he had no beauty or majesty to attract us to him') is applied to Jesus in the New Testament, some verses several times. Indeed, there is good evidence that his whole public career, from his baptism through his ministry, sufferings and death to his resurrection and ascension, is seen as a fulfilment of the pattern foretold in Isaiah 53.

One of the significant things about this passage is its emphasis on the servant's suffering on the behalf of others – wicked others at that. J. S. Whale, in *Victor and Victim,* says:

> The song makes twelve distinct and explicit statements that the servant suffers the penalty of other men's sins: not only vicarious suffering but penal substitution is the plain meaning of its fourth, fifth and sixth verses. These may not be precise statements of Western forensic ideas, but they are clearly concerned with penalty, inflicted through various forms of punishment which the Servant endured on other men's behalf and in their stead, because the Lord so ordained.

I will look at this theme further when we consider the prepositions used in the New Testament to describe Jesus' death for us and our sins.

Also significant is the language of the priestly sacrifices. In verse 10 we read that "**the Lord makes his life an offering for sin**". The word for "offering for sin" is the Hebrew *asam.* Tom Wright, in his impressive volume *Jesus and the Victory of God,* says of this word:

---

1 Luke 23:34; cf. 53:12.
2 John 10:11,15,17; cf. 53:10.

The word asam, translated in the LXX [the Greek translation of the third century BC] with peri hamartias, the regular phrase for 'sin-offering', may originally have had a wider range of meaning; by the first century we are safe in assuming that the Levitical, i.e. sacrificial, meaning would have been the first, and probably the only, meaning to be 'heard'.

As Isaiah 53 is so important to the New Testament understanding of the cross, I would like to make a few other observations before moving on. I have often wondered whether the sentence, "**He had no beauty or majesty to attract us to him, nothing in his appearance that we should desire him**" (v. 2), refers to his normal appearance which was not particularly striking, or to his appearance as a result of scourging and crucifixion. If the former is the case, it is the only reference in scripture to the human appearance of Jesus. However, the statement that comes earlier, "**Just as there were many who were appalled at him – his appearance was so disfigured beyond that of any human being and his form marred beyond human likeness – so he will sprinkle many nations, and kings will shut their mouths because of him**" (52:14) seems to refer to his sufferings immediately prior to, and on the cross. I wonder if this verse had an influence on Mel Gibson when portraying the sufferings of Jesus in *The Passion of the Christ*?

Referring to verse 1, "**Who has believed our message and to whom has the arm of the Lord been revealed?**", Arthur Wallis makes the comment in *Pray in the Spirit*, "These two questions are really one. Those who believed the report concerning Christ are those to whom Christ (the arm of the Lord) has been revealed. There is no faith without revelation."

I like the thought of Ed Marks in the magazine *Affirmation & Critique* with reference to the statement, "**He grew up before him like a tender shoot, and like a root out of dry ground**"(v. 2). He says, "His environment was 'parched ground,' but His root was in the life of His Father."

Verse 9 states that, "**He was assigned a grave with the wicked, and with the rich in his death**". Jesus was buried in the tomb of a rich man, Joseph of Arimathea. However, the New English Bible renders this as, "**He was assigned a grave with the wicked, a burial-place among the refuse of mankind**". F. F. Bruce comments in *The Books and the Parchments*, "[This] depends... on deriving the Hebrew word translated 'the rich' in the A.V. from another Semitic root which yields a meaning which fits the poetic parallelism better."

The final statement, "**Therefore I will give him a portion among the great, and he will divide the spoils with the strong, because he poured out his life unto death, and was numbered with the transgressors**" (v. 12), clearly seems to anticipate the resurrection and ascension of Jesus.

In *Jesus and the Victory of God* Tom Wright sums up the reasons for identifying Jesus with the "servant" of Isaiah as follows:

1) Jesus announces and enacts the kingdom of YHWH [the Hebrew letters for God], doing and saying things which dovetail very closely with the message of Isaiah 40-55 as a whole.
2) The kingdom-programme of Isaiah 40-55 as a whole is put into effect through the work of the servant, specifically his redemptive suffering.
3) Jesus acts symbolically as though he intends to put his kingdom-programme into effect through his sharing of Israel's suffering, and speaks as if that is indeed what he intends.
4) One of the relevant sayings quotes Isaiah 53 directly [Luke 22:37], and others can most easily be explained as an allusion to it.

5) It is therefore highly probable that, in addition to several other passages which informed his vocation, Jesus regarded Isaiah 53, in its whole literary and historical context, as determinative.
6) Jesus therefore intended not only to share Israel's sufferings, but also to do so as the key action in the divinely appointed plan of redemption for Israel and the world.

Before leaving Isaiah altogether, though it is not directly relevant to our theme, there is one other thing I would like to share. I love to point out to people that in Isaiah 41:10 the Lord says, "**So do not fear, for I am with you… I will uphold you with *my*[1] righteous right hand.**" In 41:13 he is the Lord who "**takes hold of *your*[2] right hand and says to you, Do not fear**". In 49:16 he says, "**I have engraved you on the palms of my hands**". In 51:16 he says, "**I have… covered you with the shadow of my hand**". In 52:12 he says, "**The Lord will go before you, the God of Israel will be your rear guard.**" As someone has said, if you are engraved on the palms of his hands, and you are covered in the shadow of his hand, then you have no business sticking your head out! I love the story of the village lady who was always praising God as she went about her work. One day she was challenged by the village atheist, who said, "One day, Sarah, you will slip through his fingers and then you won't be praising him any more." She replied, "Bless you. I could never slip through his fingers. You see, I am one of his fingers. Praise the Lord!"

The Psalms

Christianity shared with Judaism the conviction that many of the

---

1 Italics mine.
2 Italic mine.

Old Testament Images of the Cross

Psalms are Messianic – that is, they look forward to the coming of the Christ, God's Anointed One. About 15 of the Psalms are quoted in the New Testament with reference to Christ. The following are some examples:

His manhood: Psalm 8:4,5; Hebrews 2:6-8.
His Sonship: Psalm 2:7; Acts 13:33; Hebrews 1:5; 5:5.
His character: Psalm 45:6,7; Hebrews 1:8,9.
His zeal: Psalm 69:9; John 2:17.
His obedience: Psalm 40:6-8; Hebrew 10:5-7.
His sufferings: Psalm 69:9; Romans 15:3.
His betrayal: Psalm 41:9; John 13:18.
His crucifixion: Psalm 22; The Gospels (see below).
His resurrection: Psalm 16:8-11; Acts 2:25-28; 13:35.
His ascension: Psalm 68:18; Ephesians 4:8.
His exaltation: Psalm 110:1; Matthew 22:43,44; Acts 2:34,35; Hebrews 1:13.
His priesthood: Psalm 110:4; Hebrews 5:6; 7:17,21.
His conquests: Psalm 110:5,6; Revelation 6:15-17.
His eternity: Psalm 102:25-27; Hebrews 1:10-12.
His coming to judge the world: Psalms 96:13; 98:9 – not directly quoted, but spelled out in such passages as 2 Thessalonians 1:7-10.

The writers of the book of Acts and the letters of the New Testament, as well as Jesus himself, all look back to the Psalms in particular when seeking to explain or interpret the sufferings and the cross of Christ. In this respect I could not do better than quote from Derek Kidner in the first of his two books on the Psalms in the *Tyndale Old Testament Commentaries*[1] series:

---

1 *Psalms 1-72,* Inter-Varsity Press, Illinois, 1973, ©.

Most of our Lord's references to the psalms are in fact to this element in them; indeed the tragic Psalm 69 is the New Testament's largest quarry of quotations and allusions to Christ in the whole collection, six or seven different verses or phrases being drawn from it to interpret His cross and passion. From this psalm and its companions (notably 22, 35, 40, 41, 109, 118) the Gospels, Acts and Epistles find their most telling words to highlight such matters as His reforming zeal (69:9a), His deliberate self-offering (40:6-8), His experience of isolation (69:8), betrayal, hatred and rejection (41:9; 69:4; 35:19; 118:22), His suffering of reproach (69:9b), mockery (22:7f.; 69:21), stripping (22:18) and, it may be, nailing (22:16). They treat many of these explicitly as prophecy fulfilled; indeed Peter tells us that in Psalm 16 David, "being a prophet... foresaw and spoke of the resurrection of the Christ" (Acts 2:30ff.). In Acts 1:16-20 and Romans 11:9f. the apostles also show us predictions of the fate of Judas (109:8; cf. 69:25) and of unbelieving Israel (69:22ff.). Jesus himself on the cross, found words in the psalms for His darkest hour and for his last breath (22:1; 31:5).

No doubt Jesus would have turned to some of these references, when, in his appearance to his disciples on the day of his resurrection, he said, "'**This is what I told you while I was still with you: Everything must be fulfilled that is written about me in the Law of Moses, and Prophets and the Psalms.' Then he opened their minds so they could understand the Scriptures. He told them, 'This is what is written: The Christ will suffer and rise from the dead on the third day, and repentance and forgiveness of sins will be preached in his name to all nations, beginning at Jerusalem'**" (Luke 24:44-47 – see also verse 27).

Before leaving the Psalms, it is worth having a look at Psalm 22. This Psalm was written several hundred years before crucifixion

Old Testament Images of the Cross

was thought of, yet it would be hard to find a more realistic, poetic description of someone being crucified. It was to this psalm that Jesus turned in the moment of his greatest need, quoting the first verse, "**My God, my God, why have you forsaken me**" (see Matthew 27:46; Mark 15:34). The words "**I cry out by day, but you do not answer, by night, but I find no rest**" (v. 2), with a little imagination, could illustrate the alternate periods of light and darkness experienced by one undergoing such intense agony. The sentences "**I am a worm, not a human being, scorned by everyone, despised by the people**" (v. 6), "**all my bones are out of joint**" (v. 14) and "**All my bones are on display; people stare and gloat over me**" (v. 17) underline the shame of a man exposed naked (which I presume Jesus was) and writhing in pain on a wooden cross. The words "**'He trusts in the Lord,' they say, 'let the Lord rescue him. Let him deliver him, since he delights in him'**" (v. 8) echo the very words spoken in mockery by the chief priests and Jewish elders (Matthew 27:41-43). The sentence "**From birth I was cast upon you; from my mother's womb you have been my God**" (v. 10) could only have been spoken honestly by the sinless Son of God. The expressions "**I am poured out like water**" (v. 14) and "**my tongue sticks to the roof of my mouth**" (v. 15) speak of the profuse sweating and intense thirst of one exposed to the midday sun. The statement "**They divide my clothes among them and cast lots for my garment**" (v. 18) is quoted by John as being literally fulfilled (19:23,24). "**They pierce my hands and my feet**" (v. 16) was also literally fulfilled (Luke 24:39; John 20:27).

It is significant that from verse 22 of this psalm the theme changes and anticipates the resurrection. Verse 22, "**I will declare your name to my people** (or "brethren" – Hebrew *'ach*); **in the assembly I will praise you**" is quoted by the writer of Hebrews (2:12) as words spoken by Jesus himself with reference to the fact that he shared our human nature. If we accept the reconciliation provided by his death on our behalf, then he delights to call us "brothers and sisters". Verse 24, "**he has not despised or scorned the suffering of the afflicted one; he has not hidden his face from him but has listened to his cry for help**", was demonstrated to be true by his being raised from the dead by his Father on the third day. Verse 27, "**All the ends of the earth will remember and turn to the Lord, and all the families of the nations will bow down before him**", anticipates his universal authority and the spread of the gospel to the ends of the earth. The words "**all who go down to the dust will kneel before him – those who cannot keep themselves alive**" (v. 29) give us the hint that he will be the one appointed to judge the living and the dead. The final statement of the psalm, "**future generations will be told about the Lord. They will proclaim his righteousness, declaring to a people yet unborn: He has done it**" (vv. 30,31), looks forward to future generations of his people telling what he has accomplished by his death and resurrection. The Gelineau translation entitles this psalm "The suffering servant wins the deliverance of the nations."

Death leading to resurrection

In the New Testament the believer is often spoken of as being identified with his Lord in his death and resurrection. For instance, Paul speaks of the ceremony of baptism as being "**buried into his death**" (Romans 6:3). It is the burial of our old self-centred life, in order that "**just as Christ was raised from the dead through the glory of the Father, we too may live a new life**" (Romans 6:4). In making this truth a reality in our experience we are told that those who want to be disciples of Christ must "**deny themselves and take up their cross and follow [him]**" (Matthew 16:24; cf. Luke 14:27). In those days a person only "took up their cross" to die on it. Jesus is here speaking of that commitment in which we choose to live unreservedly for him, rather than for our own selfish ends. This "death" to our own selfish goals is presented as one of the key secrets of living a fruitful life for God. Paul goes into further detail about this in Romans 6. We are to "**count ourselves dead to sin but alive to God in Christ Jesus**" (v. 11). It is as our commitment to Christ deepens that we begin to experience more of the touch of his risen life. Paul was willing to suffer for his devotion to Christ because he found that in doing so he experienced more of that power and entered into a deeper relationship with his Lord. He puts it like this, "**I want to know Christ and the power of his resurrection and the fellowship of sharing his sufferings, becoming like him in his death…**" (Philippians 3:10).

This truth of death resulting in life is beautifully illustrated in a number of places in the Old Testament. The clue to finding them is to look for the phrase "the third day", which often points to the resurrection. The following are the three most vivid examples.

1) The "promised land" of Canaan has often been presented in Christian literature as a picture of heaven, to which we are all journeying through the barren desert of this life. Take for example the words of a popular hymn:

When I tread the verge of Jordan,
bid my anxious fears subside:
Death of death, and hell's destruction,
land me safe on Canaan's side.

However, this is to miss the main point. Canaan in the Bible is a picture of our present life in Christ as it is meant to be lived. It was a "**good land – a land with streams and pools of water, with springs flowing in the valleys and hills; a land with wheat and barley, vines and fig trees, pomegranates, olive oil and honey; a land where bread will not be scarce and you will lack nothing; a land** where the rocks are iron and you can dig copper out of the hills" (Deuteronomy 8:7-9). In other words, a land of abundant refreshment and provision for every need. It was also a land "**that drinks rain from heaven… a land the Lord your God cares for; the eyes of the Lord your God are continually on it from the beginning of the year to its end**". It did not have to be "**irrigated by foot**" which required hard work on the treadmill to bring water up from the Nile, an experience they had endured in Egypt (Deuteronomy 11:10-12). This is the life Jesus was talking about when he declared, "**I have come that they may have life, and have it to the full**" (John 10:10). So Canaan represents that life of faith where I trust in the one who cares for me and where I have learned to "drink of the rain from heaven". There are still battles to be fought, as was the case with the Israelites in the promised land, but I am learning the secret of victory.

However, to enter this land the Israelites had to cross the Jordan. They had already left Egypt, a picture in the Bible of the life lived in this world without God. They had crossed the Red Sea, which symbolises our baptism and union with Christ (see 1 Corinthians 10:1-4). They had experienced God's guidance and provision on their journey through the wilderness. But now they were faced with a deeper experience of God's love and power. Jordan does symbolise our death – not physical death, but that which we have been looking at above, our unreserved commitment to Christ, the taking up of our cross to follow him.

It is significant that, after 40 years wandering around in the wilderness, it was in "**three days**" that the Israelites were to cross Jordan and possess the promised land (Joshua 1:11). The ark, carried by the priests and symbolising God's presence with his people, made the journey first (3:3,6), as Jesus has done for us. When the priests placed their feet in the water, the river immediately stopped flowing, possibly the result of an earthquake temporarily blocking the river as has happened several times in Jordan's history. They went through on dry ground and were immediately in the new land. As we take our stand with Christ, whatever this may involve, we begin to experience something of the touch of his risen life. This may happen through a crisis experience or as a gradually deepening understanding.

2) A second beautiful illustration of this principle is given in the book of Esther. In order to save her people, Esther tells her cousin Mordecai, who had brought her up, to gather the Jews to pray and fast for her for "**three days**" (Esther 4:16). At the end of that time she would go into the presence of King Xerxes to plead for her life and the life of her people. Anyone who went into the king's presence uninvited would automatically come under the sentence of death, unless the king should hold out his golden sceptre. On the third day she goes into the king's presence. He holds out the golden sceptre and she is, as it were, raised to life. The result is salvation for her people.

3) A third example is the story of the prophet Jonah, which Jesus himself spoke of as an illustration of his death and resurrection (Matthew 12:40). Jonah gets himself and others into trouble by his disobedience to the Lord. The ship they are on is in danger of sinking. Jonah confesses his sins and puts himself in the place of death by offering to be thrown overboard. He is swallowed by the whale and after "**three days and three nights**" (Jonah 1:17) is vomited onto dry land. Not only are the other sailors converted (1:16), but the city of Nineveh repents and is spared judgement (chapter 3).

George Mueller was a wonderful man of faith who fed and clothed 3,000 children in the orphanages he built in Bristol during the latter part of the nineteenth century. He also gave away thousands of pounds for Christian work – money he had received in answer to prayer. It is recorded that when someone asked the secret of his service, he replied, "There was a day when I died."

As he spoke, he bent lower, until he almost touched the floor. He continued, "Died to George Mueller, his opinions, preferences, tastes and will; died to the world, its approval or censure; died to the approval or blame even of my brethren or friends; and since then I have studied only to show myself approved unto God."

For other examples of illustrations of the resurrection where "third day" is mentioned, see:

Genesis 1:9-13: resurrection, the secret of a fruitful life.
Exodus 5:3: resurrection, the place where the journey begins.
Numbers 10:33: Jesus went before to find a resting place for us.
Hosea 6:2: where we find spiritual healing and his living presence.

The cross in the Gospels

Emphasis on the passion and cross in the Gospels

In most biographies, the death of the person concerned is a mere incident at the close of the book. In Hay's life of Abraham Lincoln there are 5,000 pages, but only 25 are devoted to the dramatic account of his assassination and death. There is certainly much of dramatic interest in the passion and death of Jesus, but when we look at the space given to these events in the Gospel writings, what do we find?

All the Gospels declare that Jesus was crucified during the Jewish feast of Passover. John adds the information that Jesus had experienced at least two previous Passovers (John 2:13; 6:4). This, together with other clues, indicates that his public ministry lasted something like two to three years. Matthew's Gospel has 28 chapters. In Matthew 21 Jesus rides into Jerusalem on the Sunday before he is crucified. That means that a quarter of Matthew's Gospel deals with the final six days of Jesus' life. An additional chapter deals with his resurrection. Mark has 16 chapters. In Mark 11 Jesus rides into Jerusalem. That means that about one-third of Mark's Gospel deals with that same period.

Luke's Gospel is a little different. Luke has 24 chapters. He gives two chapters to Jesus' conception, birth and childhood, followed by one on the ministry of John the Baptist. Then he gives six chapters to Jesus' public ministry, chiefly in Galilee. At the end of chapter 9

Jesus begins his last journey up to Jerusalem. This means that of the 24 chapters, 15 deal with the final few months of his time on earth, six of these dealing with the final few days and the resurrection.

John's Gospel is the most significant of all in this regard. John has 21 chapters. Half-way through the Gospel, in chapter 12, Jesus arrives in Bethany for that final week. By chapter 13 we have already got to his final meal with his disciples, the night before his crucifixion. Chapters 13 to 18 tell us about the events of that fateful night. Chapter 19 deals with the conclusion of his trial and crucifixion, and chapters 20 and 21 tell of his resurrection. This means that almost half of the Gospel is about the last 24 hours of his life, together with his resurrection.

In addition to the space the Gospels give to this segment of Jesus' life on earth, they describe his sufferings and death with a detail that has no parallel in their account of other events of his life and ministry.

Whatever we make of this, it clearly demonstrates that the events surrounding the cross were of the utmost importance to those who recorded these events. The German scholar, M. Kahler, rightly described these writing as "Passion Gospels with extended introductions".

Hints and references to the cross before its occurrence

There are a good number of hints and also clear statements in the four Gospels, before the event happened, to the effect that Jesus' public ministry would end at the cross. Probably the most helpful thing I can do here is to list them in the chronological order in which they occurred, as well as that can be determined. I shall add a few of my own comments. Something like thirty of these statements come from the lips of Jesus himself. You will note that when Jesus is talking about himself, he commonly calls himself "the Son of Man". It is generally understood, I believe rightly so, that Jesus is identifying himself with a figure so named who appears in the book of Daniel. "In my vision at night I looked, and there before me was one like a son of man, coming with the clouds of heaven. He approached the Ancient of Days and was led into his presence. He was given authority, glory and sovereign power; all nations and peoples of every language worshipped him. His dominion is an everlasting dominion that will not pass away, and his kingdom is one that will never be destroyed" (Daniel 7:13,14). It is debated as to whether some in the Judaism of Jesus' day interpreted this "son of man" as referring to a coming messianic individual, but Jesus clearly related this passage to himself when challenged by the high priest to tell them if he was indeed the Messiah (Matthew 26:64; Mark 14:62).

It is very significant that the first clue as to the chief purpose of his sending Jesus into this world is given to us before his birth by God himself in his appearance to Joseph in a dream. "**You are to give him the name Jesus, because he will save his people from their sins**" (Matthew 1:21). "Saving us from our sins" is always associated in the New Testament with what he achieved by his death.

When the angels appeared to the shepherds to announce the birth of Jesus, they described two "signs" by which they would recognise him: he would be "**wrapped in cloths and lying in a manger**" (Luke 2:12). Why were these two signs chosen? Could it be because the cloths would be similar to those wrapped around a body for burial? And if Jesus is indeed the "Lamb of God", sacrificed for us, then where better place to find him than in an animal's feed box! The lambs these shepherds were caring for would have been destined for sacrifice in the temple, as were all those for several miles around Jerusalem. This was a despised profession, but it was to them that the announcement was first made.

Why Did Jesus Die?

Thirty-three days after Jesus' birth, his parents took him to the temple in Jerusalem to perform the prescribed purification ceremony (Leviticus 12). The aged Simeon recognised him as the promised Messiah and gave Mary a hint of what was to come in his words, "**a sword will pierce your own soul too**" (Luke 2:35).

Maybe we have a symbolic hint of what was to come in the offering of myrrh by the wise men when they visit Jesus before his flight to Egypt. The only other places it is mention in the New Testament are when it was offered to him before his crucifixion to deaden the pain (which he refused – Mark 15:23), and its use by Joseph and Nicodemus to anoint his body (John 19:39).

Jesus began his public ministry with his baptism by John in the River Jordan. On this occasion God spoke from heaven with the words, "**This is my Son, whom I love; with him I am well pleased**" (Matthew 3:17; Mark 1:11; Luke 3:22). The first phrase in this sentence echoes the words in Psalm 2:7, "**You are my Son**", which was widely recognised as a Messianic Psalm, looking forward to the coming king. The words, "**my Son, whom I love**" echo the phrase from Isaiah 42:1, "**my chosen one in whom I delight**". This is one of the Suffering Servant passages in Isaiah that I have described above, and if Jesus had not been clear in his own mind up to this point that his destiny would be that of this "servant of the Lord", he certainly would have been from then on. Maybe this is one of the ways in which we can interpret the significance of the temptations he faced in the wilderness immediately following his baptism, as he was severely pressed to take any other way for achieving his purpose than the cross (Matthew 4:1-11). Denney comments on these words spoken by God at his baptism:

> There could be no truer index to His life than a combination of Psalm 2:7 with Isaiah 42:1ff – the Son of God as King, and the Servant of the Lord: and this combination… dates from the

high hour in which Jesus entered on His public work and is not an afterbirth of disappointing experiences.

It was right at the beginning of Jesus' public ministry that John the Baptist pointed him out as "**the Lamb of God, who takes away the sins of the world**" (John 1:29).

Jesus chose to identify himself with the person described in Isaiah 61 when announcing the nature of his mission at the beginning of his public ministry. "**The Spirit of the Lord is on me, because he has anointed me to proclaim good news to the poor**" (Luke 4:16-21 – see Isaiah 61:1,2). Though this is not one of the "Suffering Servant" passages we have described above, it comes from the same part of the Book of Isaiah. This incident reveals Jesus was fully aware that Isaiah 61 referred to his ministry. It is extremely unlikely that, after 30 years of studying the Scriptures and preparing for ministry, Jesus was unaware that Isaiah 53 did also. In claiming to be the fulfilment of Isaiah 61, he was daring to claim to be the fulfilment of all Messianic prophecy.

In one of his disputes with Jewish leaders concerning his actions in the temple, Jesus declared, "**Destroy this temple, and I will raise it again in three days**". John adds the comment, "**The temple he had spoken of was his body**" (John 2:19-21). This saying was quoted in evidence against him at his trial (Matthew 26:61).

In his conversation with Nicodemus, Jesus said, "**Just as Moses lifted up the snake in the wilderness, so the Son of Man must be lifted up, that everyone who believes may have eternal life in him. For God so loved the world that he gave his one and only Son, that everyone who believes in him shall not perish but have eternal life**" (John 3:14-16). It is possible that the second of these sentences is the comment of John rather than the words of Jesus.

John also records two other incidents, later in Jesus' ministry, in which he spoke of being "lifted up". Both occasions were in

Why Did Jesus Die?

disputes with Jewish leaders. These are obvious references to his coming crucifixion, which was then not far off. "**When you have lifted up the Son of man, you will know who I am. You will also know that I don't do anything on my own. I say only what my Father taught me... I always do what pleases him**" (8:28,29). "**I, when I am lifted up from the earth, will draw all people to myself**" (12:32). It is possible that the idea of being lifted up also includes the thought of his exultation in glory. However, where it is spoken of as the action of the Jews (8:28) and compared to the elevation of the brazen serpent on a pole, as in 3:15, the allusion to the cross is unmistakable. And John, in 12:33, specifically adds, "**He said this to show the kind of death he was going to die.**" There is an exact parallel in Ezra 6:11, where King Cyrus of Persia declares that anyone who alters his edict is to be "lifted up" and impaled on a beam from his house. Alan E. Lewis has a significant point to make on this "lifting up" in his book *Between Cross and Resurrection*:

> Long before his death, the Johannine Christ [i.e. Christ as described in the Gospel of John] had spoken, with the most powerful of double meanings, of a "lifting up" in which his physically painful and degrading suspension from a gallows would constitute exaltation and acclamation, the vanquishing of darkness and the manifestation of light. As John Marsh [in *Saint John*] points out, "It cannot be too strongly emphasised that for John the cross is the instrument and point of victory, not the point of defeat which has to be reversed on Easter morning. Here, as the Lord dies, he conquers."

It is significant that the Greek of 8:28 is simply "you will know that I am", with the "I" emphasised (*ego eimi*). This appears to be an allusion to the name of God that he gives to Moses in Exodus 3:14. It is the cross that reveals, as nothing else does, who he really is.

I will explore this further in Part 2 under the heading "The cross and the Trinity".

When Jesus said that when lifted up he would "**draw all people to [himself]**" (12:32), I believe he did not mean all people without exception, for there are many who refuse to be drawn to him. He meant rather all people without distinction, whether it be of class, race, colour, gender or anything else.

Matthew specifically quotes from Isaiah 53, which we have described above in connection with the cross, when referring to the foretelling of Jesus' healing ministry. "**This was to fulfil what was spoken through the prophet Isaiah; 'He took up our infirmities and bore our diseases'**" (Matthew 8:17 – see Isaiah 53:4).

When questioned about why his disciples did not fast as John the Baptist's did, Jesus replied, "**How can the guests of the bridegroom mourn while he is with them? The time will come when the bridegroom will be taken from them; then they will fast**" (Matthew 9:15; Mark 2:19,20; Luke 5:34,35).

In describing Jesus' humility and avoidance of unnecessary publicity, Matthew quotes from another of Isaiah's "Suffering Servant" passages, "**Here is my servant whom I have chosen, the one I love, in whom I delight; I will put my Spirit on him... He will not quarrel or cry out; no one will hear his voice in the streets. A bruised reed he will not break, and a smoldering wick he will not snuff out, till he leads justice to victory**" (Matthew 12:18-21 – see Isaiah 42:1-4).

In a dispute with the Pharisees and teachers of the law, Jesus foretold, "**As Jonah was three days and three nights in the belly of a huge fish, so the Son of Man will be three days and three nights in the heart of the earth**" (Matthew 12:40).

John describes a lengthy discussion that Jesus had with Jewish leaders in which he claimed to be the "**bread of life**" who could satisfy our deepest needs, give eternal life to people and raise them up on the last day (6:25-59). In metaphorical images he spoke of the need to personally make our own the benefits of his death. "This bread is my flesh, which I will give for the life of the world. …Very truly I tell you, unless you eat the flesh of the Son of man and drink his blood, you have no life in you. Whoever eats my flesh and drinks my blood has eternal life, and I will raise them up at the last day. For my flesh is real food and my blood is real drink. Whoever eats my flesh and drinks my blood remains in me, and I in them" (6:51-56). He precludes all possibility of religious materialism in the understanding of these words by going on to declare: "The Spirit gives life; the flesh counts for nothing. The words that I have spoken to you – they are full of the Spirit and life" (v. 63).

In his role as the Good Shepherd of his people, Jesus indicated that he would give his life for them. This would be a purely voluntary offering. "I am the good shepherd. The good shepherd lays down his life for the sheep. …I know my sheep and my sheep know me… and I lay down my life for the sheep. I have other sheep that are not of this sheep pen. I must bring them also. …There shall be one flock and one shepherd. The reason my Father loves me is that I lay down my life – only to take it up again. No one takes it from me, but I lay it down of my own accord. I have authority to lay it down and authority to take it up again. This command I received from my Father" (John 10:11-18). Denney comments:

> Christ's death is not an incident of his life, it is the aim of his life. The laying down of his life is not an accident in his career, but his vocation; in it the divine purpose of his life is revealed.

The references to his "**other sheep**" and the "**one flock**" indicate that he saw his cross having an effect far wider than just the Jewish nation and that he would unite in one family those who would "follow him".

Jesus did not talk clearly to his disciples about his coming cross until they had come to the point where they were prepared to publicly acknowledge to him that they truly believed he was the promised Messiah. This happened at Caesarea Philippi in northern Galilee, before his final journey to Jerusalem, where he put them on the spot and asked them directly who they thought he was. After Peter's acknowledgement that **"You are the Christ, the Son of the living God"** (Matthew 16:16) the record informs us that **"From that time on Jesus began to explain to his disciples that he must go to Jerusalem and suffer many things at the hands of the elders, chief priests and teachers of the law, and that he must be killed and on the third day be raised to life"** (v. 21 – see also Mark 8:31; Luke 9:22). Notice here the little word "must" (Greek *dei*). There is an inevitability or compulsion about it. He used this word also in his declaration that he **"must be lifted up"** if those who believe are to receive eternal life (John 3:14). It is a continuing theme in Luke's Gospel (13:33; 17:25; 22:37; 24:7,44). In the total context of his teaching it is plain that the necessity evident in the word "must" did not arise from the fact of outward circumstances, nor that the forces arrayed against him were so strong that his death at their hands was inevitable, but it was the "must" of inner compulsion. His suffering and death were necessary if he was to fulfil the mission his Father had given him. As Denney comments:

> When he unfolds Messiahship it contains death. This was the first and last thing he taught about it, the first and last thing He wished His disciples to learn.

Jesus added on this occasion that they, too, must be prepared to **"take up their cross and follow [him]"** (v. 24 – also Mark 8:34; Luke 9:23). This was a challenge he repeated later, on their way to Jerusalem, as a condition of discipleship (Luke 14:27). This statement would have been meaningless unless he had been thinking in terms of crucifixion as the means by which he would die. In those days one took up a cross for one reason only, to die on it. That Jesus was speaking metaphorically, in terms of death to selfish desires rather than necessarily physical death (though it *may* mean that for some), is plain by that fact that in Luke's account the expression "daily" is added. **"Those who would be my disciples must deny themselves and take up their cross daily and follow me"** (Luke 9:23).

A week after this, the event known as "the transfiguration" occurred. Peter, James and John saw Jesus in glowing garments speaking with Moses and Elijah. Luke gives us an insight into what they were talking about. **"They spoke about his departure, which he was about to bring to fulfilment at Jerusalem"** (Luke 9:31). No doubt this dramatic event was to prepare both Jesus and his inner circle for what lay ahead. At this point, however, the disciples did not have a clue as to what he was talking about. Crucifixion figured nowhere in their conception of the mission of the promised Messiah.

As they came down the mountain where the transfiguration occurred, Jesus told them, **"Don't tell anyone what you have seen, until the Son of Man has been raised from the dead"** (Matthew 17:9). They then asked him a question about a prophecy concerning Elijah, which Jesus answered by declaring that it had been fulfilled in the ministry of John the Baptist. He then said, **"In the same way the Son of Man is going to suffer at their hands"** (v. 12 – see also Mark 9:12).

Shortly after this, **"When they came together in Galilee, he said to them, 'The Son of Man is going to be delivered over to human hands. He will be killed, and on the third day he will be raised to life.' And the disciples were filled with grief"** (Matthew 17:22,23; Mark 9:30,31). Luke adds, "But they did not understand what this meant. It was hidden from them, so that they did not grasp it, and they were afraid to ask him about it" (Luke 9:45 – cf. Mark 9:32).

Matthew records a discussion between Peter and Jesus that may well contain an oblique reference to the cross. Peter asks him "**Lord, how many times shall I forgive someone who sins against me? Up to seven times?**" Jesus replies, "**I tell you, not seven times, but seventy-seven times** (or possibly 'seventy times seven')". Tom Wright, in *Evil and the Justice of God,* has an interesting comment on this statement:

> Notice the symbolic depth of what Jesus is asking for. 'Shall I forgive my brother seven times?' asks Peter. 'No,' says Jesus, 'not seven times, but seventy times seven.' For any first-century Jew who knew the scriptures, the echo would be clear. Daniel in chapter 9, asks the angel how long the exile in Babylon will go on for. Will it not be seventy years, as Jeremiah had foretold (9:2)? No, says the angel; not seventy years, but seventy times seven (9:24). This is how long it will take – note this – 'to finish the transgression, to put an end to sin, and to atone for iniquity; to bring in everlasting righteousness'. The exile in Babylon was the result of Israel's sin; God has dealt not only with the exiled state of his people but with the root causes in their own wickedness. What Jesus is saying is that the new age is here, the age of forgiveness, and that his people are to embody it.

A further link with the cross in Daniel 9 occurs in verse 26 where we read, "**the Anointed One will be put to death**".

Though not related directly to the cross, it is worth noting Wright's further comment on "seventy times seven":

> Behind this, again, lies the Jubilee commandment in Leviticus: when seven is multiplied by seven, debts must be forgiven. It

is not clear just how thoroughly this was kept at any period in ancient Israel, but it forms a clear, and to us deeply counter-cultural boundary-marker within the divinely ordered social and economic life of God's people. It is one of those commands which the church has cheerfully ignored for long years and is only now rediscovering, in the light of the massive economic inequity in today's world.

Luke tells us that "**As the time approached for him to be taken up to heaven, Jesus resolutely set out for Jerusalem**" (9:51). Mark writes, "**They were on their way up to Jerusalem, with Jesus leading the way, and the disciples were astonished, while those who followed were afraid. Again he took the Twelve aside and told them what was going to happen to him. 'We are going up to Jerusalem,' he said, 'and the Son of Man will be delivered over to the chief priests and teachers of the law. They will condemn him to death and will hand him over to the Gentiles, who will mock him and spit on him, flog him and kill him. Three days later he will rise'**" (Mark 10:32-34 – see Matthew 20:17-19; Luke 18:31-33). On this occasion, Luke tells us again that "**The disciples did not understand any of this. Its meaning was hidden from them, and they did not know what he was talking about**" (v. 34). It is interesting that, though he had explained this so many times, the angels who appeared at his tomb after his resurrection still had to remind them of it. "**Remember how he told you, while he was still in Galilee: 'The Son of Man must be delivered over to the hands of sinners, be crucified and on the third day be raised again'**" (Luke 24:6-8). Not till then did the pieces start to fall into place.

Luke records the following statement on his way to Jerusalem: "**I have a baptism to undergo, and what constraint I am under until it is completed**" (Luke 12:50). He used the same metaphor when James and John came to him requesting places of honour in his kingdom, asking them, "**Can you drink the cup I drink and be baptised with the baptism I am baptised with?**" (Mark 10:38 – see Matthew 20:22). Denney points out that "cup" and "baptism" are religious terms:

> The cup is put into his hand by the Father, and if the baptism is a flood of suffering in which He is overwhelmed, it has also, through the very name which he uses to describe it, the character of a religious act.

In the discussion with the disciples that followed, pointing out that true greatness comes by service, he declared, "**For even the Son of Man did not come to be served, but to serve, and to give his life as a ransom for many**" (Mark 10:45 – see Matthew 20:28). He does not say that he can bear to die because by doing so many would be set free. He says that this is the very purpose of his coming. Jesus said he had come to do what the Psalmist declared no human could do for another (Psalm 49:7-9) – that which only God could do (v. 15).

On the journey to Jerusalem, indicating his determination not to be put off, Jesus said, "**I must press on today and tomorrow and the next day – for surely no prophet can die outside Jerusalem!**" (Luke 13:33).

Further on, when talking about his future coming again, he said, "**The Son of Man in his day will be like the lightning, which flashes and lights up the sky from one end to the other. But first he must suffer many things and be rejected by this generation**" (Luke 17:24,25).

In the Parable of the Vineyard, which Jesus told when the chief priests and elders came to question him in the temple courts, the owner of the vineyard sent his son to collect the fruit. The tenants "**said to each other, 'This is the heir. Come, let's kill him and take his inheritance.' So they took him and threw him out of the vineyard and killed him." The priests and elders recognise that Jesus is talking about their attitude towards him. Jesus immediately follows this by quoting Psalm 118:22, "**Have you never read in the Scriptures: 'The stone the builders rejected has become the cornerstone; the Lord has done this, and it is marvellous in our eyes**" (Matthew 21:33-46; Mark 12:1-12; Luke 20:9-19).

Six days before the Passover, at the home of her brother Lazarus, Mary anointed Jesus with expensive perfume. When criticised, Jesus defended her action and declared, "**Leave her alone! It was intended that she should save this perfume for the day of my burial**" (John 12:7 – see Matthew 26:12; Mark 14:8).

In reply to a request from some Greeks who wished to see Jesus, he said, "**The hour has come for the Son of Man to be glorified.**" That he was speaking about his death is plain, as he went on to say, "**Very truly I tell you, unless a kernel of wheat falls to the ground and dies, it remains only a single seed. But if it dies, it produces many seeds... Now my soul is troubled, and what shall I say? 'Father save me from this hour?' No, it was for this very reason I came to this hour**"[1] (John 12:23-27).

We may well ask what it means for Jesus to be "glorified"? (See also John 13:31,32; 17:1). No doubt he partly had in mind his resurrection and ascension to the place of honour at his Father's right hand. But there appears to be some emphasis in the statement above on being glorified by death. The best definition of "glory" I have come across is that it is the outward, visible manifestation of an inward character. Nowhere are the character of Jesus, his devotion to his Father and his sinless, loving nature more visible than during his trial and crucifixion. It is against the backdrop of all

---

1 For other references to this "time" or "hour", see John 7:6,30; 8:20; 13:1; 16:32; 17:1; Matthew 26:45.

the evil he endured, human and satanic, that his inward goodness shines brightest. If you squeeze an orange and there is no badness in it, only pure juice will come out. In spite of the suffering Jesus endured, only goodness came out because that was all there was within. Consider the fact that, of the seven sentences Jesus spoke while enduring the incredible pain of the crucifixion (after having endured an extremely painful scourging), the first three were the expression of his concern for others – his concern for his enemies (Luke 23:34), his concern for his mother (John 19:26,27) and his concern for his fellow-sufferer (Luke 23:39-43). His glory is revealed in his death, and all that it entails, more than in all his miracles.

Writing of the refusal of many to believe in Jesus, in spite of the clear signs he had given them, John quotes from Isaiah 53, the chapter which we have seen focuses on Jesus' suffering for the sins of others. "**Lord, who has believed our message and to whom has the arm of the Lord been revealed?**" (John 12:38 – see Isaiah 53:1).

As the deadline approached, Jesus said to his disciples, "**As you know, the Passover is two days away – and the Son of Man will be handed over to be crucified**" (Matthew 26:2).

The Last Supper

The last meal that Jesus shared with his disciples is full of references about what was to come. Consider the following:

"**Jesus knew that the hour had come for him to leave this world and go to the Father**" (John 13:1).

"**I have eagerly desired to eat this Passover with you before I suffer. For I tell you, I will not eat it again until it finds fulfilment in the kingdom of God**" (Luke 22:15,16).

"**I am not referring to all of you; I know those I have chosen.

But this is to fulfil the scripture: 'He who shares my bread has lifted up his heel against me' [Psalm 41:9]. I am telling you now before it happens, so that when it does happen you will believe that I am who I am"... After he had said this, Jesus was troubled in spirit and testified, "Very truly I tell you, one of you is going to betray me" (John 13:18-21). Matthew adds, "The Son of Man will go just as it is written about him. But woe to that man who betrays the Son of Man! It would be better for him if he had not been born" (26:24 – also Mark 14:18-21; Luke 22:21,22).

"Jesus told them, 'This very night you will all fall away on account of me, for it is written: "I will strike the shepherd, and the sheep of the flock will be scattered," [Zechariah 13:7]. But after I have risen, I will go ahead of you into Galilee.' Peter replied, 'Even if all fall away on account of you, I never will.' 'Truly I tell you,' Jesus answered, 'this very night, before the rooster crows, you will disown me three times'" (Matthew 26:31-35 – also Mark 14:27-30; Luke 22:31-34; John 13:37,38).

"While they were eating, Jesus took bread, and when he had given thanks, he broke it and gave it to his disciples, saying, 'Take and eat; this is my body.' Then he took the cup, and when he had given thanks, he gave it to them, saying, 'Drink from it, all of you. This is my blood of the covenant, which is poured out for many for the forgiveness of sins'" (Matthew 26:26-28 – also Mark 14:22-24). Luke adds the command of Jesus, "**Do this in remembrance of me**" (Luke 22:17-20). Paul repeats this command in his recounting of the Last Supper in 1 Corinthians 11 and adds the comment that "**whenever you eat this bread and drink this cup, you proclaim the Lord's death until he comes**" (vv. 23-26). After he comes, we will have no need of this reminder of his death, as in heaven his risen body always bears the marks of his suffering in his hands, side and feet (Luke 24:39; John 20:27).

It is noteworthy that Jesus commanded us to keep only two

ceremonies. The first is baptism, which symbolises our identification with Christ in his death and burial (Romans 6:3,4) and the cleansing from sin that is available to us through the gospel (Acts 22:16). The second is the Lord's Supper, which focuses on his body given and blood shed, the means of forgiveness.

Before leaving the Upper Room for the Mount of Olives, Jesus quoted another prophecy, again from that significant chapter, Isaiah 53 (v. 12), **"It is written: 'And he was numbered with the transgressors'; and I tell you that this must be fulfilled in me. Yes, what is written about me is reaching its fulfilment."** (Luke 22:37).

For a summary of the significance of all that Jesus was doing at this last meal with his disciples, in the context of his total mission, I could not do better than quote from Tom Wright's book *Simply Christian*:

> He spoke of the Passover bread as his own body that would be given on behalf of his friends, as he went out to take on himself the weight of evil so that they would not have to do so. He spoke of the Passover cup as his own blood. Like the sacrificial blood in the temple, it would be poured out to establish the covenant – only, this time, the new covenant spoken of by the prophet Jeremiah. The time had now come when, at last, God would rescue his people, and the whole world, not from mere political enemies, but from evil itself, from the sin which had enslaved them. His death would do what the Temple, with its sacrificial system, had pointed towards but had never actually accomplished. In meeting the fate which was rushing towards him, he would be the place where heaven and earth met, as he hung suspended between the two. He would be the place where God's future arrived in the present, with the kingdom of God celebrating its triumph over the kingdoms of the world by refusing to join in their spiral of violence. He would love his

enemies. He would turn the other cheek. He would go the second mile. He would act out, finally, his own interpretation of the ancient prophecies which spoke, to him, of a suffering Messiah.

Gethsemane

Leslie Newbiggin, in *Sin and Salvation,* contrasted the ease of creation with the cost of redemption:

> The Son of God, the Word of God made flesh, kneels in the Garden of Gethsemane. He wrestles in prayer. His sweat falls like great drops of blood. He cries out in agony: "Not my will, but thine be done." That is what it cost God to deal with man's sin. To create the heavens and the earth costs Him no labour, no anguish; to take away the sin of the world cost Him His own life-blood.

Jesus suffered such agony in the Garden because he knew that what he would face in bearing the sins of the world involved much more than physical pain. Martin Luther commented on Jesus in Gethsemane, "Never man feared death like this man." Jesus prayed, **"My Father, if it be possible, may this cup be taken from me"** (Matthew 26:39; Mark 14:36; Luke 22:42). What was the "cup" he was referring to? It was the **"cup of… wrath"** (Isaiah 51:17; cf. Jeremiah 25:15; Psalm 75:8). As there was no other way to gain our salvation, he drank it down to the dregs.

John Stott aptly says:

> What Jesus shrank from was not death as an experience of pain, but death as the penalty for sin; not physical death at the hands of the Romans, but spiritual death at the hands of his Father; not the nails which would tear his flesh, but the sins which he

would bear upon his soul. It wasn't the moment when all his disciples would forsake him, but a far worse experience of being forsaken which would force from his lips that awful cry, "My God, my God, why have You forsaken me?" Jesus knew that he was to endure the wrath or judgement of God – the Godforsakenness which we deserve because of our sin and guilt. No wonder he cried out to be spared from it! It is a prayer we can never echo. Suffering and pain we have to bear, but not the anguish of sin-bearing. Only Jesus, the spotless God-man, could do that.

Someone has written:

Death and the curse were in that cup,
O Christ, 'twas full for Thee;
But Thou hast drained the last dark drop,
'Tis empty now for me.
That bitter cup, love drank it up,
Now blessing's draught for me.

Stott, in *The Cross of Christ*, comments again:

B. B. Warfield wrote a careful study entitled 'On the Emotional Life of Our Lord', in the course of which he referred to the terms employed by the synoptic evangelists in relation to Gethsemane. Luke's word *agōnia* he defines as 'consternation, appalled reluctance'. Matthew and Mark share two expressions. The primary idea of 'troubled' (*adēmoneō*), he suggests, is 'loathing aversion, perhaps not unmixed with despondency', while Jesus' self-description as 'overwhelmed with sorrow' (*perilypos*) 'expresses a sorrow, or perhaps we would better say, a mental pain, a distress, which hems him in on every side, from which there is therefore no escape.' Mark uses another word of his own, 'deeply distressed' (ekthambeomai), which has been rendered 'horror-struck'; it is 'a term', Warfield adds, 'which more narrowly defines the distress as consternation – if not exactly dread, yet alarmed dismay'.[1] Put together, these expressive words indicate that Jesus was feeling an acute emotional pain causing profuse sweat, as he looked with apprehension and almost terror at this future ordeal.

The place was appropriately named Gethsemane. The Hebrew word Geth (*gath*) means "press", and semane (*shemen*) means "oil" or "richness". This was where olives were crushed until the rich juices flowed out. Maybe Isaiah's expression "**he took our pain and bore our suffering**" (53:4) includes the idea that he experienced that whole range of human emotions, not only those that bring joy, but here particularly, the very worst that we could feel. Maybe also, it is not too far-fetched to include that thought in the truth Paul is seeking to convey in Ephesians when he says: "**What does 'he ascended' mean except that he also descended to the lower, earthly regions? He who descended is the very one who ascended higher than all the heavens, in order to fill the whole universe.**" (4:9,10). It certainly means that, though he is God, he fully understands every experience I might have to cope with, even death itself.

Though Jesus was aware of the suffering that lay ahead, in Gethsemane the full horror of what it meant to bear the sins of the world was impressed upon him. It was also in Gethsemane that the die was cast and he deliberately committed himself to his Father's will. Tom Wright, in his commentary on Mark's Gospel, *Mark for Everyone*, puts it like this:

---

1 These particular Greek words occur in Matthew 26:37; Mark 14:33 and Luke 22:44. B. B. Warfield's essay was published in *Person and Work*.

Gethsemane invites us to consider... what it meant for Jesus to be, in a unique sense, God's Son. The very moment of greatest intimacy – the desperate prayer to "Abba, Father" – is also the moment where... he is set on the course for the moment of God-forsakenness on the cross.

Perhaps this is also the moment when his fully human nature is most truly revealed. Though he was fully God, the Second Person of the Divine Trinity,[1] in taking human nature he chose to live his life on earth as all the rest of us are supposed to live, in obedience to our loving heavenly Father. This is the point at which that obedience was put to the utmost test. The writer of Hebrews put it like this: "**Son though he was, he learned obedience from what he suffered and, once made perfect, he became the source of eternal salvation for all who obey him...**"(5:8,9). He was perfect in his obedience and therefore perfect in his humanity, something that can be said of none other. The writer of Hebrews also declares that "**he offered up prayers and petitions with loud cries and tears to the one who could save him from death, and he was heard because of his reverent submission**" (5:7). I have often wondered what is meant by "**he was heard**", as he obviously wasn't saved from death. I assume it means that he was heard in the sense that he was given strength to go through with it. When it appears that our prayers are not answered in the way we would wish, it is often because God has something greater in mind for the long term. Our task is to submit and trust.

When Jesus was arrested, Peter tried to defend him and cut off the ear of the high priest's servant. Indicating his commitment to his Father's will, as expressed in the prophetic Scriptures, Jesus responded, "**Put your sword back in its place, for all who draw the sword will die by the sword. Do you think I cannot call on my**

---

1 I explore this theme in the booklet *Understanding the Trinity.*

Why Did Jesus Die?

Father, and he will at once put at my disposal more than twelve legions of angels? But how then would the Scriptures be fulfilled that say it must happen in this way?" (Matthew 26:52-54). I understand that there were twelve legions of Roman soldiers in Palestine at that time, hence the allusion. God's resources are always greater than those of humans!

To the men who had come to arrest him, Jesus said, "**Am I leading a rebellion, that you have come out with swords and clubs to capture me? Every day I sat in the temple courts teaching, and you did not arrest me. But this has all taken place that the writings of the prophets might be fulfilled**" (Matthew 26:55,56 – also Mark 14:48,49).

One thing seems clear from all the above references. These numerous hints and clear references to the coming cross scattered throughout the teaching of Jesus indicate that he fully understood the implications of the Old Testament Scriptures which he regarded as referring to himself. If he did not really say these things but instead they were merely words put in his mouth at a later date by New Testament writers, then we have been left with a complete misrepresentation of Jesus' own understanding of the Old Testament writings – who he was, and why he had come into this world. Indeed, such a viewpoint leaves us with a distorted view of the gospel message we are to proclaim.

Ben Meyer, in *The Aims of Jesus,* asks and answers an important question:

> What, in the end, made Jesus operate in this way, what energised his incorporating death into his mission, his facing it and going to meet it?
>
> The range of abstractly possible answers is enormous... But... it is above all in the tradition generated by Jesus that we discover what made him operate in the way he did, what made

him epitomise his life in the single act of going to his death: He 'loved me and handed himself over for me'... 'having loved his own who were in the world he loved them to the end'... If authenticity lies in the coherence between word (Mark 12:28-34 parr.) and deed (Galatians 2:20; Ephesians 5:2; John 13:1; Revelation 1:5), our question has found an answer.

The trial

A careful analysis of the events of the trial indicates the following order of events:

Appearance before Annas: This is only mentioned by John (18:12-24) who was probably the "**other disciple, who was known to the high priest**" (v. 16) and who accompanied Peter into the courtyard. Annas had been deposed from the priesthood in A.D. 15 but five of his sons had been high priests, and now Caiaphas, his son-in-law, held that position. He still had much influence and still, apparently, maintained the title "high priest" (v. 19). During his questioning, Jesus was struck in the face by one of the officials (v. 22). John tells us that he was "**bound**" (v. 12) when taken to Annas and still bound when sent on to Caiaphas (v. 24).

Appearance before Caiaphas: Caiaphas was high priest from A.D. 18 to 36, which included the period of persecutions described in the early chapters of Acts. This part of the trial took place in Caiaphas's house (Luke 22:54) where the "**teachers of the law and the elders**" and the "**chief priests and the whole Sanhedrin**" (the Jewish spiritual and civil governing body) were gathered (Matthew 26:57,59; Mark 14:53,55).

False charges were made. When questioned about these charges, Jesus remained silent (Matthew 26:59-63; Mark 14:55-61).

Why Did Jesus Die?

He was put under oath by Caiaphas to declare whether he was the **"Christ, the Son of the living God."** Jesus affirmed this, identifying himself with the **"Son of Man"** of Daniel 7:13 (Matthew 26:63-66; Mark 14:61-64). Luigi Santucchi, the Italian novelist, has a perceptive comment on this religious leader's response to Jesus:

> We can minister to God and serve him in our own way but we have a horror of meeting him. If he comes too near we have only one way of defending ourselves from him, Caiaphas' way – by killing him, killing him even in the name of God, shouting at him that it's blasphemy to appear alive in our midst.

Their decision that he was worthy of death was followed by physical abuse, insults and mocking (Matthew 26:66,67; Mark 14:64,65).

Peter's denials are recorded by all four Gospels (Matthew 26:69-75; Mark 14:66-72; Luke 22:54-62; John 18:15-18,25-27).

The Sanhedrin formally sentenced him to death (Matthew 27:1; Mark 15:1; Luke 22:66-71). According to Matthew, this was **"early in the morning"**; Mark, **"very early in the morning"**; Luke, **"at daybreak"**. It seems from Luke's account that Jesus was again asked if he was the Christ. Again he affirmed this.

Under Roman occupation, any capital sentence passed by the Sanhedrin had to be ratified by the Roman governor, so it was necessary to get Pilate's approval before it could be executed.

First appearance before Pilate: The **"whole assembly"** (Luke 23:1) led Jesus to Pilate, but, to avoid ceremonial uncleanness before eating the Passover, they did not enter his palace (John 18:28).

Pilate first attempted to avoid a decision by putting it back on the Jewish leaders (John 18:29-32). They pointed out that they had **"no right to execute anyone"**.

Jesus was accused of "**subverting our nation. He opposes payment of taxes to Caesar and claims to be Christ, a king**" (Luke 23:2).

Jesus was asked by Pilate if he was the King of the Jews. He affirmed this. (Matthew 27:11; Mark 15:2; Luke 23:3). John records the response of Jesus that his kingdom was not of this world and that he came to bear witness to the truth. Pilate asked, "**What is truth?**" (John 18:33-38).

Pilate protested that he could find no charge against him (Luke 23:4).

Further accusations were made by the chief priests and elders. Jesus gave no answer to the charges, which amazed Pilate (Matthew 27:12-14; Mark 15:3-5).

Pilate made a second attempt to avoid a decision by sending him to Herod when he learnt that Jesus was from Galilee, Herod's jurisdiction (Luke 23:6,7).

Appearance before Herod: This is described only by Luke (23:8-12). This was Herod Antipas, the ablest of Herod the Great's sons. Herod at one time had a conscience, and though he had imprisoned John the Baptist because of John's criticism of him for marrying his brother's wife, Herodias, he "**protected him, knowing him to be a righteous and a holy man**" and he "**liked to listen to him**" (Mark 6:20). However, Herod's moment of decision came when asked by the daughter of Herodias for "**the head of John the Baptist on a platter**" (Mark 6:25). Because of his fear of what others might think if he failed to keep his oath, he stifled his conscience and beheaded John. It is significant that when faced with Jesus himself, Jesus had nothing to say to him (Luke 23:9).

Jesus was vehemently accused by the "**chief priests and the teachers of the law**"(v. 10).

Herod and his soldiers ridiculed and mocked him, and

Why Did Jesus Die?

"**Dressing him in an elegant robe, they sent him back to Pilate. That day Herod and Pilate become friends – before this they were enemies**" (v. 11,12). It was claimed that Herod's enmity against Pilate stemmed from the fact that previously Pilate had slain some of Herod's subjects. This could explain why Pilate had been careful to get Jesus tried before him.

Second appearance before Pilate: Pilate protested Jesus' innocence for the second time (Luke 23:14,15).

Pilate's third attempt to avoid a decision was to offer to "**punish him and then release him**" in the hope that this would satisfy them (Luke 23:17).

Pilate's fourth attempt to avoid a decision was to offer to release a prisoner, as was apparently the custom during the Passover festival, no doubt hoping they would choose to release Jesus (Matthew 27:15-26; Mark 15:6-15; Luke 23:18-25; John 18:39,40). The crowd chose Barabbas, "**thrown in prison for insurrection and murder**" (Luke 23:25). During this exchange Pilate said for the third time that there were no grounds for the death penalty and again offered to punish and then release Jesus (Luke 23:22). During this exchange, Pilate's wife sent him a message saying, "**Don't have anything to do with that innocent man, for I have suffered a great deal today in a dream because of him**" (Matthew 27:19).

Pilate's fifth attempt to avoid responsibility was to wash his hands in front of the crowd, declaring: "**I am innocent of this man's blood… It is your responsibility!**" (Matthew 27:24). The crowd said, "**His blood is on us and on our children!**" (v. 25).

Pilate ordered Jesus to be flogged (Matthew 27:26; Mark 15:15; John 19:1). A Roman flogging was a brutal affair that went beyond the Jewish limit of 40 lashes (Deuteronomy 25:3). The scourges were armed with lumps of lead or bone which tore the flesh, and victims could sometimes die as a result of the flogging.

After this torture, the governor's soldiers took him into the Praetorium and gathered the "**whole company of soldiers**" around him. They "**stripped him and put a scarlet robe on him**" (Matthew 27:27,28), probably a soldier's cloak, and wove a crown of thorns to place on his head. I comment on the symbolic significance of the crown of thorns on page 32. Mark and John call the garment a "**purple robe**" – purple being the colour of royalty. "**They put a staff in his right hand as a sceptre. Then they knelt in front of him and mocked him. 'Hail, King of the Jews!' they said. They spat on him, and took the staff and struck him on the head again and again**" (Matthew 27:27-30 – see Mark 15:16-19; John 19:2,3).

Third appearance before Pilate: John describes another appearance before Pilate after the flogging (19:4-16). For the fifth time he protested Jesus' innocence and had Jesus brought out wearing the crown of thorns and the purple robe. He declared, "**Here is the man!**" (v. 4,5). Obviously he was hoping they would feel sorry for Jesus and agree to release him. This was his sixth attempt to avoid sentencing Jesus to death. Facing a continuing demand for crucifixion from the crowd, Pilate declared for the sixth time that he found no basis for a charge against him (v. 6).

Tom Wright, in *The Resurrection of the Son of God,* has an interesting comment on this declaration of Pilate. John, in starting his Gospel with the words "**In the beginning was the Word**", with its obviously link to Genesis 1:1, underlines the point that his book is about the new creation in Jesus. On the sixth day of the original creation humans were created in the divine image. On the sixth day of the last week of Jesus life Pilate declares, "**Here is the man**". The seventh day, the day the Creator rested from his work, is the day Jesus rests in the tomb. The first day of the next week is the beginning of the new creation with Jesus' resurrection.

When the Jewish leaders accused Jesus of the charge of blas-

Why Did Jesus Die?

phemy in claiming to be the Son of God, Pilate "**was even more afraid**" and took Jesus back inside the palace to question him further (v. 7,8). On being asked where he came from, Jesus gave no answer (v. 9). When Pilate expressed annoyance at his refusal to answer and told Jesus that he had power to free or crucify him, Jesus declared, "**You would have no power over me if it were not given to you from above. Therefore the one who handed me over to you is guilty of a greater sin**" (v. 10,11).

Pilate then went out to the crowd and continued his attempt to set Jesus free. The Jewish leaders kept shouting for a death sentence and told Pilate that he was no friend of Caesar's if he released one who claimed to be a king. Eventually Pilate brought Jesus out and sat in the "**judge's seat**" (v. 13), indicating that he was about to make a decision. The Jews had already complained to the emperor about Pilate's behaviour, so no doubt he would have been sensitive to this threat.

Pilate said, "**Here is your king**" (v. 14), a statement perhaps made in mockery. He asked, "**Shall I crucify your king?**" and the chief priests revealed their hypocrisy by declaring, "**We have no king but Caesar**" (v.15). Finally, Pilate handed Jesus over to them to be crucified (v. 16).

John tells us these final events happened "**about the sixth hour**" (19:14 – literal translation). Westcott gave good reasons for supposing that John, instead of reckoning hours from 6 a.m. to 6 p.m., as was the Jewish custom, reckoned them from midnight to noon, and noon to midnight – a practice which we know from the *Martyrdom of Polycarp* was in use in Asia Minor at the time John wrote his gospel, and which is still followed in the West today. This means it was about 6 a.m. when Pilate passed sentence on Jesus. This fits in with Mark, who, following the Jewish method of reckoning hours, states that it was "**the third hour**" (Mark 15:25 – literal translation), i.e. 9 a.m., when the crucifixion began.

Alan E. Lewis has an interesting comment to make on the character of the people involved in these events, particularly from Mark's perspective:

> It has been noticed that Mark's Gospel, in particular, takes pains to implicate all the actors equally – save the principal – in the moral failure of this day. Treacherous Judas; weak disciples, first asleep and then in flight; desperate priests and abusive guards; cowardly Peter and calculating Pilate; violent soldiers and jeering passersby: truly a "solidarity in sin unites all those involved… [as] Mark brings the crucified Messiah face to face with the barriers of human guilt." [M. Hengel, *The Atonement*]. Though each claims innocence, actually all the representatives of humanity are integrated by the passion narrative into collective accountability for the death of Jesus (cf. Romans 3:23; 11:32). "No one wishes to be responsible. That is why they are all guilty." [Von Balthasar, *Mysterium Paschale*].

M. Dupin pointed out in a tract on the trial of Jesus that Jewish law was disregarded in a number of ways: he was arrested in the night, bound as a malefactor, beaten before his arraignment and struck in open court during the trial; he was tried on a feast day and before sunrise; he was compelled to incriminate himself, and this under oath or solemn judicial adjuration; and he was sentenced on the same day as his conviction.

The crucifixion

As with the trial of Jesus, I will list the events of the crucifixion in their chronological order, comparing the four accounts that we possess.

The first three Gospels simply state that the soldiers "**led him**

Why Did Jesus Die?

away" to crucify him (Matthew 27:31; Mark 15:20; Luke 23:26). But John adds that he went "**carrying his own cross**" (John 19:17), though historians tell us that this may have only been the cross-bar. The first three Gospels also tell us that on the way the soldiers compelled Simon of Cyrene (a province of North Africa), who "**was passing by on his way from the country**" (Mark 15:21 – Matthew 27:32; Luke 23:26) to carry the cross. This implies that Jesus, in his weakened state, was unable to carry it all the way. Mark tells us also that Simon was "**the father of Alexander and Rufus**". The fact that Mark mentions them by name indicates that they must have been known to the Christian community at the time Mark was writing. This suggests the possibility that Simon became a disciple of Jesus as a result of this encounter with him, and passed his faith onto his sons. He may well have stayed to see the end and would certainly have told his sons about this experience.

Luke tells us that "**a large crowd was following Jesus, and in the crowd a lot of women were crying and weeping for him.**" Jesus turned and said to them: "**Women of Jerusalem, don't cry for me! Cry for yourselves and for your children. Someday people will say, 'Women who never had children are really fortunate!'**" (23:27-31). He then quoted from the prophet Hosea: "**At that time everyone will say to the mountains, 'Fall on us!' They will say to the hills, 'Hide us!'**" (v. 30 – see Hosea 10:8). Jesus could no doubt foresee the horrible suffering the Jews would experience nearly forty years later when the Roman armies destroyed Jerusalem after a war in which, according to the historian Josephus, something like a million Jews perished.

Jesus' first word on his way to crucifixion was to women, as was his first word after his resurrection (Matthew 28:8-10; John 20:15-17). "**Don't cry for me!**" This is the only divine prohibition in the crucifixion story. Jesus is not looking for a superficial emotional response towards his physical sufferings but something much deeper.

He desires us to understand something of *why* he suffered. He wants a repentance, a turning, a longing for moral change, an obedience. Should we fail to respond to his cross appropriately, then he has a word of warning, "**Cry for yourselves…**"

The place of execution is called "**Golgotha**" (Matthew 27:33; Mark 15:22; Luke 23:33; John 19:17), an Aramaic name meaning "**the place of the skull**" – possibly receiving its name from a skull-shaped hill nearby.

Jesus was offered wine mixed with "**gall**" (Matthew 27:34) or "**myrrh**" (Mark 15:23). According to tradition, this was prepared by compassionate women to dull the pain. Jesus, after tasting it, refused to drink it. In making his greatest sacrifice he wanted to be as mentally alert as possible.

Jesus was crucified (Matthew 27:35; Mark 15:24; Luke 23:33; John 19:23) and we know from the resurrection appearances that this was by nailing the hands and feet (Luke 24:40; John 20:20,27 – see Psalm 22:16). According to Mark, this happened at "**the third hour**" (15:25 – literal translation), which by Jewish reckoning would have been nine o'clock in the morning.

The soldiers stripped Jesus and divided his garments among themselves (Matthew 27:35; Mark 15:24; Luke 23:34; John 19:23,24). John tells us that they divided them into four shares, "**one for each of them**" (v. 23), indicating that four soldiers were present, and also tells us that they gambled for his tunic or undergarment which was "**seamless, woven in one piece from top to bottom**" (v. 23). I comment on the symbolic significance of this robe on pages 33,34.

"**Above his head they placed the written charge against him: THIS IS JESUS, THE KING OF THE JEWS**" (Matthew 27:37; Mark 15:26; Luke 23:38; John 19:19-22). John's account informs us that this was placed there on Pilate's orders, no doubt intended as a mockery to the Jews. John adds that the title included the words "**Jesus of Nazareth**" (v. 19), which would have been an added insult to strict Jews, who looked with scorn on Galileans (see John 7:52). He also tells us that it was "**written in Aramaic, Latin and Greek**" (v. 20). When the chief priests protested, Pilate ignored their request to change it, declaring, "**What I have written, I have written**" (19:22). The Jewish leaders had won their battle in persuading him to have Jesus crucified. At least he was going to have the last word!

Each gospel writer mentions that he was crucified with two others, Jesus being in the middle (Matthew 27:38; Mark 15:27; Luke 23:32,33; John 19:18). Matthew and Mark call them "robbers", "bandits" or "insurrectionists" (Greek – *lēstai)*, whereas Luke calls them "criminals" or "evildoers" (*kakourgoi*). Apparently they were men of violence, willing to kill as well as steal.

Jesus' first words from the cross. "**Father, forgive them, for they do not know what they are doing**" (Luke 23:34). It seems, from Luke's placing of these words, that they were spoken as he was nailed to the cross and as it was placed in its socket, before the soldiers divided his clothes. We may debate as to whether this prayer was merely for the four soldiers who carried out the sentence, or whether it was also meant to include those responsible for his sentencing. One might argue that at least some of the Jewish leaders did know what they were doing, even though they were unwilling to face the truth confronting them. However, I suspect Jesus was thinking of all those responsible. It indicates that there is nothing you or I could say or do that could put us beyond the reach of his prayers.

Matthew and Mark give us the fullest account of the mocking Jesus endured from those who watched his crucifixion, and Luke mentions it briefly (Matthew 27:39-44; Mark 15:29-32; Luke 23:35,36). Matthew tells us that "**those who passed by hurled insults at him**", "**the chief priests, the teachers of the law and the elders mocked him**" and "**the rebels who were crucified with him also heaped insults on him". Luke adds, "The soldiers also came up and mocked him". The taunting words "**Come down from the cross, if your are the Son of God!**" (Matthew 27:40; cf. Mark 15:30) echo the tempting voice that had whispered in the desert early in his ministry (Matthew 4:5,6; Luke 4:9-11).

The second word from the cross. All the Gospel writers mention that women were present at the crucifixion. Matthew tells us, "**Many women were there, watching from a distance. They had followed Jesus from Galilee to care for his needs. Among them were Mary Magdalene, Mary the mother of James and Joseph, and the mother of Zebedee's sons** [James and John]" (27:55,56). Mark adds "**Salome**" (15:40), who may have been the same person as "**the mother of Zebedee's sons**" mentioned by Matthew, and could also have been "**his mother's sister**" mentioned by John (19:25). This would make James and John first cousins of Jesus. "**Mary the mother of James and Joseph**" may have been the same person as "**Mary the wife of Clopas**" whom John mentions (19:25). Luke does not name the women present. John says, "**Near the cross of Jesus stood his mother, his mother's sister, Mary the wife of Clopas, and Mary Magdalene. When Jesus saw his mother there, and the disciple whom he loved standing nearby, he said to her, 'Woman, here is your son,' and to the disciple, 'Here is your mother.' From that time on, this disciple took her into his home**" (19:25-27).

It has usually been assumed that "the disciple whom he loved" is John himself, the author of this gospel. He speaks of himself in this way in several other places (13:23; 21:20). If "**from that time on**" means that he took her to his home immediately, then he probably returned later, as verse 35 implies he was present at the end. However, there may be another implied meaning here. In the Greek there is no word for "home" and it is doubtful if John would have had a home in Jerusalem. It simply says "he took her to his own."

Why Did Jesus Die?

Fleming Rutledge makes an interesting point in her wonderful little book *The Seven Last Words from the Cross*:[1]

> By rewriting the covenant in his own blood, Jesus has done something completely new. In giving his mother to the disciple, he is causing a new relationship to come into existence that did not exist before. The disciple and the woman are not individual people here. They are symbolic: they represent the way the *family* ties are transcended in the church by *the ties of the Spirit*. That is why Jesus calls his mother "woman" in the Gospel of John. He is setting aside the blood relationship in order to create a much wider family.

We find the same emphasis also in other places in the Gospels (e.g. Mark 3:32-34). That is not to say that family ties are unimportant. Jesus obviously cared for his mother. But here he is creating something greater. It is important to note that the Greek word for "woman" does not denote any disrespect.

As far as we know, John was the only male disciple present at the crucifixion. The rest had gone into hiding.

The third word from the cross. Luke tells us of the brief verbal encounter between Jesus and one of the dying thieves who had obviously had a deep change of heart since first insulting Jesus with the others. **"One of the criminals hanging there also insulted Jesus by saying, 'Aren't you the Messiah? Save yourself and save us!' But the other criminal told the first one off, 'Don't you fear God? Aren't you getting the same punishment as this man? We got what was coming to us, but he didn't do anything wrong.' Then he said to Jesus, 'Remember me when you come into power** [or 'your kingdom']!'

---

[1] William B. Eerdmans Publishing Company, 2005, ©.

Jesus replied, 'I promise that today you will be with me in paradise'" (23:39-43). This encounter illustrates three very important truths.

First, though truth is not unimportant,[1] we are not saved by our full understanding of the truth, but by our trust in the Saviour. We do not know whether or not this robber had heard Jesus preach before. However, what he had seen of Jesus convinced him that terms such as "the Son of God", which those around the cross were throwing at Jesus in mockery, contained something of the truth. He had no way of understanding that this man was paying the price for sin – neither could he know Jesus would rise from the dead, though he intuitively grasped that Jesus had a kingdom somewhere. But here was someone he desperately needed in his moment of death, and in desperation he sought mercy and found it.

Second, we are not saved by our good behaviour but by facing up to our sins and seeking forgiveness. The dying robber had no opportunity to make up for the harm he had done, but I have no doubt that if his life had been spared, he would have clearly demonstrated by his behaviour that his repentance was genuine. I love a thought given to us by D. L. Moody. He could imagine this condemned criminal, who had wasted his life and brought misery to others, walking arm in arm with the Saviour down the streets of the eternal city. That is what Jesus came to achieve. St. John Chrysostom observed that when Christ wished to bring the bandit into paradise, he immediately spoke the word and brought him in. Christ did not need to pray to do this. God had placed an angel with a flaming sword to guard paradise (Genesis 3:24), and by his own authority Christ opened paradise and brought in the thief.

Third, I don't think it was any accident that Jesus was crucified between two sinners, one who sought forgiveness and found it, and

---

1 See my booklet *What Is Truth and Does It Matter?*

the other who, as far as we know, never did. Wherever and whenever Jesus and his cross is proclaimed, it always causes this division between those who respond appropriately and those who don't. Paul put it like this: "**The message of the cross is foolishness to those who are perishing, but to us who are being saved it is the power of God**" (1 Corinthians 1:18). Jesus put it even more starkly: "**Do you think I came to bring peace on earth? No, I tell you, but division. From now on there will be five in one family divided against each other, three against two and two against three. They will be divided, father against son and son against father, mother against daughter and daughter against mother, mother-in-law against daughter-in-law and daughter-in-law against mother-in-law**" (Luke 12:51-53).

The fourth word from the cross. "**From noon until three in the afternoon** [literally "From the sixth hour until the ninth hour"] **darkness came over all the land**" (Matthew 27:45; Mark 15:33). Luke adds, "**for the sun stopped shining**" (23:44,45). I have always assumed that it was during these three hours that Jesus endured the awful consequences of bearing the sins of the human race. We cannot imagine what this involved. The darkness over the land may have been an eclipse of the sun, though I presume that would have been of much shorter duration. Whatever the cause, natural or supernatural, it pictured the darkness that covered Jesus' soul as he endured the separation from his Father that we need never endure.

"**About three in the afternoon** [literally "the ninth hour"] **Jesus cried out in a loud voice, '*Eli, Eli, lema sabachthani?*' – which means, 'My God, my God, why have you forsaken me?'**" (Matthew 27:46; Mark 15:34 – Aramaic). This cry, a quotation from Psalm 22:1 (see above, pp. 62-64), expressed a deep reality, not just a feeling of the moment. Dietrich Bonhoeffer, in *Letters and Papers from Prison*, wrote:

The Cross in the Gospels

It is infinitely easier to suffer in obedience to a human command than to accept suffering as free responsible men. It is infinitely easier to suffer with others than to suffer alone. It is infinitely easier to suffer as public heroes than to suffer in ignominy. It is infinitely easier to suffer physical death than to endure spiritual suffering. Christ suffered as a free man, alone, apart, and in ignominy, in body and in spirit and since that day many Christians have suffered with him.

As Fleming Rutledge suggests, this saying from the cross is the one to have if you are having only one of the various sayings. "Rightly understood... it brings the most comfort, because it plumbs the most profound depths." It speaks to what was really happening during those dark hours.

If you or I should at any time *feel* that we have been abandoned by God, it would be good to remember that when Jesus *really was* abandoned, he was still right in the centre of his Father's will.

The fifth and sixth words from the cross. John records these. "**Later, knowing that everything had now been finished, and so that Scripture would be fulfilled, Jesus said, 'I am thirsty.' A jar of wine vinegar was there, so they soaked a sponge in it, put the sponge on a stalk of the hyssop plant, and lifted it to Jesus' lips. When he had received the drink, Jesus said, 'It is finished.' With that, he bowed his head and gave up his spirit**" (John 19:28-30 – see also Matthew 27:48; Mark 15:36).

What Scripture Jesus had in mind is uncertain. Psalm 69:21 comes to mind, "**They put gall in my food and gave me vinegar for my thirst.**" However, this fits in better with the wine vinegar mixed with gall that was offered him before his crucifixion and which he refused. Perhaps we should turn to Psalm 42:2, "**My soul thirsts for God, for the living God. When can I go and meet with God?**"

Why Did Jesus Die?

A third possibility, suggested by Fleming Rutledge, is that he had in mind Psalm 22:15, "**My mouth is dried up like a potsherd, and my tongue sticks to the roof of my mouth.**" If this is the case, considering he knew "**all was now completed**", and he was acting "**so that the Scriptures would be fulfilled**", it is likely he is speaking, not primarily from his very real mortal weakness, but from the sovereign control of his own mission.

We can make the connection with two other sayings of Jesus in John's Gospel: "**those who drink the water I give them will never thirst**" (4:14) and "**whoever believes in me will never be thirsty**" (6:35). He thirsted that we may never have to. As Rutledge puts it:

> He who gives the calm of lakes and pools, the freshness of brooks and streams, the majestic depths of seas and oceans, the glory of pounding surf, the might of Niagara and the tinkling of the garden fountain, the One from whose being flows the gift of the water of eternal life – this is the One who is dying of a terrible thirst on the Cross for the love of his lost sheep.

Whatever the precise thoughts Jesus had in mind at this moment, the soldiers were moved to offer him some of the wine vinegar they kept handy for their own use. It may well be that Jesus wished to declare in a strong voice his triumphant statement that his work was now finished, and in his parched and exhausted condition it must have been hard to say anything, let alone declare it with conviction. However, having drunk the wine, and summoning what strength remained, he sent one word resounding over Calvary's hill, so expressive of the glory and triumph of his completed mission, "**It is finished**" (John 19:30). No doubt this is the second cry Jesus gave "**in a loud voice**" that is mentioned by Matthew and Mark (Matthew 27:50; Mark 15:37). In the Greek language, in which the New Testament was written and which Jesus probably spoke, this is just one word – *Tetelestai*. Unlike the English translation, it is not ambiguous. It doesn't mean, "It's over; this is the end; I'm done for." It means "It is complete; it is perfected." What he had come into the world to achieve had now been done. The one perfect, effective sacrifice for the sins of the human race had now been offered. Twice, at the very beginning of his ministry, John the Baptist had identified the main purpose of Jesus' life and work. **"Behold the Lamb of God, who takes away the sin of the world"** (John 1:29,36). Not long afterwards Jesus had told his disciples, **"My food is to do the will of him who sent me and to finish his work"** (John 4:34). Now he can declare that the work is indeed finished. The moment of his apparent defeat is the moment of his greatest victory.

Matthew tells us that **"At that moment the curtain of the temple was torn in two from top to bottom. The earth shook, the rocks split, and the tombs broke open. The bodies of many holy people who had died were raised to life. They came out of the tombs after Jesus' resurrection and went into the holy city and appeared to many people"** (27:51-53). I have explained the significance of the rent curtain under the heading "Day of Atonement – the rent curtain" on pages 48-50. Who these **"holy people"** were who were raised to life, whether they were raised at the moment of Jesus' death or later after his resurrection, when they came out of the tombs, and to whom they appeared, I would not like to speculate. One thing is certain – that by his death Jesus conquered, disarmed and disabled death, and these people were but the first trophies of that victory. It is possible that this event is an echo of Ezekiel's statement to Israel in exile that the Lord will **"open your graves and bring you up from them; I will bring you back to the land of Israel… I will put my Spirit in you and you will live"** (37:12-14). (The wording in the Greek translation of this passage is close to Matthew 27:52,53.) Matthew is indicating that through the cross and resurrection of Jesus the real return from exile is now beginning.

Why Did Jesus Die?

The final word from the cross. Luke records one more word that Jesus spoke with his dying breath as he bowed his head for the last time, " 'Father, into your hands I commit my spirit.' **When he had said this he breathed his last**" (23:46 – see Psalm 31:5). He had said previously, "**No one takes my life from me. I give it up willingly!**" (John 10:18).

It is interesting that each of the Gospel writers tells us that Jesus quoted from the Psalms while on the cross. These prayers have sustained the faith of multitudes over the last two millennia when facing trials. Jesus probably knew most of the Psalms by heart. He quotes Psalm 31:5 to reaffirm his complete trust in his Father at the moment of death. The very fact that he can still trust him as "Father" underlines for me the totally voluntary nature of a sacrifice that involved being abandoned by his Father as he bore the sins of the human race. It also underlines the understanding that existed between the two in deciding that such a sacrifice was worthwhile.

There is one other matter to note before moving on to Jesus' burial. Matthew, Mark and Luke each record the responses of people who were watching these events. Matthew reports: "**When the centurion and those with him who were guarding Jesus saw the earthquake and all that had happened, they were terrified, and exclaimed, 'Surely he was the Son of God!'**" (27:54). Mark only mentions the centurion's response (15:39). Luke's version is: "**The centurion, seeing what had happened, praised God and said, 'Surely this was a righteous man'**" (23:47). He adds, "**When all the people who had gathered to witness this sight saw what took place, they beat their breasts and went away**" (v. 48).

I don't think I could do better than finish this section with a paragraph from Tom Wright's extremely thoughtful book, *Evil & the Justice of God*:[1]

---

[1] SPCK, 2006, ©. For further commentary on these thoughts, buy this book and read it!

Jesus on his cross towers over the whole scene as Israel in person, as YHWH in person, as the point where the evil of the world does all that it can and where the creator of the world does all that he can. Jesus suffers the full consequences of evil, evil from the political, social, cultural, personal, moral, religious and spiritual angles all rolled into one, evil in the downward spiral hurtling towards the pit of destruction and despair. And he does so precisely as an act of redemption, of taking that downward fall and exhausting it, so that there may be new creation, new covenant, forgiveness, freedom and hope.

The burial

Each of the Gospel writers tells us of the burial of Jesus by Joseph of Arimathea, but it is John who fills us in with some prior details. "Now it was the day of Preparation, and the next day was to be a special Sabbath. Because the Jewish leaders[1] did not want the bodies left on the crosses during the Sabbath, they asked Pilate to have the legs broken and the bodies taken down. The soldiers therefore came and broke the legs of the first man who had been crucified with Jesus, and then those of the other. But when they came to Jesus and found that he was already dead, they did not break his legs. Instead, one of the soldiers pierced Jesus' side with a spear, bringing a sudden flow of blood and water. The man who saw it has given testimony, and his testimony is true. He knows that he tells the truth, and he testifies so that you also may believe. These things happened so that the scripture would be fulfilled: 'Not one of his bones will be broken,' and, as another Scripture

---

1 Literally "the Jews", but when John uses the term "**the Jews**", he is not referring to Jews generally, but to the Jewish leadership. This becomes obvious when observing the instances where the phrase occurs.

says, 'They will look on the one they have pierced'" (19:31-37).

The breaking of the legs was apparently a common practice to hasten death. If their feet were nailed, they would be able to prop themselves up, though with much pain, to enable breathing. Once the legs were broken breathing would be difficult, if not impossible. The Scripture referred to would probably be Exodus 12:46 which states that no bones of the Passover lamb were to be broken (see pages 37-40). Psalm 34:19,20, where it is said of the righteous man that "**[God] protects all their bones, not one of them will be broken**", may also be relevant. The second quotation is from the prophet Zechariah (12:10).

As regards the blood and water that flowed from the spear wound, William Stroud M.D., in his book *Treatise on the Physical Cause of the Death of Christ* (1884), maintained that this may be caused by a ruptured heart in which the blood flows into the pericardium where it separates into its constituent parts giving the appearance of blood and water. This view was accepted by Sir Alexander Simpson (1916), who said he had seen several such cases "in which the pericardial bag was greatly distended and the blood had separated into clot and watery serum." It would be interesting to think Jesus died of a "broken heart" but whether the person who observed this phenomenon meant us to take any spiritual significance from what he saw is left to our imagination. Augustus Toplady, who wrote the popular hymn *Rock of Ages,* obviously thought so.

> Rock of ages, cleft for me,
> let me hide myself in thee;
> let the water and the blood
> from thy riven side which flowed,
> be of sin the double cure,
> cleanse me from its guilt and power.

Who the "**man who saw it**" was, we are not told. It could well have been John himself, or if he had already left to take Mary away, it may have been someone who reported it to him. There is considerable emphasis on eyewitness testimony in the New Testament, not least in this Gospel.[1]

John gives us the most detailed description of the burial. "**Later, Joseph of Arimathea asked Pilate for the body of Jesus. Now Joseph was a disciple of Jesus, but secretly because he feared the Jewish leaders. With Pilate's permission, he came and took the body away. He was accompanied by Nicodemus, the man who earlier had visited Jesus at night. Nicodemus brought a mixture of myrrh and aloes, about seventy-five pounds. Taking Jesus' body, the two of them wrapped it, with the spices, in strips of linen. This was in accordance with Jewish burial customs. At the place where Jesus was crucified, there was a garden, and in the garden a new tomb, in which no one had ever been laid. Because it was the Jewish day of Preparation and since the tomb was nearby, they laid Jesus there**" (19:38-42).

Matthew adds that it was Joseph's "**own new tomb that he had cut out of the rock**" and that he "**rolled a big stone in front of the entrance**" (27:60). Mark adds that Joseph was "**a prominent member of the Council, who was himself waiting for the kingdom of God**" and that he went "**boldly**" to Pilate (15:43). If he had previously been a secret disciple, at least now he was prepared to nail his colours to the mast and face the consequences (as was also Nicodemus – see John 3:1-3 and 7:50-52). Luke tells us that he was "**a good and upright man, who had not consented to their decision and action**" (23:50). Luke also tells us that "**the Sabbath was about to begin**" (v. 54), which would place the burial about

---

1 For more information on eyewitness testimony in the Gospels, see my booklet *Did the Writers of the New Testament Get Their Picture of Jesus Right?*

sundown, suggesting that the burial may have been accomplished in some haste as it would not have been appropriate to do this on the Sabbath.

Matthew, Mark and Luke tell us that the burial was observed by women. Matthew mentions "**Mary Magdalene and the other Mary**", Mark mentions "**Mary Magdalene and Mary the mother of Joseph**" and Luke mentions "**The women who had come with Jesus from Galilee**" (Matthew 27:61; Mark 15:47; Luke 23:55). As far as we know, John was the only male disciple who was present at the crucifixion. The others had gone into hiding "**for fear of the Jewish leaders**" (John 20:19). The women, however, saw it through to the end.

Matthew tells us of the request of the chief priests and Pharisees to Pilate to allow a guard to be placed on the tomb lest the disciples "**come and steal the body and tell the people that he has been raised from the dead**" (Matthew 27:62-66). It is significant that Jesus' claim that he would rise from the dead was known to them. Whether it was their own guard that was used or whether they were requesting extra soldiers from Pilate is unclear. Matthew 28:14 seems to indicate that it was a guard under Pilate's control. At any rate the tomb was sealed, probably with a cord covered with clay or wax on which an official seal had been impressed, and a guard posted.

The resurrection

In the booklet *Did Jesus Really Rise from the Dead?* I have given the considerable historical evidence for the truth of this event and some of its implications. John, as we have seen, was present right through these events. Luke, a reliable historian, claimed to have received his accounts from "**those who from the first were eyewitnesses and servants of the word**" (1:2). During his two-year stay in

Jerusalem (AD 57-59) he would have known at least some of those involved, including James, the half-brother of Jesus, who was one of the leaders of the church in Jerusalem at that time. Paul, to whom Jesus personally appeared, would also have known many eyewitnesses of these events (see 1 Corinthians 15:1-8). He was certainly well acquainted with Peter and James and probably many others. It is not my intention to go over all this evidence again here, or to describe the resurrection appearances that we have in the Gospels, but in Part 2 of this book I will make some comments about how the resurrection affects our understanding of the cross.

Between resurrection and ascension

The cross is not specifically referred to in the brief accounts we have of the appearances of Jesus to his disciples during these forty days. However, he does take time on his first appearances to them to underline the necessity for it and how the three major groups of writings in the Old Testament all foretold it (Luke 24:25-27; 44-47). His opening words to his gathered friends on Easter evening were the repeated "**Peace be with you**", a peace that is now possible only through the cross. He signifies this by showing them his hands and his side (John 20:19-21 – see Ephesians 2:14-18). In the accounts of his commission to his disciples it is baptism and forgiveness of sins that are mentioned (Matthew 28:19; Luke 24:46,47; John 20:23). Baptism, the rite by which men and women are admitted to Christian society, is inseparably associated with the forgiveness of sins. So in his final instruction as to what his coming is to mean to the world, we find him focusing on those things which, both in his earlier teaching and in the subsequent teaching of the apostles, can be defined only by relation to his death.

Why Did Jesus Die?

The cross – the focus of prophecy

There are numerous passages through the Old Testament which the Bible itself claims to be in the form of prophecy. That means they are not only words from God directed to the situations that existed in the times in which the words were written, but are also looking forward to future events. Of all the quotations that are specifically referenced in the New Testament as being of this nature, the vast majority are centred on the first coming of the Christ.[1] It is noteworthy that the majority of these prophecies focus on his death and the events immediately preceding or following it. To underline this I shall list here the references to these prophecies that are recorded in the New Testament.

Jesus, to the disciples when questioned about Elijah: "**To be sure, Elijah does come first, and restores all things. Why then is it written that the Son of Man must suffer much and be rejected? But I tell you, Elijah has come, and they have done to him everything they wished, just as it is written about him**" (Mark 9:12,13 – see Malachi 4:5).

Jesus, approaching Jerusalem: "**The Son of Man did not come to be served, but to serve, and to give his life as a ransom for many**" (Mark 10:45) echoes Isaiah 53:12, "**He bore the sin of many**".

Matthew, describing the events of Palm Sunday: "**This took place to fulfil what was spoken through the prophet: 'Say to the Daughter of Zion, "See, your King comes to you, gentle and riding on a donkey, and on a colt, the foal of a donkey"'**" (Matthew 21:4,5 – see Zechariah 9:9).

Jesus, to the chief priests and elders: "**Have you never read in the Scriptures: 'The stone the builders rejected has become the

---

1   The word "Christ" is a Greek word *christos* meaning "Anointed One". The Hebrew word "Messiah" has the same meaning.

cornerstone; the Lord has done this, and it is marvellous in our eyes'" (Matthew 21:42; Mark 12:10-11; Luke 20:17 – see Psalm 118:22,23).

John, explaining the rejection of Jesus' message by many: "This was to fulfil the word of Isaiah the prophet: 'Lord, who has believed our message and to whom has the arm of the Lord been revealed?'" (John 12:38 – see Isaiah 53:1).

Jesus, when explaining at the Last Supper that one of them would betray him: "But this is to fulfil this passage of Scripture: 'He who shared my bread has lifted up his heel against me'" (John 13:18 – see Psalm 41:9).

Jesus, declaring that the disciples would desert him: "It is written: 'I will strike the shepherd, and the sheep of the flock will be scattered'" (Matthew 26:31 – see Zechariah 13:7).

Jesus, before leaving the Upper Room: "It is written: 'And he was numbered with the transgressors'; and I tell you that this must be fulfilled in me. Yes, what is written about me is reaching its fulfilment" (Luke 22:37 – see Isaiah 53:12).

Jesus, when explaining to Peter in Gethsemane that he could call angels to his assistance: "But how then would the Scriptures be fulfilled that say it must happen in this way?" (Matthew 26:54).

Jesus, to the soldiers: "This has all taken place that the writings of the prophets might be fulfilled" (Matthew 26:56 – also Mark 14:48,49).

Matthew, telling how Judas returned the thirty pieces of silver to the high priests, who used it to buy the potter's field: "Then what was spoken by Jeremiah the prophet was fulfilled: 'They took the thirty pieces of silver coins, the price set on him by the people of Israel, and they used them to buy the potter's field, as the Lord commanded me'" (Matthew 27:9,10 – see Zechariah 11:12,13).[1]

---

1 Various explanations have been given as to why Matthew quotes the passage as coming from Jeremiah, when it is from Zechariah.

Jesus, on the cross: "**My God, my God, why have you forsaken me?**" (Matthew 27:46; Mark 15:34 – see Psalm 22:1).

John, describing how the soldiers cast lots for his clothing: "**This happened that the Scriptures might be fulfilled which said, 'They divided my garments among them and cast lots for my clothing'**" (John 19:24 – see Psalm 22:18).

John, referring to the piercing of his side by the soldier with a spear: "**These things happened so that the Scripture would be fulfilled: 'Not one of his bones will be broken,' and, as another Scripture says, 'they will look on the one they have pierced'**" (John 19:36,37 – see Exodus 12:46; Psalm 34:19,20; Zechariah 12:10).

Jesus, to Cleopas and his partner on the day of his resurrection: "**'Did not the Messiah have to suffer these things and then enter his glory?' And beginning with Moses and all the Prophets, he explained to them what was said in all the Scriptures concerning himself**" (Luke 24:26,27).

Jesus, to the disciples on the day of his resurrection: "**Then he opened their minds so they could understand the Scriptures. He told them, 'This is what is written: The Messiah will suffer and rise from the dead on the third day, and repentance for the forgiveness of sins will be preached in his name to all nations, beginning at Jerusalem'**" (Luke 24:45-47).

Peter, to the crowds on the Day of Pentecost: "**God raised him from the dead, freeing him from the agony of death... David said about him: ...'you will not abandon me to the realm of the dead, you will not let your holy one see decay'**" (Acts 2:24-28 – see Psalm 16:8-11).

Peter, to a gathering in the temple shortly afterwards: "**This is how God fulfilled what he had foretold through all the prophets, saying that his Messiah would suffer... Indeed, beginning with Samuel, all the prophets who have spoken have foretold these days**" (Acts 3:18,24).

The Cross in the Gospels

The early Christians in prayer: "You spoke by the Holy Spirit through the mouth of your servant, our father David: '...The kings of the earth rise up and the rulers band together against the Lord and against his anointed one'" (Acts 4:25,26 – see Psalm 2:1,2).

Philip to the Ethiopian official: When explaining the meaning of a passage from Isaiah 53 (verses 7 and 8), which the Ethiopian had been reading, "Philip began with that very passage of Scripture and told him the good news about Jesus" (Acts 8:32-35).

Paul, preaching in the synagogue in Pisidian Antioch: "The people of Jerusalem and their rulers did not recognise Jesus, yet in condemning him they fulfilled the words of the prophets that are read every Sabbath... When they had carried out all that was written about him, they took him down from the cross [literally "tree"] and laid him in a tomb (Acts 13:27,29).

Paul, teaching in the synagogue in Thessalonica: "On three Sabbath days he reasoned with them from the Scriptures, explaining and proving that the Messiah had to suffer and rise from the dead" (Acts 17:2,3).

Paul, telling the story of his conversion before King Agrippa, Governor Festus and high-ranking military officers and prominent men of Caesarea: "God has helped me to this very day; so I stand here and testify to small and great alike. I am saying nothing beyond what the prophets and Moses said would happen – that the Messiah would suffer and, as the first to rise from the dead, would bring the message of light to his own people and to the Gentiles" (Acts 26:22,23).

Paul, years later: "For what I received I passed on to you as of first importance: that Christ died for our sins according to the Scriptures, that he was buried, that he was raised on the third day according to the Scriptures..." (1 Corinthians 15:3).

Peter, years later: "Concerning this salvation, the prophets, who spoke of the grace that was to come to you, searched intently and with the greatest care, trying to find out the time and circumstances to which the Spirit of Christ in them was pointing when they predicted the sufferings of Christ and the glories that would follow" (1 Peter 1:10; 11).

The cross in Acts

In the book of Acts, Luke continues the story he has told us in his Gospel, from the resurrection of Jesus to the imprisonment of Paul in Rome about 30 years later. It is the story of the growth of the Christian church from its first beginnings in Jerusalem, through those countries we now know as Syria and Turkey, and on to Greece and Rome. Luke records a summary of several sermons preached by Peter and by Paul, after his conversion. These and other hints allow us to assess what was at the heart of the message they preached. We do not know all the sources Luke used for this book, but he certainly knew Paul very well and probably also knew Peter and others who were closely associated with these events.

In many instances we are told that the disciples preached "**the word of God**" or the "**word of the Lord**" or simply "**the word**". In a few instances it is "**the kingdom of God**" they proclaimed. When we are given more detail as to what that "word" was all about, the focus is always on Jesus, who he was, what he had done, and what he was offering to those who would put their faith in him. The main emphasis is on his death and resurrection.

One thing becomes evident in all the references to the death of Jesus in the book of Acts – there are no direct statements concerning the atoning nature of his death. Statements such as "he died for us", "he died for our sins", "he bore our sins" or "he was made sin for us", which are so common in the letters of the New Testament, are not found here. I believe there are five reasons for this.

Why Did Jesus Die?

First, Luke was primarily a historian (and, as scholars recognise, a very good one) rather than a theologian. He records events rather than providing teaching. Though he wrote later, he was concerned to record what happened and what was preached at the time and not to record later theology.

Second, the earliest preaching of the gospel was to Jews. Most Jews of that time would have been familiar with the Old Testament writings and would have had an expectation that one day God would send his Anointed One. Though there were differing ideas about the sort of person the Anointed One would be or what he would achieve, this was a common expectation. It was natural, therefore, that the emphasis of the early Christians would be on proving to their hearers that this man Jesus, who had caused such a stir during his three years of teaching and healing around Galilee and Judea, and whom their leaders had persuaded Pilate to crucify, *was indeed the one*. And as Israel's Messiah, his resurrection also proved him to be the world's Lord. It is instructive to note all the terms used to describe Jesus in the early preaching and witnessing of the disciples.

He is the **Christ** or **Messiah**, the one foretold by the prophets (2:31,36; 3:18,20; 5:42; 9:22; 17:3; 18:5,28), or David's foretold descendant and God's "**anointed one**" (4:26), both of which are messianic concepts.

He is "**exalted to the right hand of God**" in fulfilment of Psalm 110:1 (2:33-35; cf. 5:31; 7:55,56).

He is "**Lord**" (2:36; 7:59,60) or "**Lord of all**" (10:36). The Greek word used in the New Testament for "Lord" is the same word used for God in the Greek translation of the Hebrew Old Testament of that time.

He is God's "**servant**" (3:13,26) or "**holy servant**" (4:27,30) and the "**Righteous One**" (3:14; 7:52), terms that echo the prophet Isaiah.

He is the "**author of life**", whom they had killed! (3:15).

He is **Prince** and **Saviour** (5:31; 13:23) and there is salvation in none other, there being "**no other name under heaven by which we must be saved**" (4:12).

He is the "**Son of Man**" (7:56), the figure in the book of Daniel to whom will be given "**authority, glory, and sovereign power; all nations and peoples of every language worshipped him. His dominion is an everlasting dominion that will not pass away, and his kingdom is one that will never be destroyed**" (7:13,14).

He is "**judge of the living and the dead**" (10:42) and God has given proof to everyone that "**he will judge the world with justice… by raising him from the dead**"(17:31).

He is the one who will "**bring salvation to the ends of the earth**" (13:47 – see Isaiah 49:6).

Third, there is not the same emphasis on explaining the significance of the crucifixion that we find in the letters of the New Testament, because of the settings in which the early proclamations of the gospel were made. All the settings Luke describes are evangelistic settings. In other words, apart form the early preaching in Jerusalem, they were telling the good news of the gospel to those who had never heard of Jesus, or if they had, they would have had no idea who he really was. It was natural then to focus on his person, rather than on the saving nature of his death. We read that the early converts "**devoted themselves to the apostles' teaching**" (2:42). What this teaching, which was addressed to those who had become Christians, consisted of, we do not know. I can imagine it contained much of what was later spelled out in more detail and depth in the letters that we have.

A fourth reason has to do with the nature of the death and resurrection of Jesus. Up to the point that Jesus rose from the dead, the disciples did not have much clue at all about what was going on. Jesus had told them that he had come "**to give his life as a ransom**

for many" (Mark 10:45). During his last meal with them he had clearly said that his body would be broken and his blood poured out "**for the forgiveness of sins**" (Matthew 26:28). But people die every day, often cruelly. That Jesus' death should be anything different, or have cosmological significance, was way beyond their perception. However, people don't rise from the dead every day! It is understandable that this is what got their attention and started them thinking in totally new ways. It is understandable, therefore, that it was the resurrection they would focus on in their effort to convince their fellow countrymen that Jesus was indeed the promised messiah.

The fifth reason is that the full meaning of his death is something that takes time to digest. In my own personal experience this was the case. As a lad of about seventeen I experienced the forgiveness and the presence of the Holy Spirit in my life that is offered to us in the gospel. However, it was some time before it dawned on me that it was by means of the cross that Jesus had purchased that forgiveness on my behalf. The resurrection was obvious to the first disciples. After all, they had talked and eaten with Jesus over a period of 40 days after he had been well and truly dead and buried. No doubt, the significance of his death and why that had been necessary in order to reconcile us to God was one of the things he had talked about over those 40 days. However, this was not at all as obvious as the fact that he was *alive*. It was Paul, after his conversion, possibly a year or two later, who grasped most clearly the implications of Christ's death. I will explore the reasons for this in the next chapter.

What the early disciples did do, however, was to offer men and women the *benefits* of Christ's death and resurrection. In Acts the benefits are primarily twofold – forgiveness (2:38; 5:31; 10:43; 13:38) and the gift of the Holy Spirit (2:38; 5:32; 8:17; 9:17; 10:44; 19:6). They could not only be fully reconciled to God, but he would come to live within them as a permanent abiding presence, transforming them from within and creating a new community of his people. This had been foretold by the Old Testament prophets, specifically Jeremiah (31:31-34) and Ezekiel (36:25-27). Receiving these benefits was conditional on their repentance, their trust in Jesus and their willingness to accept him as the Lord of their lives, signifying this repentance by being baptised (e.g. 2:38; 3:19; 5:31,32; 10:43,47; 17:30).

Paul's statement in 1 Corinthians 15 that "**he received**" the teaching that "**Christ died for our sins**" as of "**first importance**" (v. 3) is relevant here. He would have received this doctrine from members of the primitive church, probably within the first seven years after Jesus' death, so it would have been part and parcel of their teaching. Similarly, in the same letter he tells how he "**received from the Lord**" the tradition of the Lord's Supper with its emphasis on the body of Jesus given for us (11:23,24). "Received from the Lord" probably means that, though he got it from the apostles, the teaching went back to Jesus himself. In addition, the allusions we find to Isaiah's Suffering Servant in Acts are highly significant. He is God's "holy servant" (3:13; 4:27) and it is Isaiah 53, where forgiveness and justification through sacrificial death are so prominent, that is specifically focused on by Philip in his discussion with the Ethiopian (8:32-35). Throughout Acts it is the Jesus who has died and risen who offers men and women forgiveness and the gift of the Holy Spirit.

Before leaving Acts, it is worth commenting on an interesting passage that occurs in Peter's first sermon to the crowds in Jerusalem. He declared, "**This man was handed over to you by God's deliberate plan and foreknowledge; and you, with the help of wicked men, put him to death by nailing him to the cross**" (2:23). Here we have the mystery that we find also in other parts of the Bible – the mystery of the relationship between God's sovereign purposes and human choice. It was God's purpose from the beginning to send his Son to pay the price for our sins, in order to bring us back to himself. Indeed, the book of Revelation describes Jesus as "**the Lamb who was slain from the creation of the world**" (13:8). Octavius Winslow summed this up in a neat statement: "Who delivered up Jesus to die? Not Judas, for money; not Pilate, for fear; not the Jews, for envy; – but the Father, for love!" And yet, that in no way excuses those who were responsible for the deed. Maybe the answer to the mystery can be found in the word "foreknowledge". God is not limited to time in the way we are. After all, he created time – in a big bang about 13.7 billion years ago according to modern scientific theory. But though he can foresee the future, this does not mean that he determines our actions and that we are not responsible for the choices we make. Maybe this is a mystery we have to live with and will no doubt become plain enough when we gather round the throne in glory. The early disciples did not hesitate to put the blame for the crucifixion of Jesus where it belonged (see also 3:13-15; 4:10,11; 5:30; 7:51-53). Alan E. Lewis comments on this point:

> Note the unmistakable and unflinching linguistic connections in the NT (paradosis) between God "giving up" the Son, and the Son "giving himself up" to death, on the one hand, and, on the other, human acts of betrayal and surrender, i.e., the "betraying" of Jesus by his disciples and his being "handed over" and "delivered up" to the Jewish and Roman authorities who destroyed him. See esp. Mark 9:31; 10:33; 14:10,41,42; 15:1,15; Romans 8:32; Galatians 2:20; 1 Corinthians 11:23.

The cross in the New Testament letters

When we come to the letters of the New Testament, we find a very interesting thing. You would have thought that with someone who had lived such a wonderful life, such as no one else has ever lived before or since, that there would have been lots of things the writers of these letters could have written about. They could have written about his great compassion and the way he mixed with the outcasts of society; his remarkable healing ministry to the lame, the lepers, the blind, the tormented and even how, on occasions, he raised the dead; the confident authority with which he spoke and the wisdom of his teaching which has been unsurpassed, or the confident and unassuming way in which he challenged the civil and religious rulers of his day. We have a full account of all these things in the four Gospels, but they hardly get another mention in the rest of the New Testament.

When events from the life of Jesus are referred to, from his birth to his ascension into heaven, we find that all the emphasis is on his death and his resurrection. According to my reckoning, a rough estimate of the number of references to the cross in the letters is as follows: 18 in Romans; 11 in 1 Corinthians; six in 2 Corinthians; eight in Galatians; six in Ephesians; three in Philippians; seven in Colossians; two in 1 Thessalonians; one in 1 Timothy; two in 2 Timothy; one in Titus; 23 in Hebrews; ten in 1 Peter; five in 1 John; and if we include all the references to the Jesus as the Lamb, the animal of sacrifice, 29 in Revelation. The only letters not to mention the cross directly are James, 2 Peter, Jude, the three short personal letters of Philemon, and 2 and 3 John.

Christ's death "for our sins"

Another interesting thing to note is that all the emphasis here is on the fact that he died for "us" or "for our sins". Consider the following phrases that are typical of what we find: He died "**for many**" (Mark 10:45); "**for the ungodly**" (Romans 5:6); "**for us**" (5:8); "**for us all**" (8:32); "**for you**" (1 Corinthians 11:24); "**for our sins**" (15:3); "**for all**" (2 Corinthians 5:14); "**for me**" (Galatians 2:20); "**for her** [the church]" (Ephesians 5:25); "**to do away with sin**"(Hebrews 9:26); "**to take away the sins of many**" (9:28); "**for sins**" (1 Peter 3:18); "**for the sins of the whole world**" (1 John 2:2).

The different words that are used in the Greek language in which the New Testament was written, which are translated "for" in this context in our English translations, are significant. Four different words are used, *huper, peri, anti* and *dia*. *Huper* is the most common and is used 26 times in this way. It has the meaning "*in behalf of, for the sake of someone or something*", though many times it is shown by its context to be used in the sense of "*instead of*". For example, in another context, Paul wanted to keep Onesimus in Rome to serve him "on behalf of" his master Philemon, that is, "in his place" (Philemon 13). This meaning, in relation to the cross, is particularly clear in passages such as 2 Corinthians 5:21 and Galatians 3:13. *Peri*, used 6 times, usually has the meaning "*with regard to, with reference to*". According to the Arndt-Gingrich lexicon, when used with the Greek word for "sin" it has the sense "*to take away, to atone for*". *Anti* is used three times in connection with the Greek word *lutron*, "a ransom" (Matthew 20:28; Mark 10:45; 1 Timothy 2:6). It has the primary meaning "*instead of, in place of*", though it can develop into "*in behalf of*", similar in meaning to *huper*. Leon Morris, in *The Apostolic Preaching of the Cross*, comments: "The most common meaning of the preposition, both inside the New Testament and out, is 'instead of' or 'in exchange for'." *Dia* is used once in this context (Romans 4:25). It has the meaning "*because of*".

So it could be said, in summary, that Christ died "on our behalf", "for our sake", or "instead of us", or "with regard to", "with reference to", or "because of" our sins, or to "take them away". Patricia Hampl, in *I Could Tell You Stories*, says that redemption requires that radical evil and radical atonement collide. This happened on the cross.

The eminent theologian, Karl Barth, in his *Church Dogmatics, IV*, summed up the New Testament use of these prepositions as pointing to Christ's "activity as our Representative and Substitute." He says:

> They cannot be understood if – quite apart from the particular view of the atonement made in Him which dominates these passages – we do not see that in general these prepositions speak of a place which ought to be ours, that we ought to have taken this place, that we have been taken from it, that it is occupied by another, that this other acts in this place as only He can, in our cause and interest, that we cannot add to anything that He does there because the place where we might do so is occupied by Him, that anything further which might happen can result only from what is done by Him in our place and in our cause.

Concerning this emphasis John Stott, in *Our Guilty Silence*, says:

> Since Jesus had no sin either in his nature or in his conduct, he need never have died either physically or spiritually... Then

why did he do it? What was the rationale of his death? There is only one possible, logical, biblical answer. It is that he died for our sins, not his own. The death he died was our death, the penalty which our sins had richly deserved.

There are no doubt several reasons we could give as to why Jesus came: to show us how to live by giving us his teaching and an example to follow; to give us a purpose for living; or to give us hope for the future. However, John sums up the major emphasis of the New Testament when he declares, "**he appeared so that he might take away our sins**" (1 John 3:5).

The blood of Christ

Another significant emphasis is that which is placed on "the blood of Christ". Jesus himself, during his last meal with his disciples, had spoken of "**my blood of the covenant, which is poured out for many for the forgiveness of sins**" (Matthew 26:28). Earlier, he had declared that it was through the appropriation of his blood that we receive eternal life and enjoy a close relationship with him (John 6:53-56). This way of speaking of Christ's death occurs about 30 times in the New Testament. In the letters it is the most common way of doing so.

God had forbidden his people to eat the flesh of animals that still contained the blood, "**because the life of every creature is its blood**" (Leviticus 17:14). We now know the truth of that statement. Our bodies contain something like one hundred trillion cells, each of which requires a constant supply of oxygen, amino acids, nitrogen, sodium, potassium, calcium, magnesium, sugars, lipids, cholesterols, and hormones. All these are carried on tiny rafts of blood cells which have access to every living cell in the body through minute capillaries. Each cell has its own drawing rights and extracts what

The Cross in the New Testament Letters

it needs to fuel its amazingly complex chemical reactions. Without the life-giving quality of the blood the cells would very quickly die. Quite literally, "the life of the flesh is the blood"! When Jesus spoke of his blood being "poured out", he was referring to his life, the life of God himself, voluntarily given for us. Leon Morris, in *The Atonement: Its Meaning and Significance*, showed very clearly that this term "blood" denotes a life laid down in a violent, sacrificial death. Oswald Chambers made this comment:

> The expression "the blood of Christ" means not only that Christ shed his blood, but also that he poured it out before God. In the Old Testament the idea of sacrifice is that the blood, which is the life (see Genesis 4:4), is poured out to God, its Giver. When Jesus Christ shed his blood on the cross it was not the blood of a martyr, or the blood of one man for another; it was the life of God poured out to redeem the world.

It is significant in this respect that the Hebrew word for blood occurs 362 times in the Old Testament. In 203 of these instances it refers to death with violence of some kind. In 103 instances it refers to sacrificial blood, 78 of these occurring in Leviticus and Exodus. When the Hebrews heard the word 'blood', the most likely association to be conjured up would be that of violent death.

Another function of blood is its cleansing properties. Each cell in the body needs to get rid of its potentially hazardous waste products such as carbon dioxide, urea and uric acid. It is the blood cells that have this cleansing action, removing these wastes to the kidneys. The heart of a 70kg man will pump about six litres per minute. Twenty percent of this flows through the kidneys, which distil some thirty chemicals and promptly return 99 percent of the volume back into the bloodstream, sending the remaining one percent off to the bladder for expulsion. These remarkable blood cells survive for a quarter-million circuits and are then nudged to the liver and spleen for one last unloading. They are picked clean and broken down into amino acids and bile pigment for recycling. Every second the bone marrow produces another four million blood cells to replace these.

So the cleansing nature of blood also provides us with a very appropriate metaphor for the cross. The missionary doctor Paul Brand, who did some wonderful pioneering surgical work restoring dignity to patients deformed by leprosy, wrote the book *In His Image*, together with Philip Yancey, on this remarkable body God has given us. He says:

> I used to think it strange that the Bible keeps talking about the cleansing power of the blood (1 Peter 1:2). It seemed to me that the blood was messy stuff. I needed to wash my white lab coats if they became stained with blood.
>
> Today I love the analogy; it is so true of the body. The blood is constantly cleansing every cell, and washing away all the debris that accumulates all the time.

Consider the following statements:

We have been **bought** by his blood (Acts 20:28).
Our sins are **atoned for** through the shedding of his blood (Romans 3:25).
We are **justified** by his blood (Romans 5:9).
We have **redemption, the forgiveness of sins** through his blood (Ephesians 1:7).
We are **brought near** to God by the blood of Christ (Ephesians 2:13).
We have **peace** with God through his blood (Colossians 1:20).
We have **eternal redemption** by his blood (Hebrews 9:12).
It is the blood of Christ that will **cleanse our consciences**

from acts that lead to death (Hebrews 9:14).
We have **confidence to enter the presence of God** by the blood of Jesus (Hebrews 10:19).
It is the blood of Christ that **sanctifies us** (Hebrews 10:29).
We are **made holy** by his blood (Hebrews 13:12).
We are **redeemed from an empty way of life** with the precious blood of Christ (1 Peter 1:18,19).
The blood of Jesus **purifies us from all sin** (1 John 1:7).
He **freed us from our sins** by his blood (Revelation 1:5).
It was with his blood that he **purchased for God members of every tribe and language and people and nation** (Revelation 5:9).
Our robes are washed and made white by the blood of the Lamb (Revelation 7:14).
We **triumph over the evil one** by the blood of the Lamb (Revelation 12:11).

There appears, also, to be a progressive revelation of the remission of sin through the shedding of blood in he Bible. In the case of Abel, the blood was sufficient for the forgiveness of one man (Genesis 4:4). During the first Passover, the blood of the lamb on the doorpost was sufficient to protect a whole family (Exodus 12:3). When the tabernacle was constructed, on the Day of Atonement the blood of one goat was sufficient to atone for the guilt of the nation (Leviticus 16:15,16). But in the case of Jesus, the Lamb of God, the blood shed on the cross was sufficient for "**the sins of the whole world**" (1 John 2:2). I believe J. Behm got the New Testament emphasis on blood in this context right when he said: "'Blood of Christ' is like 'cross', only another, clearer expression for the death of Christ in its salvation meaning."

Because I like stories, I will finish with three short ones. John Bunyan, the author of *Pilgrim's Progress,* which has probably gone through more editions than any other book in history other than the Bible, wrote in his later book, *Grace Abounding*:

> I remember that one day, as I was travelling into the country, and musing on the wickedness and blasphemy of my heart, and considering the enmity that was in me to God, that Scripture came into my mind, 'He [has] made peace by the blood of his cross.' By which I was made to see, both again and again that day, that God and my soul were friends by his blood; yea, I saw that the justice of God and my sinful soul could embrace and kiss each other through his blood. This was a good day to me; I hope I shall never forget it.

When the multimillionaire J. P. Morgan died, it was found that he had made his will a year before his death. It consisted of 10,000 words, and contained 37 articles. Some of his financial transactions had involved such large sums of money that they disturbed the financial equilibrium of the whole world. Yet he left us in no doubt as to what he considered the most important clause in his will and what stood out in his mind as his most important transaction. He said:

> I commit my soul into the hands of my Saviour, full of confidence that having redeemed me and washed me with His precious blood, He will present me faultless before the Throne of my Heavenly Father. I entreat my children to maintain and defend at all hazards and at all costs personally, the blessed doctrine of the complete atonement of sin through the blood of Jesus Christ once offered and through that alone.

A story is told of Queen Victoria that is said to be authentic. When she occupied her castle at Balmoral, Scotland, she was in the habit of calling in on certain cottagers living in the neighbourhood. One aged Highland woman, who felt greatly honoured by these visits and who knew the Lord, was anxious about the spiritual state of the queen. As the season came to a close one year, Her Majesty was making her last visit to the humble home of this dear child of God. After the good-byes were said, the old cottager timidly inquired, "May I ask your gracious Majesty a question?" "Yes," replied the queen, "as many as you like." "Will your Majesty meet me in heaven?" Instantly, the royal visitor replied, "I will, through the all-availing blood of Jesus."

The poet and hymn writer, William Cowper, put it like this:

There is a fountain filled with blood,
drawn from Immanuel's veins,
And sinners plunged beneath that flood
lose all their guilty stains.

Such language may seem a little grotesque in today's society where we associate blood with all the mayhem we see constantly on television. However, to those with understanding and with the humility to recognise their greatest need, it contains the most important truth and glorious news that is available to this weary planet.

The cross in Paul's letters

Paul could well be called "the theologian of the cross". He was uniquely positioned for the remarkable ministry God gave him. A man of brilliant intellect, who had studied at the feet of the most renowned rabbi of the day (Acts 22:3), and at home in three cultures – Hebrew, Greek and Roman – he ultimately became the most prolific writer in the New Testament. Thirteen of the 21 letters are traditionally attributed to him. Scholars debate his authorship of some of these, though they are in almost unanimous agreement that he wrote seven of them. For the purpose of this study I will assume his authorship of all 13. To assume otherwise would have little effect on the results, as his insights into the meaning of the cross are clearly presented in the seven that are universally recognised as having been written by him.

An important perspective on his understanding of the cross came from his religious training. He was, by upbringing and choice, a strict Pharisee. By his own description he was "**circumcised on the eighth day, of the people of Israel, of the tribe of Benjamin, a Hebrew of Hebrews; in regard to the law, a Pharisee; as for zeal, persecuting the church; as for righteousness based on the law, faultless**" (Philippians 3:5,6). His whole training had led him to believe that one could prove oneself acceptable to God by one's own moral efforts. If anyone could have made it with God by good pedigree, proper ritual, religious observances, sincere motives and impeccable behaviour, Paul could have done so.

Another factor would have been the views he had initially held about the nature of the promised Messiah, though he nowhere spells these out. Like many of his day, he had no doubt longed for a deliverer who would save the Jews from the domination of Rome and restore the purity of Pharisaical religion. Such a messianic figure would be widely recognised and respected, at least by its religious leaders, and receive the nation's acclaim.

But Jesus had been humiliated, condemned and *crucified* – crucified between two "bandits" as Mark and Matthew call them, men of violence, prepared to kill as well as steal. A crucified person, as the Romans put it, was *damnatio ad bestias,* meaning "condemned to the death of a beast". As Rutledge points out, crucifixion was deliberately intended to be *obscene* in the original sense of that word. The Oxford Dictionary suggests "disgusting, repulsive, filthy, foul, abominable, loathsome." The crowds understood that their role was to increase, by jeering and mocking, the degradation of those who had been so designated as unfit to live. They were *supposed* to curse him – and they did. Heaping abuse on a crucified victim was part of the ritual, part of the entertainment. The crucified would be mocked, spat upon, beaten nearly to death, naked, plagued by insects, and covered with dirt, sweat, blood and excrement. Added to this was the fact that for a Jew, one so condemned came under the curse of God (Deuteronomy 21:23).

When the early Christians proclaimed a man killed in this way as the Messiah promised by all the prophets who would deliver his people from their sins and who had been appointed as judge of the human race, it was too much for Paul. For a respectable, religious, moral and passionate person like Paul, his reaction was understandable. He made it his mission to stamp out this new sect. "**I persecuted the followers of this Way to their death, arresting both men and women and throwing them into prison**" (Acts 22:4). "**I put many of the Lord's people in prison, and when they were put**

The Cross in Paul's Letters

to death, I cast my vote against them. Many a time I went from one synagogue to another to have them punished, and I tried to force them to blaspheme. I was so obsessed with persecuting them that I even hunted them down in foreign cities" (Acts 26:10,11).

Maybe, when Paul observed the manner in which the first martyr, Stephen, met his death (Acts 7:57-60), he began to have misgivings. His reaction, though, was to silence his conscience by violent anti-Christian activity. However, when he was finally confronted by the risen Christ on the road to Damascus (Acts 9:1-9), his faith in his own morality, his religious beliefs and his own learning collapsed like a pack of cards. It is little wonder that, after his conversion, he disappeared into the desert for three years to sort things out and rethink his understanding of the Old Testament from scratch (Galatians 1:17,18).

Paul emerged from this time with two unmistakable convictions. The first was that the man Jesus, who had died on Calvary's hill and who had spoken to him on the Damascus Road was indeed Lord of heaven and earth. His experience on the Damascus Road was enough to convince him of that. For one brought up in the strict monotheism of Judaism, this conviction was to form his understanding of the trinitarian nature of God. The second conviction was the fact that the key to understanding the nature of true religion lay in the cross and resurrection of Jesus. No doubt, this understanding had taken longer to resolve. However, the shock of Damascus Road must have enabled him to glimpse something of the depths of evil in the human heart, the grip of which had led him in such a wrong and violent direction. A radical problem demands a radical solution. His views on the cross, with their roots in the teaching of Jesus himself, were probably fully developed by Paul early in his Christian experience. Certainly they were by the time he began to write the earliest letters that are still in existence – that is, about A.D. 50, 20 or so years after the crucifixion and probably about 15 to 17 years after his conversion. As Denney stated, "We cannot discover in Paul's interpretation of Christ's death anything which essentially distinguishes his earliest [letters] from his latest." His gospel, the only gospel he knew, was always "**the message of the cross**" (1 Corinthians 1:18), or "**the message of reconciliation**" (2 Corinthians 5:19). So let's summarise the emphasis he gives to the cross in these letters.

The cross and sin

As with all the writers of the New Testament, the reason Paul gives for Jesus' death is that it dealt with the problem of sin and the effect sin had on our relationship with God. Whatever else we may learn from the cross – how to stick to our principles whatever the consequences, how to face suffering, how to love our neighbour, how to treat our enemies – it is the fact that Jesus died "**for our sins**" or "**for us**" that always receives the greatest emphasis. "**God made him who had no sin to be sin for us**" (2 Corinthians 5:21). He "**redeemed us… by becoming a curse for us**" (Galatians 3:13). Other truths flow from this one. He didn't die for good people but "**for the ungodly**", those who were "**God's enemies**" (Romans 5:6,10). He is the "**Passover lamb**" whose blood shelters us from judgement (1 Corinthians 5:7).

And it is not just that he died "**for us all**" (Romans 8:32). There is something very personal about the cross for Paul. "**The life I live in the body, I live by faith in the Son of God, who loved *me*[1] and gave himself for *me*[2]**" (Galatians 2:20). As someone has put it: "Jesus died on the cross – that's history. Jesus died for me – that's salvation." It never ceased to amaze Paul that Jesus should die for

---

1 Italics mine.
2 Italics mine.

him, "Even though I was once a blasphemer and a persecutor and a violent man... Here is a trustworthy saying that deserves full acceptance: Christ Jesus came into the world to save sinners – of whom I am the worst" (1 Timothy 1:13-15). The truth of what Jesus had done for him had so gripped him that the allurements of this world and its false values had no more appeal for him than they would have for a dead man. "May I never boast except in the cross of our Lord Jesus Christ, through which the world has been crucified to me, and I to the world" (Galatians 6:14). As Denney states:

> When it had dawned on his mind what the cross of Christ was, when he saw what it signified as a revelation of God and his love, everything else in the universe faded from his view.

The cross central in Paul's preaching

It was the cross that became the central plank of Paul's preaching. In reminding the Corinthian Church of his ministry among them, he declared, "I resolved to know nothing while I was with you except Jesus Christ and him crucified" (1 Corinthians 2:2). And again, "What I received I passed on to you as of first importance: that Christ died for our sins according to the Scriptures, that he was buried, that he was raised on the third day according to the Scriptures" (1 Corinthians 15:3,4). He rebuked the Galatian Christians for turning from truths he had taught them: "Who has bewitched you? Before your very eyes Jesus Christ was clearly portrayed as crucified" (Galatians 3:1). However much the example of Jesus' life may have meant to Paul, it was by his death that he "disarmed the powers and authorities, [making] a public spectacle of them, triumphing over them by the cross" (Colossians 2:15). Denney says of Paul's exposition of the meaning of the cross in

Romans and Galatians, "This death of Christ is the source of all that is Christian. All Christian inferences about God are deduced from it."

Our identification with Christ in his death

One of the major themes of Paul's teaching is the emphasis that he puts on our union or identification with Christ, particularly in death and resurrection. When we come in repentance and faith to Jesus, submitting our lives to him as Saviour and Lord, then the Holy Spirit, who is now the Spirit of the risen Christ, brings us into an intimate relationship with Christ. Paul constantly describes this relationship as being "in Christ". John Stott, in *Life in Christ*, tells us that the expressions "in Christ", "in him" and "in the Lord" occur 164 times in Paul's letters.

Baptism is the symbol of our entry into this relationship. Whereas baptism in Acts is spoken of as the washing away of sins (Acts 22:16), Paul also speaks of it as the burial service of our old way of life, symbolising our identity with Christ in his death and resurrection. "**Don't you know that all of us who were baptised into Christ were baptised into his death? We were therefore buried with him through baptism into death in order that, just as Christ was raised from the dead through the glory of the Father, we too may live a new life**" (Romans 6:3,4 – cf. Colossians 2:12). Lalu Dasgupta, who came to faith in Christ while attending an Alpha Course, described in *Alpha News* what his baptism meant to him.

> I did get the feeling of it being a new start. Just before I went under the water for baptism, I remembered all those guilty feelings and thoughts, all the things in my life that I was particularly ashamed of – the sort of things that happened five or ten years ago, that have never left me.

I had them in the front of my mind and I thought, 'What I'm about to go through now is going to cleanse me of all of this…'

I felt myself saying sorry to God for all those things and they don't exercise me any more.

So through that very simple act of baptism, I had the knowledge that despite my guilty feelings, I'd been forgiven. I felt that the old me was dead and I was now living for someone else.

This does not mean that there is anything automatic about baptism in bringing us into a relationship with God. In his letters to the Romans, the Galatians and the Colossians, Paul is concerned to underline the importance of faith in our relationship with Christ before he ever gets around to speaking about the significance of baptism. Rather, baptism is the sign and seal of the righteousness we receive by faith, as was circumcision under the old covenant (Romans 4:11).

Other passages where Paul speaks about our identification with Christ in his death are Romans 7:4 and Colossians 2:20: "**So, my brothers and sisters, you also died to the law through the body of Christ, that you might belong to another, to him who was raised from the dead, in order that we might bear fruit for God.**" "**Since you died with Christ to the elemental spiritual forces of this world, why, as though you still belonged to the world, do you submit to its rules: 'Do not handle! Do not taste! Do not touch!'?**" When Jesus died, in God's reckoning, it was just as if I had died, paying the full penalty for my own sins. The result is that the law cannot now condemn me – I am freed from guilt – and my allegiance now is not to a set of rules, do's and don'ts, but to a person to whom I now belong. Of course, allegiance to Christ has its moral demands,[1]

---

1 See further on this theme in my booklet *Does It Matter How We Live?*

but my motivation now is gratitude and my love for Jesus, and my motivator is the living Christ who has come to live within me by his Spirit.

Paul expresses this identification from God's perspective (Jesus identifying with us) in Romans 8:3: "**What the law was powerless to do because it was weakened by the sinful nature, God did by sending his own Son in the likeness of sinful humanity to be a sin offering. And so he condemned sin in human flesh, in order that the righteous requirements of the law might be fully met in us, who do not live according to the sinful nature but according to the Spirit.**" Similarly, in 2 Corinthians 5:14 Paul declares, "**we are convinced that one died for all, and therefore all died.**" Denney comments:

> This clause puts as plainly as it can be put the idea that his death was equivalent to the death of all. In other words, it was the death of all men which was died by him.

Social commentator, Os Guinness gives us one implication of this truth:

> At the supreme moment of his dying Jesus so identified himself with men and the depths of their predicament and agony that no man can now sink so low that God has not gone lower.

Or as N. T. Wright eloquently expresses it in *The Lord and His Prayer*, he went "solo and unaided into the whirlpool [of evil], so that it may exhaust its force on him and let the rest of the world go free."

In this same passage in 2 Corinthians 5, Paul goes on to state that those who believe this "**should no longer live for themselves but for him who died for them and was raised again**" (v. 15).

Denney comments again:

> It will not be easy for anyone to be grateful for Christ's death, especially with a gratitude which will acknowledge that his very life is Christ's, unless he understands the cross in the sense that Christ there made the death of all men his own.

And it is this identification with Christ in his death that is the sole ground of our salvation. Dietrich Bonhoeffer, in *Life Together*, says:

> The fact that Jesus Christ died is more important than the fact that I shall die, and the fact that Jesus Christ rose from the dead is the sole ground of my hope that I too shall be raised on the Last Day. Our salvation is "external to us." I find no salvation in my life history, but only in the history of Jesus Christ.

As Jesus represented us in his death and resurrection, so he now represents us in heaven. He is our advocate, presenting his death on our behalf before his Father and interceding on our behalf (Romans 8:34; 1 John 2:1,2). It is in this context that Paul can speak of him as **"the last Adam"**, **"the second man"** or **"the heavenly man"** whose likeness we will one day bear (1 Corinthians 15:45-49). Also relevant is 2 Timothy 2:11: **"If we died with him, we will also live with him."**

Paul underlines what the effect of this truth should have on our goals in life. **"For Christ's love compels us, because we are convinced that one died for all, and therefore all died. And he died for all, that those who live should no longer live for themselves but for him who died for them and was raised again"** (2 Corinthians 5:14,15).

Why Did Jesus Die?

Our identification with Christ in suffering

Paul can also speak of our willingness to endure suffering, because of our allegiance to Christ, as being identified with Christ in his sufferings. "**We always carry around in our body the death of Jesus, so that the life of Jesus may also be revealed in our body. For we who are alive are always being given over to death for Jesus' sake, so that his life may also be revealed in our mortal body**" (2 Corinthians 4:10,11). "**Now I rejoice in what I am suffering for you, and I fill up in my flesh what is still lacking in regard to Christ's afflictions, for the sake of his body, which is the church**" (Colossians 1:24). It is our willingness to be identified with Christ and his purposes in this world, whatever it might cost, that releases the resources the living Christ makes available to us in order to fulfil those purposes. Paul expresses his passion to know Christ and experience his resurrection power in these terms: "**I want to know Christ – yes, to know the power of his resurrection and participation in his sufferings, becoming like him in his death, and so, somehow, attaining to the resurrection from the dead**" (Philippians 3:10,11).

The cross and the wisdom of God

Another major emphasis in Paul is how the cross challenges human pride and human ideas of wisdom. God has deliberately chosen a way of reconciling us to himself which perfectly meets our real needs, but which undermines human pride, "**so that no one may boast before him**" (1 Corinthians 1:29). From a human perspective, "**he was crucified in weakness**" (2 Corinthians 13:4). The idea that God should save humankind by allowing his Son to die a shameful death is "**a stumbling block to Jews**" (to put it in a more general context – those who, in their pride, refuse to admit their deep need of forgiveness and think they can earn God's acceptance by their good works and religious observances) "**and foolishness to Gentiles**" (those who are too proud to admit that their Creator knows more than they do and to learn from him – 1 Corinthians 1:23). "**For the message of the cross is foolishness to those who are perishing, but to us who are being saved it is the power of God**" (1 Corinthians 1:18). Paul deals with this theme in extended passages in 1 Corinthians 1:18-2:16; 3:18-23).

The cross and the challenge of godly living

It is to the cross that Paul appeals to when encouraging Christians to lead godly lives. It is because "**Christ, our Passover lamb, has been sacrificed**" that we are to "**keep the Festival, not with the old bread leavened with malice and wickedness, but with the unleavened bread of sincerity and truth**" (1 Corinthians 5:7,8 – for seven days after the Passover festival the people were to eat only unleavened bread and have no yeast in their homes. See Exodus 13:3-7). Paul was particularly concerned that at the Lord's Supper, the meal which commemorates Christ's death for us, the Corinthian Christians were showing lack of love and concern for one another. He warns that "**those who eat and drink without discerning the body of Christ**" (the body of fellow believers) "**eat and drink judgement on themselves**" (1 Corinthians 11:17-33).

We are to forgive one another "**and walk in the way of love, just as Christ loved us and gave himself up for us as a fragrant offering and sacrifice to God**" (Ephesians 5:1). Husbands are to "**love [their] wives, just as Christ loved the church and gave himself up for her**" (Ephesians 5:25). Our fellow believer now becomes "**your brother or sister for whom Christ died**" (Romans 14:15). This is what gives them infinite value and we are to treat them accordingly. Unless we hold to the belief in a "limited atonement", that Christ only died for those he knew would accept his salvation (a view I find hard to accept as there seems to be so much emphasis in the New Testament that he died for all people, regardless of what their response would be) then we can no doubt apply this principle to all human beings. Even though the Scripture indicates that many will reject the Saviour and suffer eternal loss,[1] we should still regard them as "those whom Christ loves and for whom he died" and work and pray for their conversion.

Paul tells us that "**Christ died for us so that, whether we are awake of asleep, we may live together with him.**" Because of this we are to "**encourage one another and build each other up**" (1 Thessalonians 5:10,11). He also "**died and returned to life so that he might be Lord of both the dead and living**" (Romans 14:9).

Christ's death and our death

It is through his death and resurrection that Jesus has "**destroyed death**" (2 Timothy 1:10). It is not that death no longer exists. The word "destroyed" (Greek *katargeô*) would be better translated "made ineffective or powerless". So Paul can encourage his Christian friends in Thessalonica who are grieving: "**Brothers and sisters, we do not want you to be uninformed about those who sleep in death, so that you do not grieve like the rest, who have no hope. We believe that Jesus died and rose again, and so we believe that God will bring with Jesus those who have fallen asleep in him**" (1 Thessalonians 4:13,14). When dying Christians pray, they are seeking help from one who knows what they are going through – because he himself has died.

---

1 For a detailed discussion on this theme see my book *Life After Death: The Christian's Hope and Challenge*.

The death of Christ and his exultation

It is because Christ voluntarily "made himself nothing by taking the very nature of a servant, being made in human likeness," and because he "humbled himself by becoming obedient to death – even death on a cross!" that "God exalted him to the highest place and gave him the name that is above every name, that at the name of Jesus every knee should bow, in heaven and on earth and under the earth, and every tongue acknowledge that Jesus Christ is Lord, to the glory of God the Father" (Philippians 2:6-11). If God places such value on the death of his Son, should we do less?

Benefits of the cross

The New Testament gives a number of significant benefits stemming directly from the cross for those who put their trust in Jesus. These have their roots in the teaching of Jesus himself, but Paul, more than any other writer, develops these ideas further.

Forgiveness

Forgiveness for our sins is an obvious first benefit to flow from the cross, and is the necessary prerequisite for all the other benefits. The forgiveness of sins by God or by Jesus is mentioned about 44 times in the New Testament. The majority of these occur in the Gospels, but also six times in Acts (2:38; 5:31; 8:22; 10:43; 13:38; 26:18), three times in Paul's letters (Romans 4:7; Ephesians 1:7; Colossians 1:14), three times in Hebrews (8:12; 9:22; 10:18), once in James (5:15) and twice in 1 John (1:9; 2:12). Paul, as we shall see, prefers the word "justified".

G. Campbell Morgan, the prominent pastor of Westminster Chapel in London, said in one of his sermons on the cross:

> The etymology of the Greek word translated "forgiveness" [aphesis] suggests freedom. The root idea is that of being "sent out, sent forth". This particular word is variously translated in the New Testament, "deliverance", "liberty", "remission", "forgiveness"... It is a word which recognises all the bondage into which

our sins have brought us, of guilt, of pollution, of power; and declares that by this redemption we are set free therefrom. Not free merely from the penalty... Forgiveness is to be set loose from sins, their guilt gone, their pollution ceased, their power broken.

The new covenant between God and his people is essentially concerned with the forgiveness of sin. This was foretold in the Old Testament (Jeremiah 31:33-34, a passage that is quoted twice by the writer of Hebrews, in 8:10-12 and 10:16,17). Jesus inaugurated this covenant at the Last Supper, relating our forgiveness directly to his blood shed for us (Matthew 26:28), as does Paul (Ephesians 1:7), the writer of Hebrews (9:22-24), and John (1 John 1:7-9).

One of India's great Christian leaders, Bakht Singh, was once asked what aspect of the gospel he stressed when preaching to those of other faiths. Did he preach the love of God? He replied, "No. The human mind is so polluted that if you talk about love it immediately thinks of sex." Did he talk about the wrath of God? "No. Indians believe that all the gods are angry. An extra one makes no difference." He was then asked what his main message was. "I preach the forgiveness of sins. That is what all of us deep down inside are longing for."

When God forgives he does it well. "**Their sins and lawless acts I will remember no more**" (Hebrews 10:17 – also 8:12). When I surrender my life to Jesus, as far as God is concerned, the information that would have condemned me has been erased.

Justification

The word "justified", in the sense of sinful human beings being justified by God, is used about 34 times in the New Testament. For example, it was used by Jesus in the Parable of the Publican and the Tax Collector – the tax collector, who admitted his sinfulness and cast himself on the mercy of God "**went home justified before God**" (Luke 18:9-14). However, 29 uses of this word are found in Paul's letters. He obviously prefers it to the idea of forgiveness, as it includes forgiveness, but means much more. (He uses the related words "righteous" and "righteousness" 66 times). It is a word that comes from the law courts, though T. W. Manson, in his book on Paul and John, suggested that Paul's use of the word was also taken from the throne room. Paul's usage goes beyond any conception of human justice. George Carey, in his book on the cross, *The Gate of Glory*,[1] says:

> The Old Testament word for *justification* (Hebrew *tsadeq*) comes from a root which probably means 'that standard which God wants to see in the world'. The verb 'to justify' has a definite legal meaning, that is, 'to declare righteous'. This is undeniable in Deuteronomy 25:1: 'When men have a dispute, they are to take it to court and the judges will decide the case, acquitting (justifying) the innocent and condemning the guilty' (see also Exodus 23:7; Isaiah 43:9; Psalm 143:2).
>
> The Greek word in the New Testament, *dikaioō*, has the meaning, "to be vindicated, acquitted, pronounced and treated as righteous." It is basic to Paul's whole idea of what it means to be a Christian. John Stott, in his commentary *The Message of Galatians*, goes as far as to say, "Nobody has understood Christianity who does not understand this word."

My favourite illustration of the meaning of the word comes from the case of Dreyfus, a captain in the French army towards the end of the 19th century. In 1894 he was accused of selling military secrets

---

1 Hodder and Stoughton, 1986, ©

to Germany. Though the evidence pointed to his innocence, the fact that he was a Jew went against him and he was convicted, stripped of his rank, and sent to the infamous penal colony on Devil's Island. His friends believed in his innocence and clamoured for a retrial. In 1898 Emile Zola wrote his famous "J'Accuse…!" dealing with the case, which was published by the Paris daily, *L'Aurore*. Because of the outcry, Dreyfus was tried again in 1899 before the Council of War. In spite of evidence to the contrary he was found guilty again, but with "extenuating circumstances". However, to save the face of France the President offered him a pardon. His friends were not satisfied with this and pressed for a third trial. In 1906 a civil court appeal exonerated him completely. Dreyfus returned to the army and was named Chévalier de la Légion d'Honneur. His rank was restored and he served with honour in World War I.

In 1899 Dreyfus was officially "forgiven", but in the eyes of the law he was still guilty. However, in 1906 he was "justified". It was publicly recognised that he was innocent and this decision involved reconciliation and restoration. This is the meaning of justification. As H. C. G. Moule put it in *The Fundamentals*, "Our Justification means not merely a grant of pardon, but a verdict in favour of our standing as satisfactory before the Judge."

Of course, Dreyfus could be justified because he was innocent. You and I cannot be justified before God on that basis because we are not innocent. However, God is one who "**justifies the ungodly**" (Romans 4:5). Through the sacrifice of Jesus, God has provided a means whereby he is able "**to be just and the one who justifies those who have faith in Jesus**" (Romans 3:26).

Perhaps another illustration would be helpful here. A story is told of the Napoleonic wars. A man who did not want to serve was balloted as a conscript. But he had a friend who wanted to go to war and so went in his place. The friend was killed in battle and buried on the battlefield. Some time later there was another ballot to obtain conscripts. By some mistake the first man was balloted a second time. He refused to go on the grounds that he was already dead and buried. He asked them to check the records and they found he was right. The authorities could not accept this, and the case was actually taken to Napoleon. He ruled that the man was right. Legally, even though through a substitute, he had died and was buried on the battlefield. France had no claim on him. Similarly, the moral law now has no power to condemn me as I have already paid its penalty in the person of Jesus. "**Since we have now been justified by his blood, how much more shall we be saved from God's wrath through him!**" (Romans 5:9). "**Who will bring any charge against those whom God has chosen? It is God who justifies. Who then can condemn? No one. Christ Jesus who died – more than that, who was raised to life – is at the right hand of God and is also interceding for us.**" (Romans 8:33,34).

In this latter passage, Paul links the resurrection with the cross as the means by which we are justified. Though it is the cross that makes our justification possible, it is the risen Christ who does the justifying. This is the emphasis also in Romans 4:25: "**He was delivered over to death for our sins and was raised to life for our justification.**" When the advocate of a guilty person represents him in court, he may appeal to the person's sincere repentance, his normally good character or the lack of evidence against him. When Jesus represents us before the Father, I guess it goes something like this: "Yes, he or she is guilty and deserves nothing but the just sentence. However, you cannot punish them because I have paid for their sins and they are trusting in me." As someone once put it: "He paid a debt He didn't owe, so we could be released from a debt we couldn't pay."

Here we find the answer to the age-long question that bothered Job, "**How can mere mortals prove their innocence before God?**" (Job 9:2 – see also 15:14; 25:4) and has bothered countless thinking people since. Trusting in Jesus and all he has done for us is the only means by which we can receive this amazing gift of perfect standing in God's sight. It has nothing to do with our inherent worthiness or deserving and therefore cannot be earned by good behaviour. "**A person is justified by faith apart from observing the law**" (Romans 3:28). "**By observing the law no one will be justified.**" (Galatians 2:16). It is God's grace alone, his undeserved goodness, that has provided this means of acceptance. We "**are justified freely by his grace through the redemption that came by Christ Jesus**" (Romans 3:24 – see also Titus 3:7). It is the Holy Spirit coming into our lives that makes all of this a living reality. Paul, writing to believers at Corinth, some of whom had been "**sexually immoral… idolaters… adulterers… male prostitutes… practising homosexuals… thieves… the greedy… drunkards… slanderers… swindlers**", goes on to say, "**But you were washed, you were sanctified, you were justified in the name of the Lord Jesus Christ and by the Spirit of our God.**" (1 Corinthians 6:9-11).

And lest we should think there is something wrong about God declaring us righteous by himself suffering the consequence of our sins, Paul states that in the very fact of doing so he is revealing his own commitment to justice. "**He did this to demonstrate his justice, because in his forbearance he had left the sins committed beforehand unpunished – he did it to demonstrate his justice at the present time, so as to be just and the one who justifies those who have faith in Jesus**" (Romans 3:25,26).

There is one passage where Paul sums up the heart of his teaching about justification, though he does not use that word in this instance. In 2 Corinthians 5:21 he declares, "**God made him** [Christ] **who had no sin to be sin** [or 'sin offering'] **for us, so that in him we might become the righteousness of God.**" Here is the amazing transaction. Jesus was wholly identified with our sin in order that we might have his righteousness credited to us. J. Scott Lidgett, in *The Spiritual Principle of the Atonement,* says of the emphasis here:

Christ enters into our sin, takes it upon Himself, is wrapt in it. He stands for us and with us, as though a sinner, and in that capacity He dies on our behalf.

John Stott, in *The Cross of Christ,* comments:

> What was transferred to Christ was not moral qualities but legal consequences… In consequence Christ had no sin but ours, and we have no righteousness but his.

It is worth noting that this verse declares that Christ "**had no sin**". Under the Old Testament law, the animals that were offered for the sins of the people were required to be "**without defect**" (e.g. Leviticus 4:28). When a worshipper brought his lamb for the offering it did not matter if that worshipper was badly dressed, or that his clothes were torn or dirty. All eyes were on the lamb. Would the priest find fault with the lamb? If the lamb was perfect, he was accepted. So it was necessary for Christ to live a life of perfect obedience to his Father, that he might offer the perfect sacrifice to make atonement for our sins. It is that perfect righteousness which is now credited to us. Robert Haldane (1764-1842), author of a masterful commentary on Romans, wrote these words about the righteousness of Christ:

> To that righteousness is the eye of the believer ever to be directed; on that righteousness must he rest; on that righteousness must he live; on that righteousness must he die; in that righteousness must he appear before the judgement-seat; in that righteousness must he stand for ever in the presence of a righteous God.

Forgiveness has been likened to subtraction, and justification has been likened to addition. That is, when we were forgiven the penalty was removed; when we are justified there is imputed to us, put on our account, the very righteousness of God himself. And Paul declares that having received "**God's abundant provision of grace and of the gift of righteousness**" we are to "**reign in life through the one man, Jesus Christ**" (Romans 5:17).

John Bunyan described how this truth came home to him. He was crossing a field, thinking in fear about his standing in God's sight, when a sentence flashed through his mind:

> "[Your] righteousness is in heaven." [I thought] that I saw with the eyes of my soul Jesus Christ at God's right hand: there, I say, is my righteousness. …I also saw that it is not my good frame of heart that made my righteousness better, nor yet my bad frame that made my righteousness worse: for my righteousness was Jesus Christ himself, the same yesterday, today and forever.

Bunyan went home with a heart full of joy and began to search for that sentence in the Bible. But he could not find it and his heart sank again until he got to the words "**Christ Jesus, who has become for us wisdom from God – that is, our righteousness, holiness and redemption**" (1 Corinthians 1:30). That told him that the sentence was true, even if it was not in the Bible:

> There was nothing but Christ before my eyes… Now I could look from myself to him and reckon that all those graces of God that now were green in me were yet but like those cracked groats and fourpence half-pennies that rich men carry in their purses when their gold is in their trunks at home. Oh, I saw my gold was in my trunk at home! In Christ my Lord and Saviour! Now Christ was all; all my wisdom, all my righteousness, all my sanctification, and all my redemption!

As Captain Dreyfus was restored to his rightful position as a result of his being justified, so Paul describes the result of our being justified by Christ. "**Therefore, since we have been justified through faith, we have peace with God through our Lord Jesus Christ, through whom we have gained access by faith into this grace in which we now stand. And we boast in the hope of the glory of God.**" (Romans 5:1,2). "**Those he justified, he also glorified.**" (Romans 8:30). "**He saved us through the washing of rebirth and renewal by the Holy Spirit, whom he poured out on us generously through Jesus Christ our Saviour, so that, having been justified by his grace, we might become heirs having the hope of eternal life**" (Titus 3:5-7). Having been brought into right standing with God we are at peace with him, we have access to his grace, we have become heirs of his kingdom and look forward to sharing his glory! As R. A. Webb put it in *The Reformed Doctrine of Adoption*, "Justification is that act of grace whereby we sinful subjects of God's government are received into the number of, and given the right and title to, all the privileges of the kingdom of God."

Salvation

God is given the title "Saviour" seven times in the New Testament (five times by Paul) and Jesus is so called 17 times (eight times by Paul). The process of being brought into a right relationship with God is described as "being saved" 57 times (26 times by Paul). Every writer of the New Testament uses this language. This, then, is the most common way of speaking about what Christ came into the world to achieve, and what happens when we put our faith in him.

Obviously, a "saviour" is a person who saves people, and when a person is "saved" they must be saved *from* something. We talk about people being saved from burning buildings or sinking ships or other dangerous situations. So what do God and Jesus save us from?

It is certainly true that they can save people from drug or alcohol addiction, a meaningless existence, the fear of death, and lots of other things. They are doing this constantly. However, the New Testament gets to the heart of the matter. The angel declared to Mary concerning the child that would be conceived in her womb, **"You are to give him the name Jesus, because he will save his people from their sins"** (Matthew 1:21 – The name "Jesus" is the Greek version of the Hebrew "Joshua" and means "God saves"). Paul states, **"Christ Jesus came into the world to save sinners"** (1 Timothy 1:15). It is our self-centredness and the problem this causes in our relationship with God that he came to save us from. Other problems stem from this one. Jesus contrasted being **"saved"** with being **"lost"** (Luke 19:10), and Paul contrasted those who are being **"saved"** with those who are **"perishing"** (1 Corinthians 1:18).

Paul can also speak of being saved from the wrath of God. **"Since we have now been justified by his blood, how much more shall we be saved from God's wrath through him. For if, while we were God's enemies, we were reconciled to him through the death of his Son, how much more, having been reconciled, shall we be saved through his life!"** (Romans 5:9,10). As with justification, though it is the death of Christ that makes our salvation possible, it is the risen Christ who does the saving. The argument in the above passage goes something like this: if the death of Christ reconciles us to God, turning his enemies into his friends, how much more is the resurrection going to do for those who are now his friends. So salvation has to do with the whole process of bringing us from a position where we are guilty before God and facing a certain judgement, to that place where we are fully reconciled and can look forward to a continuing relationship with him through all eternity.

Concerning this process, it is interesting to note that the verb "to be saved" is used in the past, the present and the future tenses. If we have put our faith in Jesus, then he **"has saved us"** (e.g.

2 Timothy 1:9), we are "**being saved**" (e.g. 1 Corinthians 1:18) and we "**shall be saved**" (e.g. Romans 5:9). We could say that when we accept Jesus as our Saviour and Lord, then we are saved from the *penalty* due us because of our sins. As we grow in our faith, and the Holy Spirit does his work in our hearts, we are more and more saved from the *power* of sin in our lives. One day we can look forward to being saved from the very *presence* of sin, when he will "**present you before his glorious presence without fault and with great joy**" (Jude 24). As the writer of Hebrews puts it, Jesus "**is able to save** *completely*[1] **those who come to God through him**" (7:25).

Reconciliation

Jesus had plenty to say about our need to be reconciled to God and to our neighbour. However, he did not use the particular word "reconciled" except in one instance, in Matthew 5:24. For Paul, it is another of his favourite terms and he uses it 14 times in his letters.

Again, the cross is the means by which we are reconciled. "**We were reconciled to him by the death of his Son**" (Romans 5:10). He speaks of our condition before we are reconciled as being "**enemies in your minds because of your evil behaviour**" (Colossians 1:21 – see also Romans 5:10) and calls the preaching of the gospel "**the ministry of reconciliation**" and the gospel itself "**the message of reconciliation**" (2 Corinthians 5:18,19). In the light of what Jesus has done for us on the cross he urges the people in the church at Corinth to "*Be* **reconciled to God**"[2] (v. 20).

It is significant that God is never said to be reconciled to humans. Almost always, he is the subject of the verb and is said to reconcile us to himself. This puts emphasis on the truth that the process of

---

1 Italics mine.
2 Italics mine.

reconciliation always originates with God. Paul says in Romans 5:11 that reconciliation is something that we have received. There is therefore some sense in which reconciliation is independent of us. The New Testament view is that reconciliation was wrought on the cross before there was anything in our heart to respond. As Cromwell said of the covenant, it is a work "outside of us". God has dealt with the sin of the world in such a way that it no longer needs to be a barrier between himself and us. Obviously, though, to be effective, it must be "received". In this sense we are commanded to "be reconciled". T. J. Crawford long ago pointed out that the Greek words for reconciliation are used in the biblical writings "to signify the removal of enmity, not from the *offending*, but from the *offended* party"; and again he says "when one party is said 'to be reconciled to another' or 'to reconcile himself to another,' the offended party, according to the Hellenistic idiom, is the one whose friendship and favour are conciliated." Or, as James Denney put it in *Studies in Theology*:

> The thing that has to be dealt with, that has to be overcome, in the work of reconciliation, is not man's distrust of God, but God's condemnation of man.

P. T. Forsyth, in *The Work of Christ*, draws a distinction between "a change of feeling and a change of treatment", and he goes on to say, "God's feeling toward us never needed to be changed. But God's treatment of us, God's practical relation to us – that had to change." In other words, God's love never varied. But the atonement wrought by Christ means that we are no longer treated as enemies (as our sins deserve), but as friends. God has reconciled himself. Elsewhere Forsyth says: "The Cross meant more change in God than in man… Real and thorough religion is theocentric more than anthropocentric."

Paul not only talks about the cross reconciling us to God, but also reconciling humans to one another. "**For he himself is our peace, who has made the two one and has destroyed the barrier, the dividing wall of hostility, by setting aside in his flesh the law with its commands and regulations. His purpose was to create in himself the one new humanity out of the two, thus making peace, and in one body to reconcile both of them to God through the cross, by which he put to death their hostility. He came and preached peace to you who were far away and peace to those who were near. For through him we both have access to the Father by one Spirit**" (Ephesians 2:14-18). Paul is speaking here specifically of the division between Jews and Gentiles (the Jewish term for all who are not Jews), though the principle applies to all our fellow human beings. Because the Jews had been chosen by God to prepare for Christ's coming, and they had the privilege of having received God's laws and commands, many had come to believe they were superior to others. They missed the point that they had been given these privileges in order that they might share them with others, and not because they were in any way superior. They also missed the point that God's laws reveal to us our faults. Just knowing his commandments does not make us better than those who don't know them. The more strict Jews would not associate with Gentiles and considered them ritually unclean.

However, the cross breaks down these man-made barriers in two ways. First, it declares that we are all sinners in need of forgiveness, but that forgiveness is now available to all equally through the cross. Secondly, the cross makes the indwelling Spirit of God equally available to all so that all may become sons and daughters of God with equal access to him and with all the privileges that go with being a child of God. National, economic, social and gender barriers don't count in God's reckoning when it comes to our worth and our relationship to him. "**There is neither Jew nor Greek,**

Why Did Jesus Die?

neither slave nor free, neither male nor female, for you are all one in Christ Jesus" (Galatians 3:28 – see also Colossians 3:11).

Paul goes beyond merely applying Christ's reconciling work to humans when he declares in Colossians 1:19,20, "**God was pleased… through [Christ] to reconcile to himself all things, whether things on earth or things in heaven, making peace through his blood, shed on the cross.**" He leaves it to our imagination to decide what he means by "things on earth or things in heaven." C. H. Dodd commented on this verse: "Through Christ God has chosen to put an end to all the distressing disharmonies within his universe and bring all under one effective rule." This is similar to Paul's statement in Ephesians 1:10 when he says that God will **"bring unity to all things in heaven and on earth under Christ."** No doubt this includes the transformation of all the discordant things in the physical universe as well as the living universe, something he enlarges on further in Romans 8:19-25.

Before leaving the theme of reconciliation, it would be appropriate to consider the word "peace", which is closely associated with both justification and reconciliation in Paul's writings. Of the 92 times the word occurs in the New Testament, 15 refer to peace as opposed to war, personal strife, or confusion, while in all the others it is possible to see implied the thought that God is the giver of it. Peace is specifically associated with the Father or the Son about 40 times, including the greetings in the letters. God is "**the God of peace**" (Romans 15:33; 2 Corinthians 13:11; Philippians 4:9; 1 Thessalonians 5:23) and "**the Lord of peace**" (2 Thessalonians 3:16). Bringing about peace is a characteristic feature of his activity. Paul speaks of "**peace *with* God**"[1] which is associated with our justification (Romans 5:1) and with our reconciliation (Colossians 1:20) through the cross. He speaks of peace with one another as a

---

1   Italics mine.

result of the cross (Ephesians 2:14-17). Foerster, in *Theologisches Worterbuch zum Neuen Testament* (ed. G. Kittel), says:

> When Christ abolished the law He did away with the double disorder in mankind, that with one another and that against God. *Eirēnē* denotes peace with God and peace with one another and therewith a comprehensive "order": a salvation of all relationships.

So completely is Christ identified with this process of making peace that he can be said to be "**our peace**" (Ephesians 2:14).

Paul also speaks of "**the peace *of* God**"[1], that peace which is given by God and which "**will guard your hearts and your minds in Christ Jesus**" when we gratefully put all our problems in his capable hands (Philippians 4:6,7). The argument in this passage is as follows: "If you do the trusting, I will guard your heart from things that rob you of this peace." The Greek word for "guard" is a military word. E. de W. Burton, in *The International Critical Commentary*, defined this peace as: "Tranquillity of mind, which comes from the assurance of being reconciled with God and under his loving care."

The peace we have been describing in the New Testament is very closely related to the Hebrew word for peace (*shalom*) in the Old Testament. I have given a summary of the meaning of *shalom* at the end of the last chapter of my book *God's Plan for His Family, The Church*.

Redemption

The language of redemption is common in the Old Testament.

---

1 Italics mine.

Why Did Jesus Die?

To redeem someone (or something) means to deliver someone (or something) from a distressing situation. Prisoners of war could be redeemed from captivity. Slaves could be redeemed and set free. If a poor man was forced to sell some of his property, his nearest relative was obliged to redeem it for him (e.g. Leviticus 25:25). If he was forced to sell himself into slavery, then a relative could redeem him (e.g. Leviticus 25:47,48). God redeemed his people from slavery in Egypt (e.g. Deuteronomy 7:8). God is referred to as the Redeemer, particularly in chapters 40-66 of Isaiah where he is so called 13 times.

The Greek word group used for redemption, both in the Greek translation of the Old Testament and in the New Testament, always implied some cost in that a ransom price was to be paid. In fact, it was this idea of payment as the basis of release which was the reason for the existence of this whole word group.[1] Other words would be used which meant "loosing" or "releasing" when no cost was involved.

In the Old Testament, when God is the one who is doing the redeeming, there is a slight difference in that there is greater stress on the idea of deliverance than on the means by which it is brought about. It is inconceivable that God would need to pay a ransom to humans (or the Devil!). Yet the words used imply that the deliverance is at some cost. However, in the New Testament the cost is very specific. The cost is to God himself and it is the sacrifice of his Son.

Such language is used about 20 times in the New Testament of the redemption purchased for us by Jesus. It was used by Jesus himself when he declared on his final journey to Jerusalem, "**The Son of Man did not come to be served, but to serve, and to give**

---

[1] This fact is thoroughly researched in Leon Morris' excellent book *The Apostolic Preaching of the Cross*, Tyndale Press, 1955 ©.

his life as a ransom for many" (Matthew 20:28; Mark 10:45). One of the Greek words used, *agoradzō*, simply means to "purchase" or "buy", and is often so translated rather than as "redeemed".[1] Paul says that we are "**bought at a price**" (1 Corinthians 6:20; 7:23). The price paid is the blood of Christ. "**For you know that it was not with perishable things such as silver or gold that you were redeemed from the empty way of life handed down to you from your ancestors, but with the precious blood of Christ, a lamb without blemish or defect**" (1 Peter 1:18,19 – see also Acts 20:28; Ephesians 1:7; Revelation 5:9). Paul is clear about what we are redeemed from. "**Christ redeemed us from the curse of the law by becoming a curse for us**" (Galatians 3:13). "**[Christ] gave himself for us to redeem us from all wickedness**" (Titus 2:14).

Redemption and the idea of freedom have much in common. Redemption is being set free from our sin, our guilt, our false views of reality, and the consequences of this slavery. Peter describes it as being redeemed from vanity and custom, "**the empty way of life handed down to you from your ancestors**" (1 Peter 1:18). The New Testament speaks of us as being slaves to sin (Romans 6:17), to other humans (1 Corinthians 7:23), and to the elemental spiritual forces of the world (Galatians 4:3), while those without the revelation of the true God are said to be slaves to their gods (Galatians 4:8). The New Testament concept of freedom is not freedom to do what we want, it is freedom to be what we should be and do what we should do. It is freedom to love God and our neighbour. This is what we were created for. Jesus said that "**everyone who sins is a slave to sin**" (John 8:34) but added, "**If the Son sets you free, you will be free indeed**" (v. 36). D. A. Carson, in *The Gospel According to John*, comments on this statement of Jesus:

---

1 Acts 20:28; 1 Corinthians 6:20; 7:23; 2 Peter 2:1; Revelation 5:9; 14:4.

Jesus not only enjoys inalienable right as the unique Son of God, but exercises full authority vested in him by the Father to liberate slaves. Those whom Jesus liberates from the tyranny of sin are really (*ontos*) free. True freedom is not the liberty to do anything we please, but the liberty to do what we ought; and it is genuine liberty because doing what we ought now pleases us.

If we have been "bought with a price" then we now belong to God and don't have any right to live as we please. We are under new ownership. In this respect, it is worth noting that in Galatians 3:14 we are told that the purpose of redemption is "**that by faith we might receive the promise of the Spirit**", and Galatians 4:5 says we are redeemed "**that we might receive adoption to sonship.**" Leon Morris aptly comments:

> It is wrong to separate the legal status, gained by the complete discharge of the claims the law had upon us, from the resultant life. The only redemption Paul knew was one in which the redeemed had received the gift of the Holy Spirit, and in which they lived as those who had been adopted into the family of God…

In the Scripture we see the price paid, the curse borne, in order that those who are redeemed should be brought into the liberty of the sons of God, a liberty which may paradoxically be called slavery to God. The whole point of this redemption is that sin no longer has dominion; the redeemed are saved to do the will of their Master.

But in this new slavery lies the secret of true fulfilment. Jesus said, "**I have come that they may have life, and have it to the full**" (John 10:10).

As with other benefits of the cross, the idea of redemption has both a present and a future application. In most instances the New Testament declares that if we have put our trust in Christ, then we have already been redeemed. However, the Bible looks forward to the time when our redemption will be complete. Paul can speak of the "**redemption of our bodies**", something that we "**wait eagerly for**" (Romans 8:23). It is the gift of the Holy Spirit, living within us, who is the guarantee of this final and glorious event. He is "**a deposit guaranteeing our inheritance until the redemption of those who are God's possession – to the praise of his glory**" (Ephesians 1:14). It is the Holy Spirit "**with whom [we are] sealed for the day of redemption**" (Ephesians 4:30). These last two verses emphasise the fact that our redemption is not only by blood. Through the cross we receive forgiveness, but it is by the power of the Holy Spirit our redemption is brought to completion. This is in line with Old Testament passages where God is said to deliver his people "**with a mighty hand and an outstretched arm**" (Deuteronomy 26:8). Orr, in *A Dictionary of Christ and the Gospels* (ed. J. Hastings), comments:

> Redemption has the two aspects, which can never be separated – redemption by "ransom," i.e. from sin's guilt and condemnation; and redemption by power, from sin's bondage and other evil effects. The Apostolic Gospel comprehended both.

Sanctification

Another significant word is "sanctification" or "sanctified". It is very common in the Old Testament, particularly in Exodus and Leviticus, and is used 24 times in the New Testament to describe what happens when we put our trust in Christ. It could be translated "to consecrate, dedicate or make holy". Its basic meaning is "to set apart a thing or a person for a special purpose". In this sense it is often used in the Old Testament of setting apart certain vessels for use in the worship of God, such as those used in the temple. In this sense they can be described as "holy".

It comes from the same Greek root word as "saints" which is used about 60 times in the New Testament to describe Christians, particularly by Paul. So Christians are people who have been set aside by God for belonging to him and for service to him. Because we have entered into this relationship with one who is "holy" in character, then we too are called to be holy. And so the word "sanctification" also comes to describe that process by which we grow in character. Peter says we "**participate in the divine character**" through the indwelling presence of the Holy Spirit. He continues, "**For this reason, make every effort to add to your faith goodness; and to goodness, knowledge; and to knowledge, self-control; and to self-control, perseverance; and to perseverance, godliness; and to godliness, mutual affection; and to mutual affection, love. For if you possess these qualities in increasing measure, they will keep you from being ineffective and unproductive in your knowledge of our Lord Jesus Christ. But if any of you do not have them, you are nearsighted and blind, and you have forgotten that you have been cleansed from your past sins.**" (2 Peter 1:4-9). It is this cleansing which we receive through the cross that should motivate us to be worthy of the one we claim to represent. We should not forget that we are sinners saved by grace.

The New Testament declares that we are "sanctified" or "made holy" through Christ's **blood** (Hebrews 9:13,14 – see also 10:10), by the **Holy Spirit** (Romans 15:16; 1 Corinthians 6:11; 2 Thessalonians 2:13; 1 Peter 1:2) and by the **truth**, that is, **God's word** (John 17:17). We grow as we immerse ourselves in the Bible and allow its truths to penetrate our lives.

Propitiation

Another word in the New Testament that is used several times in connection with the cross is the word "propitiation". To propitiate someone is to appease their anger. If you have an argument with your spouse and they are angry with you, you may go out and buy them a gift in order to propitiate them. The Greek word *hilastērion* occurs in Romans 3:25 where we are told that "**God presented Christ as a sacrifice of atonement** [literally 'a propitiation'], **through the shedding of his blood – to be received by faith.**" The word *hilasmos* occurs in 1 John 2:2: "**He is the atoning sacrifice** [propitiation] **for our sins, and not only for ours but also for the sins of the whole world**" and in 1 John 4:10: "**This is love: not that we loved God, but that he loved us and sent his Son as an atoning sacrifice** [propitiation] **for our sins.**" Though this group of words occurs in only these instances, the idea of propitiation is often present where this particular terminology is not, for example in passages dealing with the wrath of God. This line of reasoning is so persuasive that S. R. Driver, in *A Dictionary of the Bible* (ed. J. Hastings) can regard propitiation as one of the three main categories used in the New Testament to interpret the death of Christ. In view of the emphasis in the New Testament that the death of Jesus averted the threat of divine judgment, noted theologian James Packer has this to say about propitiation in his significant book *Knowing God*:

> Not only does the truth of propitiation lead us to the heart of the New Testament gospel; it also leads us to a vantage-point from which we can see to the heart of many other things too. When you stand on top of Snowdon, you see the whole of Snowdonia spread out round you, and you have a wider view than you can get from any other point in the area. Similarly, when you are

on top of the truth of propitiation, you can see the entire Bible in perspective, and you are in a position to take the measure of vital matters which cannot be grasped on any other terms.

Scholars debate the meaning of these Greek words. For many modern writers the concept of the wrath of God is anathema. In my book *Life After Death: The Christian's Hope and Challenge* I have given a full account of the biblical emphasis on the anger or wrath of God and its meaning. I don't have the space to deal with that here. Because of a dislike of the idea that our sins *deserve* to be punished and that God will actually punish sin, there is a tendency to translate these two Greek words as "expiation" rather than "propitiation". As the term "expiation" is commonly used, it signifies the removal of sin or guilt, but neither of these is a *thing* that can objectively be removed. We propitiate a person and expiate only a fact, or act, or thing. The word here can only be given an intelligible meaning when we move into the realm of personal relations. If the cross results in God's grace rather than his wrath, then this is only another way of saying that propitiation has taken place. After an extensive study of the use of the relevant Greek words in the Greek translation of the Old Testament, and by pagan, Jewish and Christian writers of the first century, Leon Morris has this to say:

> In view of the... invariable Greek use it would seem impossible for anyone in the first century to have used one of the *hilaskomai* group without conveying to his readers some idea of propitiation.

This meaning of the word is strengthened when we look at the context in which Paul uses it in Romans 3:25. The whole force of the preceding two and a half chapters of this letter has been to demonstrate that all people, Jews and Gentiles alike, lie under the condemnation and wrath of God, and there is nothing other than this word, in this section of the letter, to express the turning away of that wrath.

Surely R. W. Dale was right when he stated in *The Atonement*:

> St. Paul's intention was to demonstrate that the whole world is exposed to the divine wrath, and that if men [and women] are to be saved, that wrath must be somehow averted. That this was his intention, becomes clearer the more rigorous the examination to which the whole argument is subjected.

This would be thoroughly consistent with Paul's statement in Galatians that "**he redeemed us by becoming a curse for us**" (3:13).

Of course, if what Jesus achieved for us by his death on the cross in some way made it possible for God to act towards us with grace rather than in wrath, we must avoid the idea of a loving Son placating an angry Father. Through the New Testament, as we shall see, it is the love of the Father, just as much as the love of the Son, that made reconciliation possible. Leon Morris sums up the difference between propitiation in pagan worship from that expressed in the New Testament:

> Among the heathen, propitiation was thought of as an activity whereby the worshipper was able to provide that which would induce a change of mind in the deity. In plain language he bribed his god to be favourable to him. When the term was taken over into the Bible these unworthy and crude ideas were abandoned, and only the central truth expressed by the term was retained, namely that propitiation signifies the averting of wrath by the offering of a gift. But in both Testaments the thought is plain that the gift which secures the propitiation is

from God Himself. He provides the way whereby men [and women] may come to Him. Thus the use of the concept of propitiation witnesses to two great realities, the one, the reality and the seriousness of the divine reaction against sin, and the other, the reality and the greatness of the divine love which provided the gift which should avert the wrath from men [and women].

P. T. Forsyth, in *The Work of Christ*, has a relevant comment on the Old Testament statement, "**For the life of a creature is in the blood: and I have given it to you to make atonement for yourselves on the altar**" (Leviticus 17:11):

> Given! Did you ever see the force of it? "I have given you the blood to make atonement. This is an institution which I set up for you to comply with, set it up for purposes of My own, on principles of My own, but it is My gift." The Lord Himself provided the lamb for the burnt offering.

Adoption

The ultimate benefit of all the above blessings is that we are now adopted as full members of the family of God forever. John and Peter speak of being "born" into God's family, an expression that John uses 13 times and Peter twice.[1] This conveys the idea of sharing in "**the divine nature**" (2 Peter 1:4) through the receiving of the Holy Spirit. Paul, however, with his more legal approach, prefers the idea of "adoption" (Romans 8:15,23; 9:4; Galatians 4:5; Ephesians 1:5), though he uses the term "born" once (Galatians 4:29). Being born into God's family underlines the inward and

---

1 John 1:13; 3:3,5,6,7,8; 1 Peter 1:3,23; 1 John 2:29; 3:9; 4:7; 5:1,4,18.

spiritual transformation that occurs when we receive the Spirit, whereas being adopted points to the new legal status, with all the rights, privileges and responsibilities of being a son or daughter of God. Paul speaks of the Spirit as the agent of this change of status. **"The Spirit you received brought about your adoption to sonship"** (Romans 8:15).

In a Jewish household, when a child came of age, if he had proven himself to be responsible and mature, in a public ceremony before witnesses, he was officially placed in his father's house. This could be spoken of as adoption. This gave him the power of attorney, full legal use of his father's name. When he signed his father's name it was as if his father had signed it. All his father's resources were now at his disposal. In the Graeco-Roman world, the child and heir of the family went through a similar ceremony at the age of 14. He would be presented with the toga virilis, the robe of adulthood. He then had the right to choose a wife, serve in the army, manage estates, enter into business, and participate in politics.

The adoption of a member of another family was a Roman rather than a Jewish custom. Under Roman law, when this occurred, the adopted son had all the rights of a natural son, including the inheritance. Even if other sons were born later, his position was not affected. I suspect Paul had in mind the Roman rather than the Jewish model when he spoke of us being adopted into God's family, though Paul's argument in Galatians 4:1-7 could perhaps apply to either. There is one clear difference, however. In those days, it was the male members of the family who held most of the legal rights. When Paul speaks of our adoption as sons, it is clear that he has in mind the legal rights of all the children of God without regard to gender. This is obvious from the rest of his writings. God has no gender favourites.

The privileges we have as God's children include:

1) Access to our heavenly Father at all times (Romans 5:2; Ephesians 2:18).
2) Abundance of love (Romans 5:5; Ephesians 3:17-19).
3) His strength and encouragement in the trials of this life (2 Corinthians 12:7-10; Philippians 4:6,7,11-13).
4) His ultimate, total protection. "**Not a hair of your head will perish**" (Luke 21:18).
5) His guidance. "**I will instruct you and teach you in the way you should go**" (Psalm 32:8).
6) His discipline and training (Hebrews 12:7-11).
7) An eternal inheritance. "**Now if we are children, then we are heirs – heirs of God and co-heirs with Christ, if indeed we share in his sufferings in order that we may also share in his glory**" (Romans 8:17. See also 1 Peter 1:3-5).

Ruth Graham Bell, in *Decision*, told the story of a young Bedouin, who, in a fit of anger, struck and killed a friend. Fearing swift justice, he fled across the desert to the sprawling black tent of the tribal chief. Confessing his crime, he asked for protection. According to custom, the old chief put his hand on one of the ropes of the great tent, swore before God, and took the young man under his protection – until the affair could be settled legally.

The next day the young man's pursuers arrived and demanded that the murderer be handed over to them. "I have given my word," the old chieftain said. "But you don't know who he killed!" they answered. "I have given my word." "He killed your son!" was the reply. The chief was shaken. He stood, head bowed, for quite some time. The accused and the accusers looked on breathlessly. Finally the old man raised his head. He stood upright. "Then he shall become my son," he said, "and everything I have will one day be his."

So it is with us. Our sins sent God's own Son to the cross,

though in his case the act was of his own choosing in order to make our adoption possible. As a result, we are welcomed into his family – now and forever.

The cross in Hebrews

The major theme of the central chapters of Hebrews (4:14-10:39) is how Christ fulfilled, in his life, death and resurrection, the symbolism of the sacrificial rituals of the first covenant established with the Israelite people at Mount Sinai. I have gone into this in some detail under the headings "The smitten rock – God in the dock", "Animal sacrifices" and "Day of Atonement – the rent curtain" in the chapter on the cross in the Old Testament (pp. 42-45, 48-50) I won't repeat that here. However the writer of Hebrews has several other significant references to the cross that I have not mentioned there.

In the first chapter, verse 3, he summarises who Christ is and what he achieved by coming to earth. "**The Son is the radiance of God's glory and the exact representation of his being, sustaining all things by his powerful word. After he had provided purification for sins, he sat down at the right hand of the Majesty in heaven.**" It is significant that, of all the achievements of Christ that he could have mentioned, he focuses on this – the way our sins were dealt with. The idea of purification, or cleansing, was the main focus of Jewish religious rituals, and the word was used for either ritual or moral cleansing. Whether as a verb or a noun, it is also used with reference to the cross (directly or by implication) in Hebrews 9:14,23; 2 Peter 1:9 and 1 John 1:7. As the writer of Hebrews declares, the cross can do what the sacrifices provided under the old covenant could never do, that is, "**cleanse our consciences from acts that lead to death, so that we may serve the living God!**" (9:14).

Why Did Jesus Die?

The writer of Hebrews speaks of Christ's identification with us, both in our humanity and in our suffering. Both of these occur in the context of speaking of his suffering in death. The first passage is in chapter 2, verses 9-18. In verse 9 he declares that Jesus "**tasted death for everyone.**" He then says that Jesus was made "**perfect through what he suffered**" (v. 10). He goes on to say that the reason he shared in our full humanity of flesh and blood was that "**by his death he might break the power of him who holds the power of death – that is, the devil – and free those who all their lives were held in slavery by their fear of death**" (vv. 14,15). Finally he says: "**Because he himself suffered when he was tempted, he is able to help those who are being tempted** (v. 18).

The main point of this passage goes something like this: to achieve what he came to do, Jesus, though not ceasing to be God, the Second Person of the divine Trinity, fully identified with us in every respect. This meant that he not only became fully human in a physical sense, he also chose to be identified with us in our human suffering. He is "**Like [us]… in every way**" (v. 17). He went to the limit of human obedience by submitting to a level of suffering that no other human has ever endured. He was "**made perfect**" in the sense that he demonstrated perfect obedience to God. It was in this role as a perfect man, and our representative, that he was uniquely fitted to experience death for us all – the ultimate consequence of our sin. In doing so he broke the power of the devil's hold over us. Satan has the power of death, as he is the one who would lure us into sin and its consequences. However, he can no longer accuse us of our sins and point to our ultimate condemnation. We are freed by our forgiveness to face death without fear of what may lie beyond. Jesus, also, because of his sufferings, is perfectly fitted to understand and support us in our temptations (or "trials" – the Greek uses the same word for both). He is perfectly equipped to be a "**merciful and faithful high priest**" (V. 17).

In chapter 5, verses 7-9, the writer gives a similar emphasis where he says: "**Jesus... offered up prayers and petitions with fervent cries and tears to the one who could save him from death, and he was heard because of his reverent submission. Son though he was, he learned obedience from what he suffered and, once made perfect, he became the source of eternal salvation for all who obey him.**" I understand the phrase "**he was heard**" to mean that his Father gave him the strength to go through with his sufferings, as he was obviously not saved from death itself. Maybe it looks forward to the resurrection beyond. His submission to his Father's will is an example for us who may also be called to suffer in obedience to his will (see 1 Peter 4:19). Jesus "**learned obedience**" in that he was called to experience obedience to a degree that he had never experienced before – obedience to the point of death. It is significant that the theme of Christ's "obedience" in the New Testament always occurs in reference to his suffering and death.

As in the writings of Paul (Philippians 2:8,9) and John (Revelation 5), Christ's exultation is directly associated with his cross. "**He is crowned with glory and honour because he suffered death**" (Hebrews 2:9).

As for Paul it is "access" to God that he emphasises as a primary blessing of justification (Romans 5:2; Ephesians 2:18; 3:12), so the writer of Hebrews speaks of the privilege of being able to "draw near" to God through the great High Priest who has dealt with our sins (4:16; 7:19-25; 10:22).

In chapter 12 the writer also looks on the cross as an example of patient endurance in the face of evil – endurance that he calls us to imitate. "**For the joy set before him he endured the cross, scorning its shame, and sat down at the right hand of the throne of God. Consider him who endured such opposition from sinners, so that you will not grow weary and lose heart**" (v. 2,3).

This emphasis on the shame of the cross, and on looking beyond suffering to its joyful outcome, is an emphasis he repeats in chapter 13. "The high priest carries the blood of animals into the Most Holy Place as a sin offering, but the bodies are burned outside the camp. And so Jesus also suffered outside the city gate to make the people holy through his own blood. Let us, then, go to him outside the camp, bearing the disgrace he bore. For here we do not have an enduring city, but we are looking for the city that is to come" (vv. 11-13). There are plenty of instances today where, even in our secular Western society, we can be regarded as "outsiders". We are to embrace this for Jesus' sake – providing, of course, that the shame is caused by our goodness rather than our badness! Peter has more to say about that (1 Peter 3:15-17; 4:14-16). R. T. Kendall in an article in the magazine *Christianity*, has a poignant comment on the above passage:

> Had you walked into Jerusalem on Good Friday and asked the religious people, 'What is God doing here today?' they would have answered, 'It's Passover and we can hardly wait to celebrate it – if only that wicked thing on the cross outside the gate would hurry up and die.' No one remotely dreamed at the time that God was in Christ reconciling the world to himself by the death of his Son (2 Corinthians 5:19). Never forget that Jesus was crucified outside the city of Jerusalem and God has continued to manifest his glory outside the camp. We therefore must be willing to go outside the camp – continually – and bear his reproach. Some would even say, 'The further out the better.'

At the end of his letter, the writer has an interesting turn of phrase in which he closely links the death of Christ with the resurrection. They are part of one package in the salvation story. **"Now may the God of peace, who through the blood of the eternal covenant brought back from the dead our Lord Jesus, that** great Shepherd of the sheep, equip you with everything good for doing his will, and may he work in us what is pleasing to him, through Jesus Christ, to whom be glory for ever and ever. Amen" (v. 20,21). With reference to this passage, I find the following paragraph in Thomas Hewitt's commentary on Hebrews in the *Tyndale New Testament Commentaries* series helpful:

> Frequent references have been made in the Epistle to the ascension and glorification of Christ, but *brought again from the dead* is the only direct allusion to His resurrection.[1] The fact that Christ was raised from the dead in virtue of the eternal covenant is proof that His redeeming work had been accepted and that salvation for His people is assured. In other words, all that is said about Christ in this Epistle is genuine, for God has set His seal upon it. The phrase itself may be reminiscent of Isaiah 63:11, which refers to the bringing up of Moses, the shepherd of the sheep, out of the sea, which, Westcott suggests, 'was a shadow of Christ's ascent from the grave.' The Lord Jesus became the one and only great Shepherd of the sheep in virtue of His shed blood by which the eternal covenant was sealed. He had performed an act which could be repeated by no other, and He received a position which could be held by no other.

It is worth stating in summary, that the main aim of the writer of Hebrews is to present Christianity as the final and absolute religion because it does perfectly what all religion aims to do. This aim is expressed in the use of one of the writer's favourite words: "eternal" (Greek *aiōnios*). John, in his Gospel and letters, uses this word 23 times, but usually in connection with "life", and it is the com-

---

1 Though it is implied often enough and there are many references or hints in the letter to the resurrection of believers in the future.

bination of these words, rather than its use as an adjective that is characteristic. But in Hebrews "eternal" is used more significantly, though less frequently. Jesus is the author of "**eternal salvation**" (5:9). This salvation is final – and nothing more is needed. There is no peril beyond it. The gospel includes the proclamation of "**eternal judgement**" (6:2), that is, judgement from which there is no appeal. Christ has obtained "**eternal redemption**" for us (9:12), the validity of which lasts forever. Those who accept this Saviour and his salvation receive an "**eternal inheritance**" (9:15), a city with foundations that God's people will never leave. And finally, the blood of Christ is the blood of an "**eternal covenant**" (13:20). Through the death of Christ a definitive relationship is established between God and humans. God has spoken his final word on the matter and has left nothing in reserve. The foundation has been laid for a kingdom that can never be removed or shaken (12:25-29). It is this finality, achieved both because of who Jesus was, and what he did on the cross, that dominates the book of Hebrews.

The cross in Peter

Peter's first letter was written to offer encouragement and guidance to Christians who were suffering persecution for their faith. Because of this, it has a good deal to say about the sufferings of Christ and how his example should inspire, motivate and encourage us. For this reason Peter seems to prefer the term "sufferings" to "death" when referring to Christ – giving his message a more general application to our own lives. It is for this reason also that references to the cross tend to crop up incidentally in the letter. Peter does not set out to deliberately discuss a theology of the cross as Paul and the writer of Hebrews do. However, whenever he speaks of Christ's innocence and patience in suffering, he moves on in every instance to Christ the sacrificial lamb, Christ the bearer of sin, Christ who died – the righteous for the unrighteous. He describes himself as "**a witness of Christ's sufferings**" (5:1). The Greek word for "witness", *martus,* from which comes our word "martyr", is no doubt used here in its full meaning – one who is not only a spectator, but also one who bears testimony to an event.

Another point worth noting is that Peter was steeped in the Old Testament, and this comes through in the direct quotes, ideas and the phraseology that he uses. By the use of a phrase such as "**sprinkled with his blood**" (1:2) and in speaking of Christ as a "**lamb without blemish or defect**" (1:19 – see Numbers 28:3, etc.), he demonstrates his belief in the death of Christ as the fulfilment of the symbolism of the Old Testament animal sacrifices. In speaking of being sprinkled with Christ's blood, after the reference to obedience in 1:2, Peter no doubt has in mind the confirmation of the covenant performed by Moses in Exodus 24:7,8. In his use of Psalm 118:22, "**The stone the builders rejected has become the cornerstone**" (2:7), he sees the rejection of Christ by the Jewish elders as the fulfilment of Old Testament prophecy. Jesus himself had quoted this verse in the same context (Matthew 21:42) and no doubt Peter was present with him on that occasion. In particular, he saw Christ's sufferings as the fulfilment of Isaiah's prophecy in Isaiah 53. Chapter 2, verses 22-25 of 1 Peter contain one direct quote and several phrases from Isaiah. His statement that "'**He himself bore our sins in his body on the cross**" (literally "tree"), echoing Isaiah 53:11, could not express more clearly what he believed to be the true significance of the cross. The order of the Greek words in this sentence puts emphasis on the fact that Christ bore our sins, not his own, on Calvary. (The same point is clear from 3:18, "**the righteous for the unrighteous**"). The Greek word for "tree" here, *xulon*, which is used as a poetic term for the cross, no doubt with reference to the curse of Deuteronomy 21:23, is literally "timber" or dead wood.

Paul singled out the death of Christ and his resurrection as the heart of the gospel message and the fulfilment of the Old Testament Scriptures (1 Corinthians 15:1-4). In a similar way, Peter mentions "**the suffering of Christ and the glories that would follow**" as the focus of Old Testament prophecy (1:10,11). The "**Spirit of Christ**" or "**the Holy Spirit**" was the one who both inspired the prophets and now inspired those who proclaimed the gospel message (vv. 11,12).

Like Paul and John, Peter speaks of the cross as providing the greatest motivation for godly living. It is because we have a Father who "**judges each person's work impartially**" and because we were redeemed at such cost from our "**empty way of life**" "**with the precious blood of Christ", that we are to live "**in reverent fear**" (1:17,18). Christ "**bore our sins**... **so that we might die to sins and live for righteousness**" (2:24). "**It is better, if it is God's will, to suffer for doing good than for doing evil. For Christ also suffered once for sins, the righteous for the unrighteous, to bring you to God**" (3:17,18). The verb "bring" here is the same word Paul uses as a noun to describe our access to God made possible by the cross and a reality by the Spirit (Romans 5:2; Ephesians 2:18; 3:12).

In his instruction to slaves, Peter speaks of Christ's behaviour in the face of unjust suffering as an example for us to follow (2:18-23). This is an emphasis found also in Paul and the writer of Hebrews. Peter adds that we may be "**called**" to this suffering (2:21) and that it may be "**God's will**" (3:17; 4:19). If we are so called to suffer, then we "**participate in the sufferings of Christ, so that you may be overjoyed when his glory is revealed**" (4:13).

It is worth noting that whenever the New Testament speaks of Christ's behaviour as an example for us to follow, it always relates it to the cross. John Howard Yoder goes as far as to say, "Only at one point, only on one subject – but then consistently, universally – is Jesus our example: in his cross." (1 John 2:6 is perhaps one exception to this).

Peter makes another interesting comment. After declaring that we were "**redeemed with the precious blood of Christ**" he continues with the statement that "**He was chosen before the creation of the world, but was revealed in these last times for your sake**" (1:20). It seems that in the counsels of the Trinity of Father, Son and Spirit, back in eternity, it was planned that God would enlarge his family. In creating humans in his own likeness, and giving humans the freedom and dignity choose either a relationship with their loving Creator, or of going their own selfish way, it was planned that the Son would suffer in order to ensure that the choice could be freely made. If this assumption is correct, then Paul's statement in

Ephesians 1:4 – "**he chose us in him before the creation of the world**" – seems to indicate that God knew beforehand who would make that choice. There are mysteries here that no doubt we will sort out in eternity. Someone has said that Christ crucified is an eternal fact realised at a certain date, but touching all time with equal closeness.

Scholars differ as to whether or not 2 Peter was written by Peter the disciple. There is no direct mention of the cross in this letter. It is plain that the writer had it in mind, however, when he declared that if we are not growing in our faith and character we "**have forgotten that [we] have been cleansed from [our] past sins**" (1:9), and also when he speaks of those who "**secretly introduce destructive heresies, even denying the sovereign Lord who bought them – bringing swift destruction on themselves**" (2:1).

The cross in 1 John

Like the writers of Hebrews and 2 Peter, John uses the metaphor of cleansing or purification through the cross. "**If we walk in the light, as he is in the light, we have fellowship with one another, and the blood of Jesus, his Son, purifies us from all sin**" (1:7). The tense of the verb "purifies" here has the meaning "keeps on purifying". Denney has a relevant quote on this emphasis:

> The forgiveness of sins has to be received again and again as sin emerges into act. But when the soul closes with Christ the propitiation, the assurance of God's love is laid at the foundation of its being once for all. It is not to isolated acts it refers, but to the personality; not to sins, but to the sinner; not to the past only, in which wrong has been done, but to time and eternity.
>
> There will inevitably be in the Christian life experiences of sinning and of being forgiven, of falling and of being restored. But the grace which forgives and restores is not some new thing, nor is it conditioned in some new way. It is not dependent upon penitence, or works, or merit of ours. It is the same absolutely free grace which meets us at the cross. From first to last, it is the blood of Jesus, God's Son, which cleanses from sin. The daily pardon, the daily cleansing, are but the daily virtue of that one all-embracing act of mercy in which, while we were yet sinners, we were reconciled to God by the death of his Son.

Jesus illustrated this truth beautifully when he said to Peter at the Last Supper, "**Those who have had a bath need only to wash their feet; their whole body is clean**" (John 13:10). In other words, the feet need daily cleansing as you walk about in sandals in a hot climate, but once you have truly accepted Christ as your Saviour you may stay in the bath. Confess sin whenever you are conscious of it, thanking him for that cleansing. Keep short accounts with God. Maintain the fellowship. That's what it means to "**walk in the light**".

As Paul does in Romans 3:25, John uses one of the terms in the "propitiation" word group. "**He is the atoning sacrifice** [propitiation] **for our sins, and not only for ours but also for the sins of the whole world**" (2:2 – also 4:10). We explored the meaning of this term earlier under the subheading "Propitiation" in the chapter "Benefits of the cross".

Like Paul, John speaks of the love of the Father in sending his Son to die for us. "**This is love: not that we loved God, but that he loved us and sent his Son as an atoning sacrifice** [propitiation] **for our sins**" (4:10). And it is the cross, above all else, that should motivate us to love one another. "**Dear friends, since God so loved us, we also ought to love one another. No one has ever seen God; but if we love one another, God lives in us and his love is made complete in us**" (4:11,12). It is interesting to compare this last verse with John's statement in his Gospel, "**No one has ever seen God, but the one and only Son… has made him known**" (1:18). In both verses he states that no one has ever seen God. But in the Gospel he says we can see what God is like by looking at the Son, whereas in his first letter he says that people should be able to see his love by looking at us, those who claim to be recipients of his love given to us through the cross.

The other references to the cross in 1 John occur in 5:6,7 where he says that Jesus came "**by water and blood**" and that "**the Spirit,**

the water and the blood" testify to the truth. The "water" in this instance is usually taken to refer to Jesus' baptism. Both in submitting to baptism by John at the very start of his public ministry (he had no need of repentance – Matthew 3:13-16) and through his death at the end, Jesus identified fully with sinful humanity. These acts testify to his great love and the main purpose of his coming. No doubt John also had in mind the two sacraments of baptism and the Lord's Supper, both of which testify to the significance of the cross.

The cross in Revelation

John, in Revelation, speaks of us as being "**freed... from our sins**"(1:5) and "**purchased for God**" (5:9) by the blood of Jesus, as do other New Testament writers. In the latter verse he adds that those so purchased are "**members of every tribe and language and people and nation.**" This is the scope of his saving work.

We noted that Peter spoke of Jesus being chosen "**before the creation of the world**" (1:20). John has a somewhat similar statement when he speaks of "**the Lamb who was slain from the creation of the world**" (13:8). It seems that human rebellion was foreseen and God's solution was purposed from the very beginning. Maybe this implies that there is something in the eternal being of God, in his total self-giving nature, that made the cross inevitable. P. T. Forsyth commented:

> It was not the failure, but the fulfilment of God's plan, for there was a cross in the heart of God long before there was a cross on Calvary's hill... There was a Calvary above, the mother of it all.

However, by far the most significant allusions to the cross in Revelation are in the use of the term "**the Lamb**", which is applied to Jesus 29 times throughout the book. As "**the Lamb**" he fulfils all the sacrificial images of the Old Testament – the lambs that were offered daily in the temple for the sins of the people, the lamb whose blood was sprinkled on the doorposts, providing protection for the fugitives from Egypt (Exodus 12:3-7), and Isaiah's Suffering Servant who "**was led like a lamb for the slaughter**" (53:7). Lest we should miss the sacrificial significance of the term, John describes him as "**a Lamb, looking as if it had been slain**" (5:6 – see also v. 12) and speaks of the "**blood of the Lamb**" (7:14; 12:11). The Greek word for "slain", *esphagmenon,* is literally "with its throat cut" and yet it is "**standing in the centre before the throne**"(5:6). It has the character that sacrifice confers, but it is alive. Although Jesus lives as Lord, everything that is expressed by his death is part and parcel of his nature.

Revelation is the final book of the Bible. Rightly understood, it gives, in a series of pictorial visions, the principles by which God governs history from Christ's first coming until his final appearance to judge the world and inaugurate his kingdom. Numbers have symbolic significance in the book. For instance, the number seven, which occurs 54 times, symbolises fulfilment or completeness. It is significant that in this book, which emphasises the completeness of God's purposes and his total victory over evil at the end of this age, there should be so much focus on Christ in his sacrificial role. Consider the following passages:

- It is "**because [he] was slain**" that he is considered worthy to reveal the hidden secrets of God's purposes in history (5:9 – also 6:1,3,5,7,9,12; 8:1).
- It is the "**Lamb who was slain**" who is "**Worthy... to receive power and wealth and wisdom and strength and honour and glory and praise**" (5:12).
- It is "**the Lamb**" who shares his Father's throne and who is jointly worshipped with his Father by the redeemed multitudes from every nation (7:9,10).
- It is "**the Lamb**" to whom salvation belongs (7:10).

- It is "**the blood of the Lamb**" that washes clean our stained garments and fits us to live in the presence of a holy God (7:14).
- It is "**the Lamb**" who paradoxically "**will be [our] shepherd**", our sustainer, protector and encourager in glory (7:15-17).
- It is the "**blood of the Lamb**" that enables God's people to overcome the accusations of Satan and "**they did not love their lives so much as to shrink from death**" (12:10,11). This is similar to Paul's statement that, in view of the cross, those compelled by the love of Christ live for him rather than themselves (2 Corinthians 5:14,15). It is the cross above everything else that provides the motivation for our devotion to Christ against all odds and difficult outcomes. Denney comments, "It is because it is an incomparable demonstration of love that it is an irresistible motive".
- It is "**the Lamb**" who is "**Lord of Lords and King of Kings**" and who triumphs over the forces of evil (17:14).
- It is in his role as "**the Lamb**" that he will be united with all his people at "**the wedding of the Lamb**" (19:7,9).
- It is "**the Lamb**" and his Father who illuminate their renewed creation and their presence there will do away with any need for centres of worship (21:22,23).
- Those who will be there to enjoy this creation are "**those whose names are written in the Lamb's book of life**" (21:27 – cf. 13:8). In recognising their need for forgiveness, they are those who have put their trust in him for his saving work. Denney significantly comments here:

> In this book the names are written of those who are to inherit life everlasting: those whose names are not found there die the second death [20:14,15]. Nothing could express more strongly the writer's conviction that there is no salvation in any other than the Lamb, that in Jesus Christ and him crucified is the whole hope of a sinful world.

- The "**river of the water of life**", which I assume to be the life-giving Spirit, flows from "**the throne of God and of the Lamb**" (22:1). It is the cross that unlocks the reservoir and enables the glorified and risen Saviour to impart his blessings to us through the Spirit (John 7:38,39).
- "**The throne of God and of the Lamb**", the centre from which all God's power and love and goodness radiate, will be present "**in the city**" where his people dwell (22:1,2).

"Blessed" indeed "**are those who are invited to the wedding supper of the Lamb!**" (19:9)

Part 2:
Related Issues

The cross and the Trinity

In my booklet *Understanding the Trinity*, I give the reasons Christians believe God is a Trinity of Persons, Father, Son and Holy Spirit. I also give reasons why this makes sense. The Biblical reasons have to do with such things as the number of times they are all mentioned together in the New Testament; the way in which they are given different functions, though all working together; the relationships that are said to exist between them; the claims that Jesus made such as only God could make, though he constantly spoke of his Father as someone separate from himself; and the obvious personal characteristics that are assigned to each of them.

As we have seen from the book of Acts, the first Christians used terms for Jesus that could only rightly be applied to God. Not only was he the promised Messiah, he was the Lord and the one appointed to judge the living and the dead. Whatever doubts they may have had about who he really was, the resurrection had convinced them he was no *mere* human being. However, though they did not hesitate to proclaim him as Lord and the only Saviour of men and women, and though Jesus must have taught them a great deal during the 40 days he spent with them after his resurrection (see Acts 1:3), there were still many issues to work through. Jesus had indicated during his last meal with them before his crucifixion that it would take time to work it all out, but that the Spirit would guide them into the truth (John 16:12,13).

Over the first three centuries of the Christian Church some

issues were hotly debated – usually in response to heresies and false views that sprang up from time to time. Most of the controversies centred round the person of Jesus, his divine and human nature and his relationship with the Father and the Holy Spirit. After many disputes, upheavals and changes of fortune between the Councils of Nicea in A.D. 325 and Constantinople in 381, the church finally turned its face unambiguously away from Arianism, the belief that Jesus, though superior to humans, had originally been created by the Father and was thus an inferior being, a view still held by Jehovah's Witnesses today. The Council of Chalcedon (451) rejected the view that Jesus' human nature was separate from his divine person, stating that he was "one person in two natures" which are united "unconfusedly, unchangeably, indivisibly, inseparably"! Debate also centred around the person and ministry of the Spirit, who, as Nicea affirmed, "with the Father and the Son is to be worshipped and glorified."

It is not my purpose to go over these debates, even if I could understand them all. I don't claim to be a theologian. However, there are some issues here that are important for a true appreciation of Christianity and the Trinitarian nature of God. Over the last century the cross and grave have become determinative in theological circles for our understanding of the doctrine of the Trinity. Karl Barth was one who gave a lead in this. In volume IV of *Church Dogmatics* he insisted that we look directly upon Christ's cross and grave in order to discern the truth of God's nature. This truth was explored further by the two prominent theologians of the Trinity – Eberhard Jungel and Jurgen Moltmann – and has been looked at by others since. What follows is my own attempt to deal with these issues from my own simplified understanding, particularly as they relate to the significance of what actually happened on the cross. The source of my deductions is always what I believe to be the teaching of the New Testament. I will touch on some of the early

The Cross and the Trinity

church debates again in the chapters *The Cross and the Problem of Suffering* and *Why Easter Saturday?*

I would select as the three most important issues that relate both to the nature of the Trinity and our understanding of what happened on the cross: first, the full divinity of Jesus; second, the full humanity of Jesus; and third, the relationship that existed between the Father and the Son as Jesus bore our sins.

1) George Carey, former Archbishop of Canterbury, sums up the basic reason the full divinity of Jesus is so important in Christian thinking in his book on the cross, *The Gate of Glory*:

> "To claim that Jesus Christ is not God himself become man for us and our salvation" writes Professor Tom Torrance, "is equivalent to saying that God does not love us to the uttermost." Indeed, if God's love stops short of Calvary we may have a God who loves – but not one whose love is complete …
>
> We can now begin to see why the early Christians fought so tenaciously for the doctrine that Jesus was truly God, because any other option spells the death of the atonement. Jesus does not need to be God to set a moral example; he does not need to be God to be a brilliant and inspiring teacher. But he does need to share the nature of God if he is the Saviour in the sense of reconciling man to God and restoring man to his former dignity. At this point we can, perhaps, begin to answer Bultmann's famous question: "Does Jesus help me because he is the Son of God or is he the Son of God because he helps me?"

The late Methodist leader Dr Donald English once observed, "The wonder of the cross is not the blood, but whose blood it was and to what purpose it was shed." If we try to explain away all the emphasis in the New Testament that Jesus is a fully divine being,[1] and to be worshipped as such, then we devalue the constantly affirmed statement that what happened on the cross was due to the love of God. God did not send a subordinate to do his work for him, he came himself in the person of Jesus. Peter can declare to the crowds in the temple, "**You killed the author of life**" (Acts 3:15). Paul states that "**the rulers of this age**" had "**crucified the Lord of glory**" (1 Corinthians 2:8). To put it bluntly, they put God to death. Again, Paul explains, "**God was reconciling the world to himself in Christ**" (2 Corinthians 5:19). It is the fact that the one hanging on the cross was truly God which safeguards the truth that "**God is love**" (1 John 4:8).

2) It is our understanding of the cross which also safeguards for us the true humanity of Jesus. Unless he had been truly human, then he could not have borne our sins as our representative in our place. Paul underlines this when he declares that Jesus was "**born of a woman, born under the law, to redeem those under the law, that we might receive adoption to sonship**" (Galatians 4:4,5). It was only as one who was fully under the demands of his Father's moral requirements, as we ourselves are, that he could redeem us sinners who had failed to live up to those demands.

However, it is the writer of Hebrews who develops this theme most fully. In chapter 2 he explains how it was necessary for Jesus to be made "**lower than the angels for a little while**" (v. 9). In order to bring "**many sons and daughters to glory**", it was necessary that he should suffer and become "**of the same family**" as us (vv. 10,11). He is therefore "**not ashamed to call [us] brothers and sisters**" (v. 11). And it is particularly in relation to the cross that it was necessary for him to become part of his own creation in becoming fully flesh and blood. "**Since the children have flesh and blood, he too**

---

[1] I deal with this more fully in the booklet *Is Jesus Really God?*

shared in their humanity so that by his death he might break the power of him who holds the power of death – that is the devil – and free those who all their lives were held in slavery by their fear of death… For this reason he had to be made like his brothers and sisters in every way, in order that he might become a merciful and faithful high priest in service to God, and that he might make atonement for the sins of the people" (vv. 14-17). Later he adds that, being fully human, Jesus was "**tempted in every way, just as we are – yet he did not sin**" (4:15).

This means, of course, that God in the person of Jesus was willing in becoming human, and particularly by his crucifixion, to identify with and be united to what is essentially alien and different to his own nature – that is our mortality and fallenness, even to the point of death. This is a point that is emphasised by theologian Eberhard Jungel.

So if Jesus is both fully God and fully human, how do these two natures relate within his person? This was much debated in early centuries, but putting the matter as simply as I believe it can be put, I think the following points are clear enough in the New Testament. First, in becoming fully human in the womb of Mary, Jesus did not cease to be God. After all, God cannot stop being God! Second, during his time on earth he was indeed "**lower than the angels**" and "**like his brothers and sisters in every way**" (Hebrews 2:9,17). In other words, it was his choice to submit to his Father in heaven and rely only on those resources that are available also to us. The unusual things he did, such as calming the storm and healing the sick, were not from his own resources, but were the work of his Father through the Spirit within him. This is a constant theme of John's Gospel (e.g. 5:19; 14:10). Though Jesus was both fully God and fully human, he was obviously one person and not a split personality. At least on this point I believe the Council of Chalcedon, quoted above, got it right.

So it is in his role as being Son of God yet fully human that he is perfectly fitted to be the "**one mediator between God and human beings**" (1 Timothy 2:5).

3) Concerning what happened to the relationship between the Father and Jesus as he bore our sins on the cross, I believe it is necessary to accept that the cry of Jesus, "**My God, my God, why have you forsaken me?**" represents a reality about what had actually happened, rather than a mere feeling. His Father had indeed forsaken him at this time. In the light of all the emphasis we have in the New Testament letters that he "**bore our sins**", was "**made sin**" and "**became a curse**" for us, I don't see how it is possible to deny that there must have been a real rending asunder of the divine family as the Father dealt with all the world's evil once and for all. Jurgen Moltmann, in *Crucified God*, speaks of the awful experience which "divides God from God to the utmost degree of enmity and distinction". We have to recognise that both Father and Son suffer the cost of their surrender, though differently.

> The Son suffers dying, the Father suffers the death of the Son. The grief of the Father here is just as important as the death of the Son. The Fatherlessness of the Son is matched by the Sonlessness of the Father.

How could this be? After all, the members of the divine Trinity enjoyed a relationship of such closeness and intimacy that they could be described as being one God (Deuteronomy 6:4) – though the Hebrew word used here, *echad*, can speak of a plurality within a singularity. Jesus described this relationship in these terms: "**I am in the Father and the Father is in me**" (John 14:10) and this kind of phrase occurs about 18 times in John's Gospel. The early church used the word *perichoresis* to describe this unity or interpenetration that existed within the Godhead, without losing their relational distinctiveness. Roger Forster, in his excellent book *Trinity*,[1] says:

---

1 Ichthus, 2004, ©.

This is a transliterated Greek word, probably deriving from *peri*, meaning "around" and *choreuo*, meaning "to make room", "go forward", or "give way" – in other words, meaning 'to dance', or 'dance around'. This word was used in pagan worship when dancing around a particular altar.

I believe the answer to the above question must lie in the ministry of the Holy Spirit. The Spirit is closely associated with the life and ministry of Jesus. It was through the activity of the Spirit that he was conceived in the womb of Mary (Luke 1:35). It was the Spirit who empowered his ministry (Matthew 3:16; Luke 4:18; Matthew 12:28). He was sustained by the Spirit (Luke 10:21). It was by means of the Spirit he was raised from the dead (Romans 1:4; 8:11; 1 Peter 3:18). The writer of Hebrews tells us that it was also **"through the eternal Spirit"** that he **"offered himself unblemished to God"** (9:14). It must have been the Spirit who not only gave Jesus the strength to go through hell for us, but also to maintain the link between Father and Son. Alan Lewis, in *Between Cross and Resurrection*, argues powerfully for this and makes the connection between Jesus' separation from his Father and our own alienation from God:

> For the Spirit is revealed between the cross and the grave to be the unifying go-between who holds the Father and the Son together when in self-abandonment to sonlessness the Father gives up the Beloved One to death and hell. And because the eternal Son, fatherless and liquidated, is flesh of our own flesh, God united to the utmost of our perishableness, the Spirit who unites the Father and the Son through their separation also holds together humanity and God, the Creator and the creatures. Thus does death within the living Trinity secure God's even closer union with humanity in its mortality and guilt, on

the very boundary of their deepest alienation and furthest separation.

Jungel, in *Mystery,* speaks of this relationship that existed between the Father and Son, even in Jesus' godforsakenness and hellish isolation, from a slightly different perspective:

> Pointedly, and yet expressing the heart of the matter, the Johannine Christ says, "For this reason the Father loves me, because I lay down my life that I may take it again" [John 10:1]. And thus he is the beloved Son who, in the midst of his separation from the Father, relates to him.

But, as Lewis adds, "It is the Spirit, proceeding from the Father and the Son, who both preserves their differentiation and prevents their disintegration."

There are truths here that are far beyond human understanding, but one thing is clear; it is the doctrine of the Trinity that makes some sense of the cross and provides some foundation for beginning to appreciate the amazing love of God, a subject to which we now turn.

The cross and the love of God

It is interesting that the New Testament nowhere defines what love is. Paul, in his great chapter on love, 1 Corinthians 13, tells us about the absolute importance of love. He describes how love behaves and he speaks of its lasting value, but he does not actually say what it is. However, we are left in no doubt as to what love is when the Bible speaks of the love of God.

It is significant that when the New Testament mentions the love of God it usually does so in the context of the cross. Consider the following examples: "**God so loved the world that he gave his one and only Son**" (John 3:16); "**God demonstrates his own love for us in this: While we were still sinners, Christ died for us**" (Romans 5:8); "**This is love: not that we loved God, but that he loved us and sent his Son as an atoning sacrifice for our sins**" (1 John 4:10). Note John's statement "*This* is love". In the Old Testament, one of the most common words used to describe God is the Hebrew word *chesed*. It occurs 148 times, 90 of these in the Psalms. This is a composite word including ideas such as "loving kindness", "long-suffering", "gentleness" and "goodness", and is often translated as "love". In the New Testament John goes a step further and tells us "**God *is* love**"[1] (1 John 4:8,16). Emil Brunner called this "The most daring statement that has ever been made in human language." But that statement alone tells us nothing. It is the cross that unpacks

---

1 Italics mine.

its meaning. As Eugenia Price says in *Share My Pleasant Stones,* "God's mercy was not increased when Jesus came to earth, it was illustrated! Illustrated in a way we can understand." Or as John V. Taylor puts it in his thoughtful book on the crucifixion, *Weep Not for Me,* "The crucified Jesus is the only accurate picture of God the world has ever seen."

Love is self-giving for the benefit of others and in God's case the "others" were those who had rebelled against him. The proof of genuine love is not merely a feeling; it is an action. In Dillistone's beautiful book, *Jesus Christ and His Cross,* he mentions that someone once asked the incomparable dancer, Pavlova, what she meant by a certain dance she had performed. She replied, "Do you think I would have *danced* it if I could have *said* it?" We tend to think of love in emotional terms, but the New Testament concept of love is more focused on active self-giving. And the greater the cost of that self-giving, the greater the love. It was on the night before his crucifixion that Jesus said to his disciples, "**Greater love has no one than this: to lay down one's life for one's friends**" (John 15:13). Because there never has been, nor could be, a greater cost than that endured by Father and Son on Calvary, this is what defines for all time the true nature of love – and the true character of God. Paul Rees said: "The cross does not so much reveal God's infinite intellect as it reveals his heart." Someone else has said, "On the Mount of Beatitudes Christ opened his mouth and taught the people: on the mount of Calvary he opened his heart and showed the people."

As the Greek language had no word to express this kind of self-giving love, the early Christians invented a new one, *agapē*, to distinguish it from other words which were used of the kind of love that exists between family members and friends, or love with a sexual connotation. Leon Morris made this comment:

> Love as men understand it is usually of the nature of *eros*. It has

two outstanding characteristics. It is love of the worthy, or at least that which men think worthy, and it is a love that includes the desire to possess. The love that we see in the cross differs in both respects. It is a love of those whom God knows to be unworthy, and it is a love which seeks not so much to possess as to give. It is a love that proceeds from the essential nature of God, not from something of value in men, which attracts us to Him.

It is worth noting that the New Testament is equally divided between the emphasis it puts on the love of the Father in giving his Son and the love of the Son in sacrificing himself for us. There is a total alignment of wills between them both. It was love that sent the Son and love that brought him. And the goal of both was that we might be included in the family.

This kind of love is beyond our understanding. Alexander Whyte, in *Lord, Teach Us to Pray*, says:

> The love of Christ has no border, it has no shore, it has no bottom. The love of Christ is boundless, it is bottomless, it is infinite, it is divine. That it passes knowledge [Ephesians 3:19] is the greatest thing that ever was said or could be said about it, and Paul was raised up of all men to see that and to say it. We shall come to the shore, we shall strike the bottom, of every other love, but never of the love of Christ!

H. R. Mackintosh, in *The Christian Experience of Forgiveness*, has a significant comment on why it is beyond our understanding:

> We are constantly under a temptation to suppose that the reason why we fail to understand completely the atonement made by God in Christ is that our minds are not sufficiently profound.

And doubtless there is truth in the reflection that for final insight into the meaning of the cross we are not able or perspicacious enough. But there is a deeper reason still. It is that we are not good enough; we have never forgiven a deadly injury at a price like this, at such cost to ourselves as came upon God in Jesus' death. We fail to comprehend such sacrificial love because it far outstrips our shrunken conceptions of what love is and can endure.

But whether we understand it or not, we can begin to experience it. When we surrender our lives to Jesus, then it is this love that is **"poured out into our hearts through the Holy Spirit"** (Romans 5:5). Anglican minister, David Watson, told how he was speaking at a University Mission one evening and just before his talk started someone said to him, "Do you see that girl over there. She's the toughest girl in the University." She had a reputation of being pretty tough, of sleeping around with many boys, taking drugs, doing all the usual kind of things. She came to see David when he had finished, and said she had asked Christ into her life at the end of his talk. He saw her next day and she told him what she had been doing. "I have just been crying and crying and crying," (and these were her very words) "because for the last six years I have felt as guilty as hell. And now", she said, "I can't really believe that God loves me." David comments, "During that day all that guilt was coming out and all God's love was coming in, and she couldn't believe that God loved her personally." Michael Green and R. Paul, in *New Testament Spirituality*, say:

> We are a delight to God. He desires us. He seeks our fellowship. Were it needed, he would die again for us. We never know ourselves to be truly loved until we know ourselves to be loved by God.

The Cross and the Love of God

When we have put our faith in Jesus, even when we don't *feel* this love, we can still trust him and *believe* it. In this respect it is worth noting that when the writers of the New Testament speak of God's love they tend to use the past tense – not "he loves us" but "he loved us", referring to the cross (e.g. John 3:16; Galatians 2:20; 1 John 4:10). If your circumstances lead you to doubt whether he really loves you, look to the cross – the greatest proof of his love.

When we have once experienced this love, then as Jesus' followers we are also commanded to begin practising it – loving our enemies as well as our friends, as that is what God our Father and role model is like. He expects the same of his children (Matthew 5:43-48). Ray Simpson, in *A Holy Island of Prayer,* lays down the following challenge:

> The tragedy of the second millennium was that the Cross, starting with the Crusades, became an emblem of the sword… The challenge of this third millennium is to let it be what it was and what it still is in its origin – an emblem of unconditional love.

The first Christians did this well, as we read in the early chapters of Acts. The gods feel no love for humans, Aristotle taught. "God so loved the world," Christians answered. That response changed the standard of living in this world, according to Rodney Stark, author of *The Rise of Christianity: A Sociologist Reconsiders History* (Princeton) and a professor at the University of Washington.

One final point. Sadly, this love, amply illustrated by the cross, can be rejected. True love never forces itself on anyone – it allows freedom of response. As Paul explains, "**God's kindness is intended to lead you to repentance**" (Romans 2:4). Where there is an unwillingness to respond in repentance there can be only one outcome. Robert Moyer put it like this: "A sinner may go to hell unsaved; he cannot go to hell unloved."

The cross and the justice of God

The words "just", "justice", "righteous" and "righteousness", either applying to God or to humans, occur about 650 times in the Bible. The word "judgement" occurs about 400 times and the verb "to judge" over 200 times. The same Hebrew and Greek words are translated as either justice or righteousness, depending on the context. It is not necessary for my purposes to go into the different words that are so translated and the shades of meaning of each. It is enough to repeat what Christopher Wright says, in *Living as the People of God*: "No idea is more all-persuasive in the Old Testament than that God is a God of righteousness and justice." One could add that this is true enough of the New Testament as well, though with the coming of Jesus, as we shall see, it is more than balanced by grace.

The Psalmist could declare of God: "Righteousness and justice are the foundation of your throne" (89:14). God governs the world by his righteous laws. The consistency of his laws is observed even in the natural world, making possible the discipline of science. The very fact that we all have a strong sense of justice, even though it may be perverted by our own self-centredness, is adequate testimony that behind it all is a being of perfect justice who created us with some of his own characteristics. Such a sense of justice did not arise from some chance evolutionary process.

E. Calvin Beisner, in a monograph *Justice and Poverty: Two Views Contrasted,* defines Biblical justice as follows:

The Biblical concept of justice may be summarised as rendering impartially to everyone his due in proper proportions according to the norm of God's moral law.

There are two important concepts in this statement. The first is that God gives to everyone what they *deserve*. If justice is to be truly impartial, there can be no exception to this. There is a strong bias in the Bible, particularly in the writings of the prophets, towards the poor. However, the reason for this is that the poor are often poor because they have first suffered *injustice*. They are still held responsible for their moral behaviour.[1]

The second point is that God's justice is always according to God's moral law, and this law is a reflection of God's own moral character. This means that if humans are to live in any meaningful relationship with God, then it is necessary for us to conform to that norm, or character. **"You are to be holy to me because I, the Lord, am holy"** is the command of both the Old and New Testaments (Leviticus 20:26 – see 1 Peter 1:15). For the prophets of the Old Testament, failure in the area of either social injustice or general wickedness was always linked with the failure to "know" God (e.g. Isaiah 1:3-17; Hosea 4:1ff.).

Both these points, taken together, present us with a seemingly insoluble problem. Voltaire once said, "Of course God forgives sin: That's his business." But there is no "of course" in the New Testament. We have all fallen so short of the norm given to us in the Bible, illustrated by such things as the Ten Commandments,

---

1 For passages that underline God's concern for social justice, see: Exodus 22:22; Deuteronomy 10:18,19; Psalm 146:7-9; Proverbs 14:31; 22,23; Isaiah 1:15-17,23; 5:1-8,22,23; 10:1-4; 58:3-12; Jeremiah 7:5-11; 22:3,13-17; Ezekiel 16:49-52; 18; 22:6-12; Hosea 4:1-3; 12:6,7; Amos 2:6-8; 5:7,10-15,21-24; 6:12; 8:4-6; Micah 2:1-3,8,9; 3:1-3,9-12; 6:8-13; 7:2-4; Zechariah 7:9-12; Malachi 3:5.

The Cross and the Justice of God

the Sermon on the Mount and the life of Jesus, that if we are to take seriously what the Bible says about the justice of God, we can expect nothing but condemnation. Charles Finney, the eighteenth-century American revivalist, made the comment that he found lawyers easier to bring to faith in Christ than other groups because they had a stronger concept of the necessity of rule by law. The Jews gloried in the fact that they were the recipients of God's moral laws. However, Paul says very clearly, "**There is no difference between Jew and Gentile, for all have sinned and fall short of the glory of God**" (Romans 3:23). Whether we are big sinners or little sinners becomes immaterial in the light of God's perfect holiness and justice. However, in a manner that goes beyond anything in our human concepts of justice, God has solved the problem in the person of Jesus Christ.

Paul spells out the solution to the problem as follows: "**God presented Christ as a sacrifice of atonement, through the shedding of his blood – to be received by faith. He did this to demonstrate his justice… so as to be just and the one who justifies those who have faith in Jesus**" (Romans 3:25,26). Denney says of this passage:

> There can be no gospel unless there is such a thing as a righteousness of God for the ungodly. But just as little can there be any gospel unless the integrity of God's character be maintained. The problem of a sinful world, the problem of all religion, the problem of God dealing with a sinful race, is how to unite these two things. The Christian answer to the problem is given by Paul in [the above] words.

How does the cross demonstrate the justice of God? It does so simply by revealing that God's attitude to evil is such that it demanded so terrible a sacrifice. R. McCheyne Edgar, in a sermon on the cross, declared:

The gathering waves of the Deluge – the flaming fire of Sodom – the sacking of Jerusalem – all famine, pestilence and agony do not proclaim so unmistakably as the Cross – how real is the wrath – how terrible is the justice of the Most High in the matter of sin!

Some of our deepest thinkers have always thought that real forgiveness is possible only when due regard is paid to the moral law. C. A. Dinsmore examined such diverse writings as those of Homer, Aeshylus, Sophocles, Dante, Shakespeare, Milton, George Eliot, Hawthorne and Tennyson, and came to the conclusion that "It is an axiom in life and religious thought that there is no reconciliation without satisfaction."

Yet, above all, as we have seen, the cross demonstrates the amazing love of a God who was willing to suffer the consequences of that sin within himself in order to fully satisfy that justice. As Alan Lewis puts it, "Here God, the Judge, becomes the malefactor, judged and sentenced, and bows to the divine verdict upon human sin and guilt." American pastor Stephen Olford says:

> The Cross expresses the divine mind, reveals the divine estimate of human sin, exhibits the divine righteousness, demonstrates the divine love, and yet does all this on a human platform so that we can appreciate the mystery of the heavenly counsels.

Emil Brunner, in *The Mediator,* put it this way: "The cross is the only place where the loving, forgiving, merciful God is revealed in such a way that we perceive that his holiness and his love are equally infinite." Calvin, echoing Augustine, was even bolder: "In a marvellous and divine way he loved us even when he hated us."

Jesus had said, in the days before his crucifixion, "*Now* **is the** time for judgement on this world"[1] (John 12:31). For one who has put their faith in Jesus, the wonderful news is that the judgement, which would have been in the future, is now 2,000 years in the past.

One objection that may be made to all this is that it can never be right for someone to pay the penalty for the sins of another. From a human perspective, maybe we can understand this better if we think in terms of Jesus as our surety, our guarantor. A guarantor is someone who is willing to assume an individual's legal obligations in the event the individual should fail to meet them. We see nothing wrong in this if it is a voluntary agreement made beforehand. From passages such as 1 Peter 1:18-21, Ephesians 1:4 and Revelation 13:8, it appears that something like this is the case in the counsels of eternity. It is also suggested from the story told in Genesis 15, which I have discussed earlier under the heading "A God who is prepared to die" in the chapter on the Old Testament. What is also relevant on this point is the identification of Jesus with us and we with him, which I looked at earlier under the heading "Our identification with Christ in his death" in the chapter on "The Cross in Paul". Paul describes the Lord Jesus Christ as the second man and last Adam, who involved us in his sin-bearing as truly as Adam involved us in his sinning (cf. 1 Corinthians 15:45ff.; Romans 5:12 ff.). At any rate, it is the unanimous testimony of the New Testament that God's way of doing it is in line with his perfect righteousness, whether we would consider it to be so or not. It is significant that in Romans 3:25,26 Paul mentions God's forbearance in the same passage as his justice. As Leon Morris says, "Neither justice nor mercy must be whittled down; but neither must they be separated."

In his book *Full Assurance,* Harry Ironside, the prominent pastor

---

1 Italics mine.

of Moody Church in Chicago, told the story of a lawyer who lay dying. He had attended church all his life but had never personally trusted Christ for his salvation. He was known to be a man of unimpeachable integrity. Yet, as he lay there facing eternity, he was troubled and distressed. He knew that upright as he had been before men, he was a sinner before God. His awakened conscience brought to his memory sins and transgressions that had never seemed so bad as then, when he knew that shortly he must meet his Maker. A friend put the direct question, "Are you saved?" He replied in the negative, shaking his head sadly. His friend asked, "Would you like to be saved?" "I would indeed," was the reply, "if it is not already too late. But" he added, almost fiercely, "I do not want God to do anything wrong in saving me!" Fortunately, God has devised a way in which he can both be "**just and the one who justifies those who have faith in Jesus**" (Romans 3:26).

Paul declares that "**in the gospel the righteousness of God is revealed**" (Romans 1:17). As Lewis states:

> God's righteousness is simultaneously that which judges sin and that which sets sin aside, with the free gift of justification apart from the law (e.g., Romans 1:16ff.; 3:21ff.; cf. 1 Corinthians 1:18ff. and the extended Johannine theme that Christ's coming means judgement for the world, e.g., John 1:10-10; 12:31).

God did it right! An old hymn puts it well:

Beneath the cross of Jesus
I fain would take my stand –
The shadow of a mighty rock
Within a weary land...
O safe and happy shelter!
O refuge tried and sweet!

> O trysting-place, where heaven's love
> And heaven's justice meet!

A moving story is told about Shamyl the Avar that illustrates this tension between justice and love. He was a remarkable leader who rallied the tribes of Dagestan in the Caucasus mountains in resisting the advance of Russia into their territory in the mid-nineteenth century. He was a giant of a man and a superb horseman and swordsman. In the process he captured the romantic imagination of Western Europe. At one time during his rule, bribery and corruption became so prevalent that he was driven to severest measures. He announced that every case discovered would be punished with 100 lashes. Not long after, a culprit was found. It was his own mother.

For two days he shut himself away in his tent, with neither food nor drink, sunk in prayer. If he made an exception for his mother, could he ever stand before his people again as a just lawgiver and a man of his word? After two days he gathered the people together and, pale as a ghost, commanded the prisoner to be brought forward and tied to the whipping post. He ordered the executioner to be ready, and gave the word for the punishment to be inflicted. This was done. But at the fifth stroke he cried, "Halt!" He had his mother released, bared his own back, had his hands tied, and directed the executioner to lay on him the remaining 95 lashes, with the sternest threats if he failed to give him the full weight of each blow. Both justice and love were satisfied. In the case of Jesus, however, he took 100 percent of the punishment.

The cross and suffering

Much of the thinking I will share in this chapter and the next comes from Alan Lewis's book, *Between Cross and Resurrection: A Theology of Holy Saturday*.[1] I am not aware of a better starting point for serious students who wish to explore these themes in greater depth. Suggestions I make here are just pointers to thinking about an area where there is much mystery. Yet there are also glimpses of truth here that can be of great encouragement as we journey through life with its ups and downs, victories and defeats, joys and sorrows, and its beckoning challenges.

First, it may be helpful to give a brief summary of one of the harmful influences that Greek philosophy has had on Christian thinking. In the third, fourth and fifth centuries, one of the issues that church leaders wrestled with, particularly as they sought to clarify their understanding of the nature of Jesus and God, was the principle of "divine impassibility" – the idea, inherited more from Greek philosophy than from the Bible, that God was not capable of passion, that he was incapable of pain or suffering, that he could not be affected with pain or uneasiness, that he was invulnerable. Lewis states:

> Almost everyone involved on all sides of the long debates

---

[1] William B. Eerdmans Publishing Company, Cambridge, U.K./Grand Rapids, Michigan, 2001, ©. Reprinted by permission of the publisher, all rights reserved.

through which [Nicene and Chalcedonian] theology took shape held it as a common axiom that even in the incarnation, God as such – the divine nature – did not and could not suffer, still less die. It proved intellectually impossible for the church in this context to muster language, conceptually, or regulative statements which corresponded to Scripture's own bold attestation that "they crucified the Lord of glory" (1 Corinthians 2:8).

Those who sought to be most faithful to Christ's full humanity, including his weakness and suffering as it is presented in the New Testament, and yet were still influenced by this thought of God's impassibility, tended, as a consequence, towards separation of Christ's two natures. It was his human, not his divine nature, which suffered for us on the cross. But the New Testament in no way divides up Christ's personality in this way – certainly not in those passages we have looked at in Hebrews which speak of his sharing our humanness in every respect.

For the influential Thomas Aquinas in the thirteenth century, God's perfection excluded all passibility. To quote Lewis again:

> Suffering or change, emotion or need, would indicate defective power or deficiency of being. God loves "without passion" or desire; and in the incarnation it is strictly by reason of his human nature, not his divine, that Christ suffers and dies.

Even Calvin said that suffering is not properly ascribed to Christ's divinity, and this thought was continued in the Reformed tradition that the eternal Word which united with Christ's human nature remained simultaneously in heaven, not forfeiting its divine, eternal Lordship.

However, the sheer force of human suffering over the last 100 years has helped to push theology towards new thinking about a suffering, crucified and buried God. After two world wars and numerous lesser conflicts, the holocaust and other major genocides, mass hunger and poverty, nuclear disasters, ecological disasters and destruction, the possibility of the death of the planet itself – and all conveyed to us constantly by the modern media – it seems as if the stench of death hangs over us today as in perhaps no previous generation.

It was Barth as much as anyone who finally broke the shackles of ancient philosophy. His insistence that theology must listen before it speaks – that we must begin with revelation, with what God himself has made known about himself in the Scriptures – enabled him to radically reconceive the nature of God in the light of the cross and grave of Jesus Christ, and hence the possibility of God's own suffering. Lewis says: "Barth overturns the Christolgical tradition as a whole by interpreting Christ's weakness and humiliation as a *divine* event and his exaltation as a *human* happening." It was God in Christ who suffered for us on the cross. It was Jesus with his resurrected human nature that was exalted to glory. Others have taken up this theme since. Lewis sums up Barth as follows:

> On the cross, not only is the Son of God rejected by humanity's violence, our blindness and ingratitude; but the Son of God sacrificed and delivered up by the Father endures the heavenly Judge's own rejection of earthly enmity and folly. Yet who is thus the victim of God's malediction but God's own very self? It is the Lord, none other, who has become the humbled servant, the repudiated cornerstone. The Son of the Father gives himself to us, "to suffer in our place the divine rejection, the divine No, the divine judgement... to fulfil the divine Yes, the divine grace." The blow of God's No first of all strikes God's own heart, who "tasted... damnation, death and hell" and did "bow before the claim and power of nothingness."

Barth eloquently says:

He elected our suffering... as His own suffering... The sentence of Pilate He elects as a revelation of His judgement on the world. He elects the cross of Golgotha as His kingly throne. He elects the tomb in the garden as the scene of His being as the living God.

Again he says:

God does not merely give himself up to the risk and menace, but he exposes Himself to the actual onslaught and grasp of evil... He hazarded himself wholly and utterly.

For Barth, it is not just the Son who suffers. There is a real sense in which God suffers too, in the mode of the Father. The humiliation of the Son is grounded in a mysterious "fatherly fellow-suffering of God," in solidarity with and substitution for human suffering, realised in the historical event of the cross.

It is true that Barth came short of attributing *death* as such to God in the light of Jesus' perishing and burial. He rejects as anthropomorphic "the idea of a God who is dead." However, I shall look at that question briefly again in the next chapter.

Jungel, another who wrote much on the subject, declared that God's freedom to exist as a created being in the person of Jesus did include a willingness to be the creature's victim, to surrender to that "opposition to God which characterises human existence. The consequence of this self-surrender of God is God's *suffering*... a suffering even to *death* on a cross."

The main point I am seeking to make is that our God is a God who has experienced suffering at its deepest level, and I believe this is thoroughly consistent with all the clues we are given in the

The Cross and Suffering

New Testament. However, it is not only true that God suffered through his coming in the person of Jesus, but that he still suffers through his identification with us in our sorrow and misery. In Paul's magnificent chapter, Romans 8, he speaks of the whole creation "**groaning in the pains of childbirth**" (v. 22). Then he says, "**we ourselves… groan inwardly**" (v. 23) as we await our final deliverance. But then he says that "**the Spirit himself intercedes for us through wordless groans**" (v. 26). Lewis declares of this passage:

> Eternally [Christ] shares humanity's infirmities as fellow sufferer, and as victim he endures re-crucifixion at their hands. He intercedes for their healing with the Father and pleads their case as advocate, and sends to comfort them the Spirit whose own beseeching, groaning, wordless prayer lifts their pain into the heart of the divine community when their own lips fall dumb in despair and numb bewilderment.

Again he eloquently says:

> The God who suffers pain and grief, death and hell, in the separation of the Father and the Son between Good Friday and Easter Saturday, is still the same suffering, grieving God, who has tasted death on Easter Day. Taking death into the Godhead, as the only way to put death to death (Hebrews 2:14), God continues to be subject to the groaning of a captive creation and the mortality of perishing humanity. Only when through the Spirit, all pain and tears have passed away will God's suffering come to an end, the ascendancy of life over death be uncontested, and what began between Easter's Saturday and Sunday be concluded.

He adds, "This is the eschatological growth and enrichment of the Trinity through God's pain and suffering in fellowship with us, and joy and delight at loving responses from us."

In Philippians 2:7 Paul tells us that Jesus "**made himself nothing**". The Greek verb *keno* means "to make empty" and can mean "to destroy; render void, of no effect". Moltmann, in his books *Trinity and the Kingdom, God and Creation,* and *The Crucified God,* conceives of the cross as a distinct and *new* event for God, when the divine experience of suffering takes on a different dimension. Until Christ returns, God through the Spirit suffers at a level of infinite intensity that did not occur before the incarnation. He sees the coming of Christ into human history and the particular event of the cross as anchor points for a much more extensive reality, a cosmic *kenosis* – a self-emptying focused not so much on the Son as on the Spirit, the Spirit immanent through all of time, in all creation. Lewis sums up his emphasis as follows:

> By the Spirit, God is the victim of everybody's pain; takes in not just one death but universal death; absorbs not only the evil done to Jesus but wickedness wherever it occurs: the godforsakenness and godlessness of not just one Easter Saturday, but of every day. That ever-repeated "Easter Saturday" experience, at the heart of every generation's suffering and grief, death and hopelessness, also belongs to the Trinitarian history of God begun at the cross.

Though we get into matters here that go further than what is spelt out in the New Testament, it does not seem to be unreasonable to me to think along such lines, taking into account the terms that are used.

So far, what we have been indicating is that, whatever suffering we may personally experience, or whatever questions we may have about the suffering we see around us, the one thing we can

The Cross and Suffering

take from the cross is that God is with us in our suffering. The Jewish author Elie Weisel relates a WW II incident that illustrates the nature of God's participation in the world. The Gestapo sadistically killed a boy before the inmates of a concentration camp. One of the onlookers cried, "Where is God now?" Another answered, pointing to the figure of the dying boy, "He is there: he is hanging on the gallows." The original speaker intended to say that God was impotent, extinguished, dead, but these words convey a profound truth for a Christian: they indicate that God was present in the situation, experiencing profoundly the horror of suffering. As Lewis puts it: "Our tears are but the slightest drop in the ocean of God's own weeping over young lives brutally curtailed, and old extended beyond all meaning, in pain, indignity, and helplessness."

Philip Yancey, in one of his thoughtful "Back Page" articles in Christianity Today,[1] tells of meeting with renowned theologian Jurgen Moltmann (whom he describes as one of his heroes) at his home in Virginia. Drafted into the war at 18, and seeing compatriots incinerated in the fire-bombings in Hamburg, the question "Why did I survive?" haunted him. He was to spend three years in prison camps in Belgium, Scotland and England. As he learned the truth about the Nazis, Moltmann felt an inconsolable grief about life, "weighed down by the sombre burden of a guilt which could never be paid off." He had no Christian background and read Goethe's poems and the works of Nietzsche, neither of which offered much hope. But an American Army chaplain gave him a copy of the New Testament and Psalms. He read, "**If I make my bed in hell, behold [you are] there**" (Psalm 139:8). As he read on, he found words that perfectly captured his feelings of desolation. He became convinced that God "was present beyond the barbed wire – no, most of all behind the barbed wire."

---

1 September 2005, ©.

On his release, Moltmann began to articulate his theology of hope. Through all his theological works run two themes: God's presence with us in our suffering and God's promise of a perfected future. As he explains in The Crucified God, in Jesus we have definitive proof that God suffers with us. (During the war in El Salvador, someone sent Moltmann a picture of one of six Jesuits murdered by a death squad, and next to his body lay a Spanish edition of this book.) But that is not the end of the story. The Gospels speak not only of the cross, but also of resurrection. Easter is the beginning of the "laughter of the redeemed... God's protest against death." Faith allows us to believe that God is not satisfied with things as they are either, and plans to make all things new. Moltmann notes that the phrase "Day of the Lord" in the Old Testament inspired fear, but in the New Testament it inspires hope, because those authors have come to know and trust the Lord whose Day it is.

God has the power to transform our present. He can heal the sick, spare us from injury, rescue us from desperate situations, and sometimes he does. Often, for his own purposes, he choses not do so, and allows us to experience this world's woes. But, as we have been arguing, he is far from indifferent. He suffers with us, and with us longs for our final transformation. However, the message of the New Testament is that there is more to come, that final deliverance for his people is certain. That certainty can strengthen us and give us confidence and hope for the journey. Before we focus on that certainty, however, let's look at the question "Why Easter Saturday?"

Why Easter Saturday?

In the last chapter we touched on the problems the church has had with the incarnation for over 1,000 years – God taking on human flesh and blood, and the implied union with dead and buried flesh. Could God still be God if touched by suffering and death? We have seen that Barth more than anyone else broke the mould of traditional teaching in this area, followed by Jungel and Moltmann and later by others. Of these, it is Jungel who is *the* theologian of the grave of Jesus Christ. With Moltmann he interprets the very being of the Trinity from the standpoint of Christ's death, burial and resurrection. But it is in his major volume, *God as the Mystery of the World,* that he, in effect, identifies Easter Saturday, the day of the burial of God, as theology's foundational, defining moment. Somehow, it is the grave, which is the guarantee of the finality of Christ's death, that silently, and almost unnoticed, presents both a problem and the gospel of Christology. The problem lies in discerning what was really happening in the tomb. Was God in Jesus really dead?[1] And if so, what are the implications of this? There are mysteries here that I do not profess to understand. However, I will

---

1 I will not attempt to interpret the difficult passage of 1 Peter 3:18-20. For serious students of such issues, I suggest you check the commentaries of those who are wiser than I for the various ways these verses have been understood, and then take your pick!

Why Did Jesus Die?

suggest some ideas that do make some sense to me.

First, it is the grave where we find that God's identity with created humanity reaches its most intense point. It has been a common understanding of biblical teaching that death entered the world as a result of sin (see Genesis 2:17; Romans 5:12). It has often been assumed that if humans had not sinned, then they would not have died physically but would have perhaps been taken eventually straight to heaven. However, the Bible clearly states that only God is immortal (1 Timothy 6:16) and that believers will be "**clothed with**" immortality only at the resurrection of the dead (1 Corinthians 15:53). This latter verse clearly states that we *are* mortal in our present state (also Romans 8:11). It may well be that the "death" referred to in Genesis 2 and Romans 5 refers only to spiritual death – separation from God – and that humans, even though they had not sinned, would still have died. Though Bible students of the past such as Augustine, Aquinas, Luther and Calvin all viewed every aspect of death as a consequence of sin, others have held a contrary view. Irenaeus was one, and in contemporary theology both Barth and Tillich reach the conclusion that humans are "naturally" mortal. Barth declares:

> Finitude, then, is not intrinsically negative and evil. There is no reason why it should not be an anthropological necessity, a determination of true and natural man, that we should one day have to die and therefore merely have been.

If this should be correct, then maybe what we see is Jesus' identification with us in every respect, *even* in our mortality. God did not leave this man's flesh (and therefore ours) at the moment when the real nature of his creaturehood and fleshliness was most apparent. As Lewis puts it:

Why Easter Saturday?

That God should say [the] resurrecting Yes to the human body only by first identifying with that body in the grave confirms that it is good and fitting not only to be fleshly, but for our flesh to perish, to come to termination and ultimate decay.

Maybe we see here the most intense example of a theme that runs through the Bible – God's promise to be with his people. It begins in the Old Testament (e.g. Deuteronomy 31:3-6; Haggai 1:13-15). Matthew begins and ends his gospel with it (1:22,23; 28:20). It culminates in the renewed heaven and earth (Revelation 21:3).

Of course, all this is totally contrary to the anti-materialistic philosophy common in the Greek philosophy of those days – Stoicism and all the varieties of Platonism – a philosophy which still persists in religions such as Hinduism and Buddhism, and which has exerted too much influence on the thinking of Christians down the ages. For the Greeks, God's identification with the Crucified and Buried One was illusory. For the Jews it was blasphemy. For the one it was impossible, for the other unfitting.

Second, the grave underlines God's identification with us in our sins. The Bible declares that "He was assigned a grave with the wicked… in his death" (Isaiah 53:9). I understand that it was during those awful three hours from midday till three in the afternoon as he hung on the cross that he actually bore the sins of the human race. However, it is the silence of the tomb on Easter Saturday that points us to the full consequences of the powers of evil. The jealousy, the pride, the selfishness, the cowardice, the cruelty, the hatred and all the other sins we can think of that led to the cross had had their say and God had allowed it to happen. He had accepted the verdict upon himself without question or defence. Now it is the silence of the tomb that impresses on us both the enormity of human depravity and the lengths to which God was willing to go in order to show his unwillingness to leave us, even in the depths of our guilt. Maybe we are to take from this the fact that even in our moral wretchedness and sin God can still be there. He himself has been a victim of that godforsakenness. Lewis says again:

> The Lord of life triumphs over death, the inimical opposite of life, not by cancelling out the adversary but by succumbing to the victory of all that God opposes. Such is the strange story we have heard, the conundrum we find so hard to solve, the shock so difficult to sustain, the abyss we find so hard to bridge, the "scandal of the cross" we would love to render comprehensible and innocuous… Only through the vulnerable victimisation at the hands of sin and death, and not by blocking, crushing, or annihilating those agents of destruction, does the triune God of righteous love flourish yet more abundantly than the luxuriant barrenness of hate and wickedness.

When Nansen was looking for the North Pole, he once found himself in very deep water. His line would not reach the bottom. He took his book and wrote the date and the length of the line and added, "Deeper than that." The next day he lengthened his line and dropped it again and again. It failed to touch bottom and he wrote down the date and the length of the line, and added, "Deeper than that." After a few days he gathered all the line that could be found on his ship, tied it together and dropped it down, but it would not reach bottom. His entry was again, "Deeper than that." However deep a person may sink morally, or however desperate a situation one may be in, the love of God in Jesus, as demonstrated by his cross and grave, is "deeper than that."

Third, there is a clear necessity for belief in the Trinity. If in some real sense God in Jesus "died", how is it possible for God to suffer the negation of death without being annihilated? Tertullian could say without hesitation, "God has died." Luther could speak of "God's passion, God's blood, God's death". Jesus himself declared, "**I was dead**" (Revelation 1:18). I believe Moltmann has got it right when he suggests that, though it is the Son who died and not the Father or the Spirit, because of the principle of *perchoresis,* the mutual indwelling of the Father, Son and Spirit in each other that I have spoken of above, there is a real sense in which death has entered into God. Death, and its division, pierces the life and heart of the triune family. Taking death into the Godhead was the only way to put death to death. Jesus "**suffered death, so that by the grace of God he might taste death for everyone**" (Hebrews 2:9). Yet it is the Spirit, whom Bishop John V. Taylor called the "Go-Between God", which somehow held the divine community together, while the devil, by means of death and hell, does his best to tear it apart. To quote Lewis again:

> For the Spirit holds the Father and the Son together in their separation, proving still more powerfully creative than death is powerfully destructive, so that in the sundered family's reuniting, the loving arms of God close over our death in an embrace of life, cancelling its fearfulness for evermore.

If it is God's absence on Easter Saturday that appears to underline a total sense of shame and failure, both human and divine, then it is his presence in the tomb through the Spirit that can begin to give us hope that even in the most desperate and seeming hopeless situations God can still be present. Could there be a bleaker situation? Not, at least, for the disciples. For two years or more they had been looking forward to the establishment of God's kingdom, however dimly they understood its nature, convinced that this Jesus was indeed the one foretold by the prophets. Now their dreams were shattered. Jesus had been no match for either the politicians and soldiers or the priests and moralists. Was the God they believed in so powerless that he could not rescue his Son from the powers that destroyed him? Had God's love and power found their limit? Was this God's last, best effort at bringing justice and peace? Had the power of death proved too much for the fragile flower of love and grace? Was Jesus not, after all, the Son of God and promised Messiah? The dreams he had inspired, the possibilities he had hinted at, had come to nothing.

Their despair is vividly portrayed by Luke in the story of Cleopas and his companion walking home to Emmaus. "**We had hoped that he was the one who was going to redeem Israel**" (24:21). Now hope was gone – possibly forever. The known end of previous Jewish liberation movements, and the fate of their claimed messiahs, would not have helped! Perhaps we can see here why God allowed the silence of Easter Saturday. We cannot ignore all those contrary signs – evil's triumph, the world's abandonment, the collapse of faith. But if God is somehow present in the worst situation that we can imagine, then he is going to have the last word, *even* if that last word may come beyond the grave. There are times when we can do little but wait until God speaks. But, however long, speak he will.

Today we are living between Good Friday and Easter Day. There will be times when there seems no ground for hope. But the story of Good Friday and Easter can assure us of two things: when God appears to be most absent, he is most assuredly present, and he will indeed have the last word. What has happened in the past will guarantee our future. As Moltmann says, "God weeps with us so that we may someday laugh with him." It is the silence of Easter Saturday that focuses our attention on these things and forces us to think through the issues at a deeper level than we would have done otherwise. And this brings us to Easter Day, which is to me the proof of all we have been saying and for which Easter Saturday provided the perfect backdrop.

God's "Yes" of Easter Day

I have dealt with historical evidence for the resurrection of Jesus from the dead in my booklet *Did Jesus Really Rise from the Dead?* and in the book *Life After Death: Christianity's Hope and Challenge.* For serious students, you won't do better than the 738 pages of *The Resurrection of the Son of God* by N. T. Wright (SPCK, 2003).

First, if the resurrection proves anything at all, it proves that, despite all evidence to the contrary, God had indeed been present through all the events of the previous two days. The empty tomb does not cancel out the cross or the occupied tomb, but it does confirm beyond all doubt that God was there.

Second, it reveals once and for all the identity of Jesus of Nazareth. When Thomas responded to Jesus' revelation of the wounds in his resurrection body by declaring, "**My Lord and my God**" (John 20:28), he was confirming what John declares in the beginning of his Gospel – the eternal God, the Word of life, had indeed become identified with mortal flesh, made from the dust of the earth and doomed to return to it (1:14). And the idea that he was indeed the promised Messiah, who had been so brutally extinguished and excluded by death, now returned with conviction and certainty, as is so apparent in the testimony of the first disciples in the early chapters of Acts. From birth to burial, God has been among us, not only with this man and in this man, but also *as* this man. Knowing now who he is, we can see more clearly what it was that was actually happening in his crucifixion, and in all that led up to it.

Third, it reveals the sufficiency of Jesus' sacrifice for the sins of mankind. Paul says, in his great chapter on the resurrection, "**If Christ has not been raised, your faith is futile: you are still in your sins**" (1 Corinthians 15:17). Commenting on this verse in an article in *Decision* magazine, John Piper writes:

> The point is not that the resurrection is the price paid for our sins. The point is that the resurrection proves that the death of Jesus is an all-sufficient price.

Death and judgement are both very personal things. We will face them both naked and alone. But the one who bore my sins in full on the cross and who endured my death in the tomb is now the living Lord who represents me in glory. In Christ I will never be alone.

Fourth, it proves that the overflowing love and power and grace of God are indeed greater than all the forces of evil, godlessness and hopelessness that can be mustered against it. The God who, at the beginning of time created the universe out of nothingness, is able to take the brokenness, defeat and alienation of the tomb and, against that backdrop, demonstrate in a single instance that he is, and has always been, the one ultimately in control. Satan had won the battle, but lost the war against God's love and grace. And God's victory over death is not a matter of smooth, ensured survival but a new existence after nonsurvival. Though God has more work to do, this demonstration is the guarantee of a greater and more final and complete victory yet to come. "**[God] has set a day when he will judge the world with justice by the man he has appointed. He has given proof of this to everyone by raising him from the dead**" (Acts 17:31).

One implication of all this is that there are no depths to which a human may sink, morally or spiritually, from which God cannot deliver him or her, where there is acknowledgement of guilt and a willingness to be identified with this Christ in his life-transforming ministry. Lewis says:

> God in humility... has triumphed *through* the grave, for its many dis-graced, defeated victims and in the form of one of them. That form, seen first in the cradle, later on a cross, and finally as a corpse, is the shape of resurrection, and there is no other. Let others dream of divine salvation for the righteous and the wise, for those able to transcend the flesh and rise to heights of timelessness and sanctity; the gospel of Christ is for the mortal and the carnal, the earthbound and the sinner. For it was just as such a one that Jesus lived, and still as such a one, fleshly, crucified, and buried, that he was raised. In him, concealed in weakness and in death, are God's true power and life at work.

Another implication of this is spelled out clearly, though briefly, in Paul's magnificent chapter, Romans 8, where he speaks of the certain future hope that is provided by the cross, the resurrection and the ministry of the Spirit. Not only will our created bodies be redeemed (v. 23) and transformed (v. 30), but the whole of creation itself, now **"groaning as in the pains of childbirth"** (v. 22), **"will be liberated from its bondage to decay and brought into the freedom and glory of the children of God"** (v. 21). As Easter Day follows Holy Saturday and did not avert it, so the ultimate victory and transformation of all creation could follow *even* such a disaster as the ecological destruction of our planet or a nuclear war and the holocaust of all humanity. As J. I. Packer says in *Your Father Loves You*, "You could speak of Jesus' rising as the most hopeful (hope-full) thing that has ever happened – and you would be right!"

Fifth, even though it often seems that evil wins the day, there is no hint of goodness prompted by the Spirit within us, no effort to show our gratitude to the Lord by our service to him, to others, or to his creation, that can ever be wasted, however much it may appear to be so. That is why Paul finished his great chapter on the resurrection, 1 Corinthians 15, with the words, "**Therefore, my dear brothers and sisters, stand firm. Let nothing move you. Always give yourselves fully to the work of the Lord, because you know that your labour in the Lord is not in vain**" (v. 58).

The cross and history's reversal of values

In another of his insightful "Back Page" articles in *Christianity Today*, "Why I Can Feel Your Pain", Philip Yancey mentions the book *Violence Unveiled* by Gil Bailie, which builds on the work of René Girard. Girard, a prominent literary critic, began to focus his work increasingly on the role of violence in human culture. In *Violence and the Sacred*, and other books, he expounded a theory of culture in which Christ's death on the cross is a single pivotal event. As Yancey explains:

> According to Girard, societies have traditionally reinforced their power through "sacred violence." The larger group… picks a scapegoat minority – or, in the case of the many societies that have practiced human sacrifice, a single individual – to direct its self-righteous violence against, which in turn bonds and emboldens the majority. The Cross, however, upset the long-standing categories of weak victims and strong heroes, for the victim emerged as the hero.

Paul was indicating something like this when he declared: **"Having disarmed the powers and authorities, he made a public spectacle of them, triumphing over them by the cross"** (Colossians 2:15). The most refined religion of the day accused an innocent man, and the most renowned justice system carried out the sentence. It was indeed a public spectacle.

Bailie points out that the gospel may not make societies less violent, but it makes them less sure about their violence. Before Jesus came, nations didn't worry about such distinctions as "just" and "unjust" wars. Moreover, the gospel set something loose that Bailie describes as "the most astonishing reversal of values in human history. Today the victim occupies the moral high ground everywhere in the Western world." As Yancey says:

> Women, minorities, the disabled, environmental and human rights activists – all these draw their moral force from the power of the gospel unleashed at the Cross, when God took the side of the victim.

It is ironic that those who criticise the church for its failures to live by its own teachings in areas such as violence, slavery, sexism and racism, do so by gospel principles. The message of the cross continues to leaven a culture when the church fails to live up to it, or even takes the wrong side. God has entrusted us flawed human beings with a gospel so powerful that it often does its work in spite of us. We best commend the gospel by humility and repentance where necessary, while continuing to point people to the source of all true goodness.

Why the cross is not popular

To the first century Christians in Corinth, Paul wrote: "The message of the cross is foolishness to those who are perishing... we preach Christ crucified: a stumblingblock to Jews and foolishness to Gentiles, but to those whom God has called, both Jews and Greeks, Christ the power of God and the wisdom of God. For the foolishness of God is wiser than human wisdom, and the weakness of God is stronger than human strength" (1 Corinthians 1:18,23-25).

At the 1988 IFES European Conference on Evangelism in Wurzburg, Germany, beneath a vast banner, "The love of Christ moves us", John Stott spoke on Paul's preaching on the cross of Christ in Corinth, and the objections to his message – intellectual, religious, personal, moral and political – to an audience of 1,000 students from across the continent. He described the first-century Corinthians as "typical" and added that the world in which we live today is just as hostile to the gospel:

> We are fooling ourselves if we imagine that we can ever make the authentic gospel popular... It's too simple in an age of rationalism; too narrow in an age of pluralism; too humiliating in an age of self-confidence; too demanding in an age of permissiveness; and too unpatriotic in an age of blind nationalism... What are we going to share with our friends? The authentic gospel or a gospel that has been corrupted in order to suit human pride?

Let's look at these five points:

Too simple in an age of rationalism. Though there is much about the cross we will never fully understand in this life, its basic message is simple enough for a small child to understand: Jesus loved me so much he was willing to die for my sins. He rose from the dead, and if I acknowledge my need, ask for his forgiveness and invite him into my life as my Lord and Saviour, then he will not only forgive me and become my friend and companion through life, but will one day welcome me into his kingdom forever. The simplicity lies in the fact that I don't have to "do" anything to become a recipient of God's grace. God has done it all. My pride tells me that I should have to do something difficult to earn such a wonderful gift. However, the New Testament declares that there is nothing I can do, and until I am prepared to acknowledge that fact I am not likely to receive it. Like a climber who is thrown a rope while clinging desperately to some protrusion from a cliff face, all I can do is to reach out and take the help offered. Jesus said, "**Truly I tell you, unless you change and become like little children, you will never enter the kingdom of heaven**" (Matthew 18:3). Though there is a place for exploring the truth of the gospel from an intellectual perspective, I need to be humble enough to acknowledge that God knows a bit more than I do. Peter Kreeft, in *Making Sense Out of Suffering*, describes God's way of saving humanity as follows:

> That God should step right into Satan's trap, Satan's world, Satan's game, the jaws of death on the cross; that he should give Satan the opportunity to cherish forever, in dark, satanic glee, the terrible words from God to God, "My God, My God, why hast Thou forsaken Me?" – this was something "no eye has seen, nor ear heard, nor the heart of man conceived" (I Corinthians 2:9). That God should take alienation away from man by inserting alienation into the very heart of God; that

he should conquer evil by allowing it its supreme, unthinkable triumph, deicide, the introduction of death into the life of God, the God of life, the Immortal One; that he should destroy the power of evil by allowing it to destroy him – this is "the foolishness of God [that] is wiser than men, and the weakness of God [that] is stronger than men" (1 Corinthians 1:25).

It is interesting that the Greek word for "foolishness" that Paul uses in 1 Corinthians 1:18 and 23 to describe the view which many hold of the gospel is *"mōria"*, from which comes our word "moron". You must be a "moron" to believe that one criminally executed, and between two bandits at that, is the Saviour of the world! Our intellectual and moral pride can keep us from accepting God's free gift of salvation. To just repent and believe seems too simple.

Too narrow in an age of pluralism. If it is true that Jesus really was God present in the flesh, the second person in the divine Trinity, and that the main purpose of his coming was to die for my sins so that I might be reconciled to God, then it is pure logic to suppose that he is the one to whom I should go for that reconciliation. Because of who he is and what he has done, he had every right to make the statement, "**I am the way and the truth and the life. No one comes to the Father except through me**" (John 14:6). The early Christians also had every right to say, "**Salvation is found in no one else, for there is no other name given under heaven by which we must be saved**" (Acts 4:12). They were merely stating the truth. However, in this postmodern age, when the greatest virtue is tolerance of every view, this is far to narrow! I explore this theme further in the booklet *What Is Truth and Does It Matter?* Of course, if you don't believe that we are sinners in need of forgiveness, then maybe there are other ways of finding God. This brings us to our next point, which, I suspect, for most people who don't like the idea that salvation is by means of the cross, is the heart of the problem.

Why Did Jesus Die?

Too humiliating in an age of self-confidence. Celsus, writing in the second century, was a formidable critic of the Christian faith. For him it was a contemptible religion and he regarded the death of its saviour its most pitiful expression. He mocked the Christian notion of the "tree of life" and "resurrection of the dead" as complete fables. "What drunken old women, telling stories to lull a small child to sleep would not be ashamed of muttering such preposterous things?" The cross in the twenty-first century is no more popular for obvious reasons. The cross, as it is presented to us in the New Testament, makes it clear that we are all guilty before God. It brings into the light of day the depths of human sin and the consequences of our pride and disobedience. The cross also makes clear that God does not like sin very much! God's purity and holiness are such that nothing tainted with evil can live in his presence. Paul tells us that the righteousness and wrath of God are revealed in the gospel (Romans 1:17,18).

Oswald Chambers died in his early 40s, but his books, published posthumously by his wife from his transcribed talks, have been a blessing to many. In his book *My Utmost for His Highest,* he warns against thinking we can have forgiveness apart from the cross:

> Never build your case for forgiveness on the idea that God is our Father and he will forgive us because he loves us! That contradicts the revealed truth of God in Jesus Christ. It makes the cross unnecessary, and the redemption 'much ado about nothing.' God forgives sin only because of the death of Christ. Conviction [of sin] is given to us as a gift of shame and repentance; it is the great mercy of God. Jesus Christ hates the sin in people, and Calvary is the measure of his hatred.

God does not balance up our good and bad deeds in determining whether he will accept us or not. As John Piper puts it:

There is no salvation by balancing records. There is only salvation by cancelling records. The record of our bad deeds (including our defective good deeds), along with the just penalties that each deserves, must be blotted out – not balanced. This is what Christ suffered and died to accomplish (Colossians 2:13,14).

The cross also reveals that we can do nothing to rescue ourselves from our predicament, which is certain judgement. We need a Saviour. This is all very humbling and too much for many to accept in an age when there is so much emphasis on our need to believe in ourselves. That is why you will find more people in church on Easter Day than on Good Friday. However, if we are to experience forgiveness and all the good things that God longs to give us, then we must accept God's verdict on our condition and reach out in humility and faith for all he has to offer.

Gypsy Smith, 1860-1947, was born in a tent, raised in a gypsy camp, never attended a school – not even for a day – yet he influenced the lives of millions of people for God through his powerful preaching. He was converted to Christ at the age of 16 and worked with General William Booth of the Salvation Army for some time before ministering as an itinerant evangelist, working with a variety of organisations all over the world, but particularly in Britain and America. In his autobiography he tells how his father was seeking God and one night dreamed he was travelling through rugged country over rocks and boulders, thorns and briers. His hands were bleeding and his feet torn. Utterly exhausted, he fell to the ground. A person in white raiment appeared and as this person lifted his hands he saw the mark of the nails. He knew it was the Lord. Jesus said, "I suffered this for you, and when you give up all and trust me, I will save you." Shortly after that, Gypsy's father found Christ.

Dominic Steele, who heads a ministry in Australia to media professionals "Christians in the Media", told in *Challenge Weekly* how he learnt this truth 20 years ago as he sought to find a relationship with God:

> What was revolutionary for me was seeing that the initiative in fixing this problem came completely from God. When God sent Jesus to die for me, Jesus paid totally for all my wrong. There was nothing I could contribute.
>
> For me this was very insulting, because I am a self-made person. I have what I have because I have earned it…
>
> I remember sitting with a friend going back and forward over this. Eventually I came to the point where I accepted what he was saying: It's all from Jesus' initiative and nothing from me. There's a powerful sentence in the Bible that puts it clearly, "For it is by grace you have been saved, through faith – this is not from yourselves, it is the gift of God – not by works, so that no one can boast (Ephesians 2:8,9)"…
>
> Understanding the resurrection of Jesus and God making him Lord of the universe was next. This was big. From now on Jesus was to be in charge – not Dominic. He was Lord of the universe, but specifically He would be Lord of me. It was January 26th, 1986 that I made the first decision to do something that I didn't want to do – that Jesus wanted me to do. That was the day I accepted Jesus as my Lord and Saviour. That was the most important day of my life.

The story is told of a mother who once saved her little girl from a burning house, but suffered severe burns on her hands and arms. When the girl grew up, not knowing how her mother's arms became so scarred, she was ashamed of the scarred, gnarled hands and always insisted that she wore long gloves to cover up the ugliness. One day her daughter asked her mother how her hands became so scarred. The mother told her, for the first time, how she had saved her life with those hands. The daughter wept tears of gratitude and said, "Oh, mother, those are beautiful hands, the most beautiful in the world. Don't ever hide them again." Whether the cross of Christ is an embarrassment to us, or whether it is the most significant event in human history, in which we glory (Galatians 6:14), depends on our understanding of who it was that hung there and what he was about.

Too demanding in an age of permissiveness. Jesus said that the most important commandments were to love God with all our hearts, souls and minds and to love our neighbours as much as we love ourselves (Matthew 22:36-40). He said lots of other things too about what he expected of those who would follow him, that I have spelled out in my booklet *Does It Matter How We Live? A Christian view of Morality.* The sort of demands he makes do not go down well in today's society.

Paul Wadell, in *Becoming Friends,* says:

> To speak of friendship with God can sound so cozy and consoling, as if we are all snuggling up to God; however, there is no riskier vulnerability than to live in friendship with God, because friends have expectations of each other, and because friends are said to be committed to the same things… Any friend of God is to faithfully embody the ways of God in the world, even to the point of suffering on account of them. There may be grace and glory in being a friend of God, but there is also clearly a cost.

I will explore further what is involved in being a disciple of Jesus in the next chapter.

Too unpatriotic in an age of blind nationalism. Though God chose one particular race of people, the Jews, to prepare for the coming of Christ, the New Testament is clear that he died for all humans of all ages. "**God so loved the world that he gave his one and only Son,**

that whoever believes in him shall not perish but have eternal life" (John 3:16). This means that people of all cultures and nationalities are equally valuable to him. God does not accept or reject people on the basis of their upbringing, gender, social standing, intelligence, political persuasion, particular beliefs, past behaviour, or any other criteria, but only on their response to his love and offer of reconciliation. Facing up to this truth and a willingness to accept those I have considered inferior to myself as of equal value to God are a necessary part of repentance in becoming a follower of Jesus.

The cross and discipleship

The most common term used to describe followers of Jesus, both in the Gospels and the book of Acts, which describes the beginnings of Christianity for the first 30 years, is the word "disciple". It occurs 264 times. In Acts it is Luke's ordinary word for "Christian", a term that only occurs three times in the New Testament and was first used by non-Christians to describe the new religion (Acts 11:26). The word "disciple" implies the commitment of a person to another individual or group. Besides the disciples of Jesus, the New Testament speaks of the disciples of John the Baptist and those of the Pharisees. The Greek word translated "disciple" also has a strong emphasis on a teacher-pupil relationship. A disciple of an individual is one who is willing to be taught or trained by that person. When we speak of Christian "discipleship" we are thinking of all that is involved in becoming an effective follower of Jesus, or, in modern terms, an effective Christian. Albert Schweitzer, the noted theologian and organist who left a promising career in those fields to study medicine, and founded a hospital and leprosy colony in the heart of Africa, said, "Discipleship is the only form in which faith in Jesus Christ can exist."

Jesus used a number of expressive images to highlight the kind of demands he would make on his followers. He spoke about the yoke of obedience (Matthew 11:29), the cup of suffering (Matthew 20:20-23), the towel of servanthood (John 13:1-17) and the cross of execution (Matthew 16:24). We could well look at each of these metaphors, but it is the last one we are primarily concerned with here. Jesus said, "**Whoever wants to be my disciple must deny themselves and take up their cross and follow me. For whoever wants to save their life will lose it, but whoever loses their life for me will find it**" (Matthew 16:24,25). Though many are called to literally give their lives for their faith in Jesus, it is plain from Luke's account of this saying that we are to take up our cross "**daily**" (Luke 9:23), that Jesus was primarily speaking of the kind of commitment which involves giving up our right to run our lives as we please, and allowing him to decide our priorities and plans and our future. Our life belongs to him, and growing as a Christian involves working out more and more what it really means to call him "Lord".

The September 2005 issue of *Christianity Today* tells the story of Chris and Cassie Haw, who, with a group of friends, moved into a house owned by Sacred Heart Catholic Church in Camden, called America's most dangerous city – and one of the most polluted. They serve the basic needs of the community, and have begun a ministry to the prostitutes and addicts living across the street from their house, who need loving neighbours more than clothes. Chris tells how he first learned about social justice at Willow Creek Community Church. A group of them "started asking questions about our way of life as contrasted with the call of the kingdom. I was taught about sweatshops, injustices, homeless people, mercy to the outsider, and other things unfamiliar to me." He learned to be a disciple of Jesus. "Willow Creek taught me that 90 percent discipleship is 10 percent short of full devotion," he says. "I took them at their word and set out to work through giving all."

When we think of discipleship in these terms, then there are very few of us who would dare to claim that we had given anywhere near "all", whatever that might mean for us personally. Even such a passionate and dedicated Christian as Paul did not claim that he had reached all he could have done in his experience of and usefulness to God (see Philippians 3:10-14). However, he could say, "**Forgetting what is behind and straining toward what is ahead, I press on toward the goal to win the prize for which God has called me heavenward in Christ Jesus**" (vv. 13,14).

When we first experience God's forgiveness and love in Jesus, then we tend to think more in terms of what he will do for us. But as we grow in our understanding of what he has done for us, and at what cost, and what he has yet planned for us in the future, then we learn to trust him more and commit ourselves at a deeper level. It is the cross and our understanding of the grace of God which flows from it that provides the motivation to join the ranks of those whose aim in life is to serve their Lord in ministering to the tremendous needs existing in this world, in whatever way he should choose. "Discipleship," says Clifford Williams, "simply means the life which springs from grace."

Discipleship, of course, not only means doing things *for* him, but growing in our relationship *with* him. Jesus said, "**I am the vine; you are the branches. If you remain in me and I in you, you will bear much fruit; apart from me you can do nothing**" (John 15:5). Only by a close relationship with him through prayer, meditation on his word, and friendship with his people can he do the work of transformation in our characters so that we grow more like him. His purpose is that we should be "**transformed into his image**" by his Spirit within us (2 Corinthians 3:18). In *The Real Jesus*, Luke Timothy Johnson has a significant point to make on the nature of discipleship. He says that the Gospels "are remarkably consistent on one essential aspect of the identity and mission of Jesus." He continues:

> Their fundamental focus is not on Jesus' wondrous deeds, not on his wise words. Their shared focus is on the character of his life and death. They all reveal the same patterns of radical

obedience to God and selfless love toward other people. All four Gospels also agree that discipleship is to follow the same messianic pattern. They do not emphasise the performance of certain deeds or the learning of certain doctrines. They insist on living according to the same pattern of life and death shown by Jesus.

Another significant point is made by Erwin McManus:

We have bought into the Christian lie that, 'the safest place to be is in the centre of God's will'... but God's desire for out lives was never to insulate us in a Christian bubble where we risk nothing, sacrifice nothing, lose nothing, worry about nothing... the Christian life was never about being safe – emotionally or physically... It has always been about engaging a dangerous cruel world... with fearless love."

In short, it has always been about carrying a cross. But it is a cross that is carried willingly and gladly with much joy thrown in.

I would like to make one other point that I have found helpful, before moving on. There is a difference between bearing a burden, and taking up a cross. Many of us have burdens we have to carry though life about which we have no choice, whether they are physical illnesses, unhappy relationships, or anything else. The New Testament gives us clues as to where we can find help with those (e.g. 2 Corinthians 12:7-10; Philippians 4:6,7; 1 Peter 5:7). However, taking up our cross to follow Jesus is a matter of choice. Richard Hays, in *The Moral Vision of the New Testament*, says:

The believer's cross is no longer any and every kind of suffering, sickness, or tension, the bearing of which is demanded. The believer's cross must be, like his Lord's, the price of social nonconformity. It is not, like sickness or catastrophe, an inexplicable, unpredictable suffering; it is the end of a path freely chosen after counting the cost. It is not an inward wrestling of the sensitive soul with self and sin; it is the social reality of representing in an unwilling world the Order to Come.

Discipleship, motivated by the love of Jesus revealed in the cross, is the pathway to a life of growing satisfaction and usefulness. And Jesus promised that, where sacrifice is involved, there are abundant rewards "**in this present age**" (Mark 10:29-31).

The cross and other religions

In the booklets *With So Many Religions, Why Christianity?* and *What Is Truth and Does It Matter?* I have outlined the main differences between Christianity and other religions. In the first of those booklets I have given personal examples from people of Hindu, Buddhist and Muslim backgrounds who have found something in the cross of Christ they have not found elsewhere. Here I will focus briefly on that, the most significant of differences.

No other religion believes in a God whose justice demands that evil is given its due penalty and yet whose love is prepared to take that penalty upon himself. And there is no other God who is prepared to give his created beings freedom to rebel against him, and yet personally enter into the sufferings and pain that is the consequence of that disobedience. Other religions which have some kind of belief in a personal god or gods (aspects of Buddhism tend to deny this), either do not accept the reality of good and evil, or do not consider evil is serious enough to present a problem that simply cannot be solved by God's mercy alone.

Muslims have an awareness of the justice of God, but they have no teaching of the love of God as it comes to us in the New Testament. John Stott, in *The Cross of Christ*, has this to say:

> One of the saddest features of Islam is that it rejects the cross, declaring it inappropriate that a major prophet of God should come to such an ignominious end. The Koran sees no need for

the sin-bearing death of a Saviour. At least five times it declares categorically that 'no soul shall bear another's burden.'[1] Indeed, 'if a laden soul cries out for help, not even a near relation shall share its burden.' Why is this? It is because 'each man shall reap the fruits of his own deeds', even though Allah is merciful and forgives those who repent and do good. Denying the need for the cross, the Koran goes on to deny the fact. The Jews 'uttered a monstrous falsehood' when they declared 'we have put to death the Messiah Jesus the son of Mary, the apostle of Allah', for 'they did not kill him, nor did they crucify him, but they thought they did'.

The Koran does speak of God's love, but only for those who in some measure deserve it. The cross, however, reveals the love of God for those who don't deserve it and never could. Also, in the light it throws on the nature of the Trinity, the cross gives us a basis for believing John's statement that indeed **"God is love"** (1 John 4:8). Love must exist in relationships, and from eternity that love has existed between the three persons of the Trinity. It is revealed and made available to us supremely through the cross.

The revelation given through the cross that God is indeed love, was something new in the ancient world. In the Greek and Roman world it was argued that love was born out of need. To link the gods with love would suggest that they lacked something and so, by implication, were imperfect and vulnerable. Zeus was the ultimate god of power, and even though Plato mistrusted the idea that the gods were arbitrarily violent, his writings reinforced the generally held opinion that the gods were invulnerable. They can do anything to anyone, but no one can affect them or cause them pain.

Of course, though the cross reveals the love of God as nothing

---

1 liii.38; xxv.18; xvii.15; xxxix.7 and vi.164.

else could, it also lays bare our desperate need. Emil Brunner, the prominent Swiss theologian, said in his classic book, *The Mediator*:

> All other forms of religion, not to mention philosophy, deal with the problem of guilt apart from the intervention of God and they therefore come to a cheap conclusion. In other religions human beings are spared the final humiliation of knowing that the mediator must bear the punishment instead of us. They are not stripped absolutely naked.

The gospel does strip us naked, and declares us bankrupt before God. However, it also provides the perfect solution to our need, and through it we can enter into an intimate relationship with him, through our adoption into his family and the indwelling Spirit within. No other religion can offer this. The Bible promises that the whole of creation will be renewed, and we can be fully assured of a future that is more certain and more real than is on offer anywhere else.

In the area of suffering in this world, the gospel also has so much to offer. In the booklet *If There Is a God, Why Is There So Much Suffering?* I have looked at the question of suffering in some detail. It is particularly the death, burial and resurrection of Jesus that gives us hope in dealing with all the questions that the problem of suffering raises. Jurgen Moltmann made a very relevant point when he wrote:

> Christ was a suffering Saviour. Statues and pictures of the Buddha show him sitting fat and contented, eyes closed in the lotus position, detached and blinded to the pain of this world. Mohammed is admired as he rides, sword in hand, inflicting wounds on the world through Jihad or 'Holy War' against 'the Infidel'. But Christ alone suffered and was wounded for that world. He is the only Saviour with wounds. He is 'The Crucified God!'

Why Did Jesus Die?

In Jesus we have a God who personally understands the worst suffering that this world can deliver. And because he understands, he can share it with us and see us through it. If we have pledged our personal allegiance to him, he will provide the motivation and strength to relieve suffering wherever that is possible. And through the victory he has achieved, he can offer the sure hope that one day it will end. Though it may not satisfy all the questions we may have about suffering, I know of no other philosophy or religion that can offer that kind of encouragement and hope.

G. Studdert-Kennedy was an army chaplain who witnessed the senseless slaughter of thousands of troops on the battlefields of France during the First World War. He was known affectionately to many of the soldiers as "Woodbine Willie". He found the cross was the only symbol which made any sense about God in the middle of that pointless suffering. In his poem, *The Comrade God*, he compares two ways we can think of God:

Dost Thou not heed the helpless sparrow's falling?
Canst Thou not see the tears that women weep?
Canst Thou not hear Thy little children calling?
Dost Thou not watch them as they sleep?

Then, O my God, Thou art too great to love me,
Since Thou dost reign beyond the reach of tears,
Calm and serene as the cruel stars above me,
High and remote from human hope and fears.

Only in Him can I find a home to hide me,
Who on the cross was slain to rise again;
Only with Him, my Comrade God, beside me,
Can I go forth to war with sin and pain.

The cross and our response

Travelling west from Lake Louise in Canada, one comes to a point where the highway is spanned by a massive wooden arch. On it is written the words, "The Great Divide". It marks the boundary between Alberta and British Columbia. The Great Divide in human history is not a wooden arch but a wooden cross. Derek Tidball, Principal of the London School of Theology, says:

> On the cross the ultimate sacrifice was offered, the High Priest died, atonement was made, healing was provided, peace was effected, redemption was purchased, access was granted, glory was manifest, a new covenant was established, a new age begun, cosmic renewal set in train.

However, the cross not only divides history into A.D. and B.C., it divides humans from one another. It divides those who respond to God's offer of salvation from those who refuse or ignore it. In New Testament terms it divides the "**children of God**" from those who "**did not receive him**" (John 1:11-13); "**the people of the kingdom**" from "**the people of the evil one**" (Matthew 13:36-43); "**whoever... has life**" from "**whoever... does not have life**" (1 John 1:12); those in whom "**the Spirit of God lives**" from those who do "**not have the Spirit of Christ**" (Romans 8:9); those who are "**not condemned**" from those who stand "**condemned already**" (John 3:18); "**whoever... has eternal life**" from those on whom

Why Did Jesus Die?

"**God's wrath remains**" (John 3:36). This division, depending on our response to Jesus Christ, is a constant and consistent theme in the New Testament. Though we have the opportunity now to respond to his love in repentance and faith, the day will come when the division is permanent – "**eternal punishment**" or "**eternal life**" (Matthew 25:46).

It is no use looking elsewhere to bridge this particular divide between us and God. Skip Heitzig, in an article in *Decision*, rightly says:

> If we go to a psychiatrist or a therapist, we'll become well-adjusted sinners. If we go to a doctor or health spa, we'll become healthy sinners. If we achieve wealth, we'll be wealthy sinners. If we join a church and decide to turn over a new leaf, we'll become religious sinners. But let us go in earnest repentance and faith to the foot of Calvary's cross, and we'll be forgiven sinners, for we will find that the cross of Jesus Christ is the only bridge that can reach God. The choice is ours. It's either separation from God or redemption by God.

Obviously, if the New Testament is true, there is no more important issue that we face in this life. If you are unsure of your relationship with God, then there are ways of making sure. There is a Jewish legend that on the night the Israelites were delivered from slavery in Egypt, the night when the firstborn of every family died unless the sacred blood had been placed on the doorposts, a young Israelite girl lay sick on her bed. As midnight approached she anxiously inquired, "Father, are you sure that the blood is there?" He replied that he had ordered it to be placed there. She was not satisfied until her father had carried her out to see for herself. They were distressed to find that the order had been neglected and there was no blood. Quickly they took steps to remedy the situation before midnight arrived. In Jesus' parable of the ten virgins, when the cry rang out at midnight, "**Here's the bridegroom! Come out to meet him!**" it was the virgins who were unprepared who were excluded from the banquet (Matthew 25:1-13).

When the call comes for you to meet Jesus, it will be insufficient to trust in your good behaviour or your religious observances, or your correct beliefs. Those things will not get you into the kingdom of God. Neither will the passing of time cancel out past sin. C. S. Lewis, in *The Problem of Pain*, said:

> We have a strange illusion that mere time cancels out sin. I have heard others, and I have heard myself, recounting cruelties and falsehoods committed in boyhood as if they were of no concern of the present speakers, and even with laughter. But mere time does nothing either to the fact or to the guilt of a sin. The guilt is washed out not by time but by repentance and the blood of Christ.

Your trust in the Saviour, who shed his blood for you, is the only sure foundation on which to build a hope of acceptance. And we have to claim for ourselves the gift of forgiveness and reconciliation that he offers. Alister McGrath, lecturer on historical and systematic theology at Wycliffe Hall, Oxford, and author of many impressive books on the Christian faith, expressed this very clearly in an article in *Decision* magazine, when looking back on his own conversion to Christ:

> Looking back on my own life as a Christian, I can see that a turning point came when I realised that the cross of Christ couldn't change me unless I allowed it to. I used to think that being a Christian meant believing that certain things were true; for example, believing that the cross of Christ really happened

Why Did Jesus Die?

in history. I didn't realise that the cross of Christ could affect me personally. I didn't understand that this event in history could turn my own history inside out, and make it "his story", that is, "God's story".

Since then, I've noticed that many people seem to have the same difficulty. They think of the cross as something that happened long, long ago and far, far away.

When I was in a situation like that, I found it valuable to close my eyes and imagine that I was there, standing amid the crowd near Calvary and watching Christ die. I imagined that I was asking myself: "Why did this wonderful Man have to die?" Gradually the crowd faded away, and I was the only one left. A voice said to me, "You are the reason that Christ had to die."

So what was God doing on the cross? The real question that each of us needs to ask ourselves are: "What did God do on that cross *for me*?" And, "Have I accepted it, and made it my own?"

Until that happens, the work of God on the cross remains unfinished in our lives.

I love a story told by Robert Coleman in his book *The Heartbeat of Evangelism* concerning an eminent preacher of a past generation, Dr Charles Berry. In his younger days, Berry had struggled with the concept of the cross and its meaning. When he began his ministry, like many people with humanistic training, he had looked upon Jesus more as a great moral teacher than a divine Saviour. He viewed Christianity as essentially living a good life.

Late one night during his first pastorate in England, while sitting in his study, he heard a knock. Opening the door, he saw a poorly dressed Lancashire girl. "Are you a minister?" she asked. Getting an affirmative answer, she continued anxiously: "You must come with me quickly. I want you to get my mother in." Imagining that it was the case of some drunken woman out on the streets, Berry said,

"Why? Go and get a policeman." "No," said the girl, "my mother is dying, and you must come with me to get her in – to heaven."

The young minister dressed and followed her through the deserted streets for more than a mile. Led into the woman's room, he knelt down beside her and began describing the kindness of Jesus, explaining that he had come to show us how to live unselfishly. Suddenly the desperate woman cut Berry off. "Mister," she cried, "that's no use for the likes of me. I am a sinner. I have lived my life. Can't you tell me of someone who can have mercy on me, and save my poor soul?"

"I stood there," said Dr Berry, "in the presence of a dying woman, and I had nothing to tell her. In order to bring something to that dying woman, I leaped back to my mother's knee, to my cradle faith, and told her of the cross, and the Christ who was able to save." Tears began running over the cheeks of the eager woman. "Now you are getting at it," she said. "Now you are helping me." And the famous preacher, concluding the story, said, "I want you to know that I got her in, and, blessed be God, I got in myself."

Of course, Jesus wants us to come to him so that we can find the greatest satisfaction and usefulness in this life, not just so that we are prepared to meet him as our Judge in the next. The danger of putting off this decision is that we will have neither the opportunity nor the desire to accept him as Saviour when our curtain call comes. All we have to do to be lost to God forever is to do nothing. After spending a whole chapter describing who Jesus really is and what he has achieved for us, the writer of Hebrews says: "**How shall we escape if we ignore so great a salvation?**" (2:3).

Though none of us are good enough to make it without God's forgiveness, you need never fear that you are so bad that he will not accept you. The only sin he cannot forgive is the failure to accept his offer. Paul, who violently persecuted Christians before his conversion, even sentencing them to death, said, "**I was once a** blasphemer and a persecutor and a violent man" and called himself the "**worst**" of sinners. However, he continued, "**But for that reason I was shown mercy so that in me, the worst of sinners, Christ Jesus might display his immense patience as an example for those who would believe in him and receive eternal life**" (1 Timothy 1:12-16).

A great prison warden, Kenyon Scudder, often told the story of a modern-day miracle. A friend of his happened to be sitting in a railway coach next to a man who was obviously depressed. Finally the man revealed that he was a convict returning from a distant prison. His imprisonment had brought shame on his family, and they had neither visited him nor written often. He hoped, however, that this was only because they were too poor to travel, too uneducated to write. He hoped, despite the evidence, that they had forgiven him.

To make matters easy for them, however, he had written to them, telling them to put up a signal for him when the train passed their little farm on the outskirts of the town. If the family had forgiven him they were to put up a white ribbon in the big apple tree near the line. If they didn't want him back they were to do nothing, and he would stay on the train, go far away, probably becoming a hobo.

As the train neared his home town his suspense became so great he couldn't bear to look out the window. His companion changed places with him and said he would watch for the apple tree. In a minute, he put his hand on the young convict's arm. "There it is," he whispered, his eyes bright with sudden tears. "It's all right. *The whole tree is white with ribbons.*" In that instance all the bitterness that had poisoned his life was dissipated.

Come to Jesus and you will find the tree white with ribbons. His outstretched arms on the cross declare, "*I love you this much! I'd rather die than live without you.*" He has promised, "**Whoever** comes to me I will never drive away" (John 6 :37). The Greek of this verse has a double negative that has the intensified meaning, "I will certainly not ever drive you away."

Another story that appeals to me is one told by the notable nineteenth century Bible teacher and evangelist, R. A. Torrey. It concerns a Mrs Bottome of New York who visited an old school friend she had not seen for 18 years. She asked the maid who met her at the door to take her card to the lady of the house. "She is not at home," was the answer. "Oh, yes she is. I saw her at the window," she replied, and she pushed past the maid into the room, where they fell into each other's arms. "What has become of you all these years?" Mrs Bottome asked her friend. "Come into this room and I will show you," was the reply. In a magnificently fitted out room, there sat a mentally handicapped boy of 17 years, scarcely able to talk, to all appearances a drivelling idiot. His mother said, "My duty lies there with my darling boy." Mrs Bottome, in a moment of carelessness, asked, "How can you endure it? I do not wonder that you are prematurely grey." "I knew you would not understand my love for my sweet boy," said her indignant friend. "It is no burden, no care, to live for and serve my boy. And if some day he will only give one sign that he recognises me as his mother, I will feel repaid for all the years of love I have lavished on him."

This is but a faint image of the love of God and I wonder how he feels when those for whom he has done so much refuse to respond to that love. Jesus said that there is much rejoicing in heaven if they do eventually respond (Luke 15:3-10 – see also vv. 23,24).

You and I are not idiots (certainly not if you have read this book this far!). The most intelligent decision you will ever make in this life is to submit your life to Jesus as your Saviour and Lord. You have everything to gain, and nothing that you lose as a result is worth keeping. Imagine four people walking down a street. One, an architect, points to a house and says, "That's one of my houses.

Why Did Jesus Die?

I designed that." Another, a builder, says, "It's my house. I built it." Another, a landlord, says, "No. It's mine. I paid for it and I hold the deeds." The last member of the group says, "That's my house. I live in it." You and I rightly belong to God. He designed us in his own likeness. He created us, though he may have taken much time to do it. But above all, we belong to him because of the price he paid for us. He holds the deeds, signed with his own blood. As C. S. Lewis says in *Mere Christianity*, "It costs God nothing, so far as we know, to create nice things; but to convert rebellious wills cost him crucifixion." He longs to take the final step of coming to live with us and in us.

Jennifer Ogilvie, in an article in *Decision* magazine, *Jesus Turned My Life Around*,[1] tells of her conversion to Christ. After graduating from college she had got involved with drink and drugs and was soon going to clubs, getting drunk Wednesdays to Saturdays. She says, "I was miserable. I couldn't get out of bed. I was drinking, getting stoned – and thinking about suicide." She got a real estate licence and one day a client she was taking to see a house shared with her how he had become a Christian eight months earlier and that Jesus had saved him from a $350-a-day cocaine habit. She thought, "Wow! He was deeper into drugs than I am, and Jesus helped *him*!" She had never heard the gospel before but wanted help so began asking God to reveal himself to her. She began listening to a Christian radio station and heard that Billy Graham was going to be in Fresno, California, to talk about Jesus. On the last night of the Crusade, 14 October, 2001, she drove 100 miles with a friend, got there late, but found seats at the top of the stadium. She says, "As Mr Graham preached about how Jesus Christ died for my sins, I felt a tug at my heart. This was the first time I had heard the full gospel – that Jesus Christ came to earth, died for me, rose again

---

1 June 2004, ©.

The Cross and Our Response

and offers me salvation. As soon as Mr Graham said, 'Come down to the field,' I got out of my seat and went down. I prayed, 'Lord Jesus, send Your Holy Spirit. Come into my heart and change me. I don't want to be me anymore. Make me new.' I felt so alive." She began reading her Bible daily, though it was some months before she found a solid church and Christian friends who enabled her to break completely free of drugs and alcohol. Today she works full-time at her church, "serving God with all my heart."

She finished the article with the words, "It's amazing that I could go twenty-four years not knowing that Christ died for me. I am so grateful for that October evening when I first learned how much Jesus loved me."

If this kind of vital relationship with God is something you are looking for, and have not yet found, then you don't have to go to some Crusade to find it. However, you do have to sort it out personally with God.

Maybe you could meditate on words from the famous hymn of Isaac Watts, "When I Survey the Wondrous Cross", written in 1707. Charles Wesley reportedly said he would give up all his other hymns to have written this one.

> When I survey the wondrous cross
> On which the Prince of glory died,
> My richest gain I count but loss,
> And pour contempt on all my pride.
>
> Were the whole realm of nature mine,
> That were an offering far too small;
> Love so amazing, so divine,
> Demands my soul, my life, my all.

You may find it helpful to pray a prayer something like this:

Why Did Jesus Die?

God, I accept that when you created this universe and thought of me, you had a great purpose for me that stretches beyond the limitations of this mortal life. Though I don't fully understand all that you may have planned for me in this life or the next, I accept that you love me and sent Jesus to die for me in order that I might be reconciled to you and become a member of your family forever.

Thank you, Jesus, for your great love.

Lord, I am coming home. I am sorry for my sins. I repent of them. I now accept your forgiveness and submit my life to Jesus as my Saviour and Lord.

Come into my life and begin the process of moulding me into all you planned that I should be and directing me in the path you have chosen for me.

Enable me to accept fully all that you have done for me and to be open to all that you want to do. Give me the courage and strength to live worthily of your love and to follow wherever you lead, so that I may grow in my relationship with you and make a difference in this needy world as your disciple.

Amen.

If this is a new experience for you, then dig into your New Testament to see what God has in store for you. Also, look around for other members of God's family who can be an encouragement to you, and for others looking for meaning to life with whom you can share your experience. And may God bless you on the journey.

God so loved the world that he gave his one and only Son, that whoever believes in him shall not perish but have eternal life. (John 3:16)

Recommended Reading

Books I have found particularly useful in putting all this together:

The Cross of Christ by John Stott, Inter-Varsity Press, U.K. 1986, ©.
Between Cross and Resurrection: A Theology of Holy Saturday by Alan E. Lewis, William B. Eerdmans Publishing Company, Cambridge, U.K./Grand Rapids, Michigan, 2001, ©.
The Death of Christ by James Denney, The Tyndale Press, London 1951, ©.
The Apostolic Preaching of the Cross by Leon Morris, The Tyndale Press, London, 1955, ©.
The Seven Last Words from the Cross by Fleming Rutledge, William B. Eerdmans Publishing Company, Cambridge, U.K./Grand Rapids, Michigan, 2005, ©.

About the Author: Dick Tripp is an Anglican clergyman with experience in parish ministry in the Diocese of Christchurch, New Zealand, and has an MA in theology from Cambridge University. He has trained people to share their faith, using the programme developed by Evangelism Explosion Ministries, and supports his wife Sally in environmental issues,  protecting New Zealand's native fauna and flora. He likes chopping wood, enjoys his family and is a director of the family farm.

Other Titles by Dick Tripp in the Series Exploring Faith Today:

The Bible: Can We Trust a Book Written Two Thousand Years Ago?
Did the Writers of the New Testament Get Their Picture of Jesus Right?
Is Jesus Really God?
Did Jesus Really Rise from the Dead?
With So Many Religions, Why Christianity?
If There Is a God, Why Is There So Much Suffering?
Understanding the Trinity: The God Revealed in Jesus Christ
The Complementary Nature of Science and Christianity
Forgiveness: What It Is and Why It Matters
How Does God Guide?
Repentance: What It Is and Why You Can't Get to Heaven Without It
What Does It Mean To Be Converted and Born Again?
The Kind of Faith That Will Get You Into Heaven
Can I Be Sure I Am Going To Heaven?
What Is Truth and Does It Matter?
Does It Matter How We Live? A Christian View of Morality
God's Vision for His Family, the Church: A Call to the Churches of the New Millenium
How Can I Find a Great Purpose for Living?
Who Am I? Finding My True Identity as a Human Being and as a Child of God
How Can I Feel Good About Myself? The Christian Basis for a Proper Self-Esteem
Life After Death: Christianity's Hope and Challenge

These may all be read online at www.christianity.co.nz

www.ingramcontent.com/pod-product-compliance
Lightning Source LLC
Chambersburg PA
CBHW050844230426
43667CB00012B/2139